# AMC
# River Guide

---

# NEW HAMPSHIRE
# VERMONT

D1012485

APPALACHIAN MOUNTAIN CLUB

RIVER GUIDES

**AMC River Guide: Maine**

**AMC River Guide: Massachusetts, Connecticut, and Rhode Island**

**AMC River Guide: New Hampshire and Vermont**
Second Edition

**New England White Water River Guide**
Second Edition
*Ray Gabler*

**River Rescue**
Second Edition
*Les Bechdel and Slim Ray*

**White Water Handbook**
Second Edition
*John T. Urban*

**The Wildest Country: A Guide to Thoreau's Maine**
*J. Parker Huber*

# AMC
# River Guide

---

# NEW HAMPSHIRE
# VERMONT

Second Edition

APPALACHIAN MOUNTAIN CLUB
BOSTON

Edited by Victoria Jas
Cover design by Joyce Weston

GV
776
.N4
A43
1989

*Library of Congress Cataloging-in-Publication Data*

AMC river guide. New Hampshire, Vermont. —2nd ed.
    p.   cm.
  Includes index.
  ISBN 0-910146-77-2 (alk. paper)
  1. Canoes and canoeing—New Hampshire—Guide-books. 2. Canoes and
canoeing—Vermont—Guide-books. 3. New Hampshire—Description and
travel—1981– —Guide-books. 4. Vermont—Description and travel—1981– —
Guide-books. I. Appalachian Mountain Club.
GV776.N4A43   1989
797.1'22'0942—dc19                                                        88-27170

Published by Appalachian Mountain Club Books, 5 Joy St., Boston, MA 02108.
Distributed by The Talman Company, 150 Fifth Ave., New York, NY 10011.

**SIXTH EDITION**

**Due to changes in conditions, use of the information in this book
is at the sole risk of the user.**

Printed in the United States of America

10 9 8 7 6 5 4 3 2 1                                        89 90 91 92 93

# CONTENTS

# PREFACE

The first extensive guidebook to New England rivers was *Quick-water and Smooth*, by John C. Phillips and Thomas D. Cabot, published in 1935. In 1965 the Appalachian Mountain Club published its *New England Canoeing Guide*. This was an updated and greatly expanded version of the earlier work, assembled by a committee of volunteers under the direction of Kenneth Henderson and Stewart Coffin. Revised editions were published in 1968 and 1971.

The *New England Canoeing Guide*, in turn, was replaced by the *AMC River Guide*, a book with a format designed for easier reference. Separate volumes were published for northeastern and south-central New England, and the text was expanded. Updated river descriptions incorporated headings giving important characteristics of each river segment. The volunteer architect for this restructuring was Philip Preston.

Conversations with users, however, revealed that arbitrary political boundaries meant more to most canoeists than did natural watershed boundaries, and so it was decided that subsequent editions of the would be organized according to state boundaries. The first *River Guide* that followed state lines was the *AMC River Guide: Maine*, which was published in 1980, followed by the *AMC River Guide: New Hampshire and Vermont* in 1983. This book is the second edition of this new format.

I'd like to thank all of the volunteer contributors to this edition: Paul Berry, Mike Burke, Fletcher Blanchard, Norton Cabell, Rod Dore, George Ellmore, Mike Fullerton, Tim Garrand, Robert and Christine Grosso, Wayne Huff, Ken Hutchins, Tim Jackson and Jane Risch, Ken Jewett, Bill Lowman, Bob Milburn, Rich Miller, Thomas Quarles, Jr., Chris Roukes, Art Sharkey, Alan Sherwood and Janis McKittrick, Don Skolfield, Len Thibodeau, George Trudel, Steve Tuckerman, Jan Van Zandt, Louise and Tim Walker, and Kyle Whitehead. Special thanks to Roioli

Schweiker, for her detailed corrections; to Vera Smith, for her patience and good humor, as always; and to Tom Hartman, for always helping me to roll up.

This team effort was challenging and rewarding. The River Guide will continue to change and grow, and I invite you to become involved in the process!

*Victoria Jas*

# INTRODUCTION

Every drop of water that falls in New Hampshire heads with reasonable expedition for the nearest southward-flowing trunk line, and then on to the Atlantic Ocean. Water from the northwestern part of the state flows west to the Connecticut River. The northeastern part of the state drains eastward into the Androscoggin and Saco rivers and through Maine to the ocean. All of the south-central part of New Hampshire drains south with the Merrimack River. Only a small bit of the coastal area rivers reach the ocean entirely through New Hampshire. Runoff on the highest mountain in the state, Mount Washington, may flow in three different ways: to the Saco, via the Ammonoosuc to the Connecticut, or via the Peabody River to the Androscoggin.

The drainage pattern in Vermont is more complicated. Surprisingly, the water to the eastern side of the Green Mountains does not all flow east to the Connecticut. Four rivers from the Champlain Watershed have pirated large drainage areas north to the Saint Lawrence River. In addition, the northern boundary of Vermont is arbitrary and was not drawn along a watershed, so another portion along the international boundary also drains north into the Saint Francis River and on to the Saint Lawrence. Finally, a small area southwest of the Green Mountains flows to the Hudson River in New York.

The rivers in this book are arranged by watersheds, from north to south and west to east.

## SAFETY

Although this book was prepared with care, no guidebook should be used on blind faith. It is a very helpful companion, along with a map, to have when you run a river, but it will not prevent every problem.

This book will not protect you from yourself. Managing a boat in current requires a degree of skill that depends on the nature of the river. Maneuvering with style and finesse is considerably different from just paddling hard. Sometimes paddling hard works, but the faster the current the less effective it is. Be realistic about your abilities and do not underestimate the power and difficulty of a river. The Safety Code of the American Whitewater Affiliation is included in the appendix; it contains many good suggestions for safe boating.

This book will also not protect you from unexpected rapids or obstacles. Many permanent changes in rivers have taken place within the last few decades, and they have often occurred when dams were washed out. New England still has many old dams that could collapse and expose whatever the millponds covered. There is always the possibility of encountering temporary or seasonal obstructions. Snowmobile bridges and ice dam nets have become a noteworthy hazard on some small quickwater streams: they are low and often awash. They usually block a river even more effectively than a fallen tree.

And lastly, this book will not protect you from sudden changes in water level. A moderate spring or autumn rainfall will significantly affect a river with a large, mountainous watershed. In a matter of hours the river can rise several feet and so become more difficult and hazardous. Unanticipated releases from dams can have the same effect.

Boating, as a sport, involves certain risks that can be minimized with the proper training, forethought, caution, and equipment.


## BE CONSIDERATE OF LANDOWNERS

Many put-ins, take-outs, and portages are open for public use. Others require that you cross private property. You will note that many landowners whose property borders popular canoeing rivers have posted their property against trespass. Paddlers can prevent additional closings by being thoughtful. Ask permission where it is possible; don't damage vegetation; park cars out of the way so they don't block roads; pick up litter. Make your portage expeditiously and leave; don't hang around picnicking and making a disturbance. Don't expect local residents to be responsible for rescuing you and your canoe. Dumping boats and getting them pinned on whitewater rivers happens to the best of us, and paddlers should prepare before launching by having suitable equipment, clothing, and a large enough group. Access to put-ins and take-outs is the right of a private landowner, and the privilege of the user. Access is becoming limited on some rivers, so it is increasingly important to maintain good relations with property owners.

## USING THE RIVER GUIDE

### Organization

Each chapter begins with a list of the rivers described. The tributaries of each river are indented and listed below it. The principal river is described first, then its tributaries in descending (downstream) order.

### Format for River Descriptions

Each description starts with general information about the river as a whole. Longer rivers are then broken into sections that are of reasonable length for a canoe trip or unrunnable sections to be omitted while paddling that river. These sections are introduced by a boldfaced heading and, in most cases, a table that summarizes significant information about that segment, such as what kind of water the paddler can expect, the recommended water level for paddling that section and the season or conditions when that level is most likely to occur, what kind of scenery the river passes through, what maps to refer to, directions and distances for portages, and total distances to be covered, in miles.

A new addition to the description is the date on which this information was verified by a volunteer river checker, with that person's initials. It is recommended that drops and other obstacles be investigated on rivers that have not been recently checked by scouting if possible before the section is run.

The tables codify the information that is usually required to plan trips rapidly. In the descriptive text that follows the tables, cumulative distances from the section starting point are placed within parentheses.

**Table Format**

| **Starting Point–Ending Point** | **Total miles** |
| --- | --- |
| Description: | (Difficulty of the river in this segment) |
| Date checked: | (Last date that information was verified as being correct, and initials of the person who verified it) |
| Navigable: | (Recommended water levels and seasons) |
| Scenery: | (What you will see from the boat) |
| Maps: | (US Geological Survey quadrangles and other maps) |
| Portages: | (Where to, when to, and how far to carry) |

**Terminology: Difficulty of River**

The following terms appear opposite the "Description" heading in the summary table and are used to describe the difficulty of the water to be paddled:

*Lake*  The segment being described flows through a lake or else it is necessary to paddle across a lake to reach the beginning of a river.

*Flatwater*  There is little or no current, and the river's surface is smooth and unbroken. Paddling upstream is easy.

*Quickwater*  The river moves fast. Its surface is nearly smooth at high water levels, but is likely to be choppy at medium water levels and shallow at low water levels.

*Marsh/swamp*  Vegetation often obstructs the river. Paddling may be slower than the distance alone would indicate.

*Class*  Difficulty of rapids in a segment is rated according to American Whitewater Affiliation classifications: I, II, III, or IV. See the appendix for a description of these classifications.

When two or more terms appear together opposite the "Description" heading in the summary table, the paddler should expect to encounter all of those conditions in that segment of the river. When one of these terms describes water conditions throughout most of the segment, it appears in boldface type.

Judging the difficulty of rapids is subjective. It depends on the type of boat, on how well paddlers read the river, and on how skillfully they maneuver their boats.

The difficulty of rapids changes with the water level. A given stretch of rapids may become easier or harder when there is more water in the river. Water level affects different parts of the same river differently. As a general rule, more water washes out a river with low gradient and small rocks, but it generates larger waves and more turbulence in a river that drops steeply through large rocks.

As water level rises, *current picks up!* Be aware of this. If the river is high and the air and water are cold, increase the rating by at least one—and possibly two—classes.

On small rivers fallen trees present a greater hazard to paddlers than do rapids, especially since their location cannot be documented in advance. Barbed wire fences frequently cross rivers in rural areas and are hard to spot. Be alert and have your boat under control.

## Terminology: Water Levels

The following terms appear opposite the "Navigable" heading in the summary tables. They describe the water level recommended for paddling a particular segment. The dates and conditions most likely to produce the recommended water level follow in parentheses.

*Low water* There is a clearly defined shoreline below the bank. Small rocky rivers will be uncanoeable, but flatter stretches and rapids in large rivers will be navigable.

*Medium water*  The river extends to the bank, and soft vegetation along the shore may be under water. Marshy areas
may be wet. Larger whitewater rivers, depending on the
type of rapids, will be navigable at this water level, and
dodging rocks will be the major entertainment.

*High water*  The river is near the top of its defined bank, and
alders along the shore may be under water. This is an acceptable water level for small whitewater rivers.

*Very high water*  Large trees or clumps of smaller ones have
their roots in the water. Reaching shore may be difficult
or impossible. This water level is recommended only for
experts who are familiar with the particular river and its
problems.

*Flood*  The river overflows its banks and makes pillows on
large trees. This stage is dangerous for everybody.

Levels lower than those recommended do not necessarily
mean that the river is not runnable; a river for which high
water is recommended may be traveled in medium water, but
it is likely to be scratchy, and paddlers may have to wade down
some sections.

## Terminology: Scenery

The following terms are used in the tables to describe the
territory that the river flows through.

*Wild*  Long sections of semiwilderness, with no more than
a few isolated camps and occasional road access. Dirt
roads may parallel the river within sight or sound but
only for short distances, and they do not noticeably alter
the semiwilderness atmosphere of the trip. These roads may
in fact be closed to the public or altogether impassable.

*Forested*  Banks on both sides of the river look densely wooded, but there are good dirt and asphalt roads that follow

along the river or are not far from it. These roads may frequently approach or cross the river. There may be farms and houses nearby, but not many of them are visible from the water.

*Rural*   Farms are visible from the river, and some fields may extend down to the water.

*Towns*   Small and isolated towns border the river. Aside from their effects on water quality, these towns have little impact on the trip.

*Settled*   There are many houses or small buildings within sight or sound of the river.

*Urban*   Multistoried buildings are visible. The shorelines are frequently unattractive.

## Maps

Each chart includes pertinent topographic maps in 7½-minute series unless followed by "15" to indicate that they are in the 15-minute series. Topographic maps may be ordered from:

> Branch of Distribution, Eastern Region
> U.S. Geological Survey
> 1200 S. Eads Street
> Arlington, VA 22202

For information on Canadian maps, write to:

> Canada Map Office
> Department of Energy, Mines and Resources
> 615 Booth Street
> Ottawa, Ontario K1A 0E9

Five-color highway maps of the states, updated annually, are available free at highway rest areas or by mail from:

New Hampshire Division of Economic Development
Concord, NH 03301

Vermont Agency of Development and Community Affairs
Information/Travel Division
61 Elm Street
Montpelier, VT 05602

Each state also produces detailed maps of all roads, which are available from the respective highway departments. The *New Hampshire Atlas* and the *Vermont Atlas,* published by the David DeLorme Company, Box 81, Yarmouth, ME 04096, available in many book, stationery, and sporting goods stores, contain a revised version of the highway department maps. Launching ramps for lakes and rivers are also marked on Vermont's official state highway map and in the New Hampshire and Vermont atlases.

## Portages

The portages in each chart are unavoidable carries, like those at dams and waterfalls, and difficult sections that usually are not runnable because of insufficient water. In addition, some rapids are listed as portages if they are significantly more difficult than the rating for that portion of the river. Unlisted portages included lift-overs to pass fallen trees and low, temporary bridges. There may also be additional carries around rapids that you do not wish to run. Portages that appear within parentheses are at the end of the river segment being described; only those who plan to paddle farther down the river need complete these portages.

## Abbreviations

The following abbreviations are used in the summary tables:

| | |
|---|---|
| ft | foot, feet |
| mi | mile, miles |
| yd | yard, yards |
| L | left |

| R | right |
| e | either |
| USGS | United States Geological Survey |
| CNTS | Canadian National Topographical Survey |

**Example: How to Read a Summary Table**

| **Smithville–Brownville** | | **3¾ mi** |
|---|---|---|
| Description: | Class I–**II** | |
| Date checked: | 1988, JS | |
| Navigable: | High water (April to early May) | |
| Scenery: | Forested | |
| Map: | USGS Waitsfield | |
| Portages: | 1½ mi   L   **dam** 15 yd | |
| | 2 mi   L   **two ledges** 100 yd | |

Smithville–Brownville
   The starting point for this imaginary segment is Smithville. The end point is Brownville.

3¾ mi
   The total distance to be covered is 3¾ miles.

Description: Class I–**II**
   Paddlers will encounter Class I and II whitewater on this segment. Most of the segment is Class II.

Date checked: 1988, JS
   Jane Smith, a volunteer river checker, verified that the description was accurate in 1988.


Navigable: High water (April to early May)
   The river is runnable at high water levels, which are most likely to occur during April and the first part of May.


Scenery: Forested
   Paddlers will pass between wooded banks, but access roads may exist in the woods, close to the river.


Map: USGS Waitsfield
   The topographic map for this segment is the US Geological Survey Waitsfield 7½-minute quadrangle.


Portages:    1½ mi   L   **dam** 15 yd
             2 mi   L   **two ledges** 100 yd
   Paddlers will have to carry their boats for about 15 yards around a dam about 13½ miles from Smithville. The best route for the portage is on the left as you face downstream. There is another portage in ½ mile, 2 miles from the starting point at Smithville. The best route is also on the left, and paddlers will have to carry their boats about 100 yards to avoid two ledges. The last portage is not the take-out point for the end of this section, however. If it were, it would appear in parentheses to indicate that only those wanting to continue downriver need to complete that portage.


## SECURITY

   Regrettably, crime has reached canoeing rivers. At put-ins for some popular rivers, close to 100 percent of the parked cars are burglarized. To discourage this, do not leave money, cameras, or other valuables in cars. The first place thieves look is in your bag of dry clothes; leave your wallet at home and take only the cash and cards that you will need; carry them in a waterproof folder in your pocket. If this is not possible (for example, on an extended trip), pay to park your car at a gas station or at a house.

## TIME

It's impossible to estimate time realistically for a canoe trip. Too many factors influence how long it will take: the water height, which affects the speed of the current; whether the boater pursues paddling as an athletic endeavor or prefers to float silently with the current, observing. A small, well-qualified party may scout nothing, while an instruction trip may scout everything. Paddlers may spend time bailing out canoes, taking pictures, or negotiating blowdowns.

On a large river with the current and wind favorably behind, the miles whiz by. A paddler may take hours to travel a single mile on a small stream blocked with alder thickets and fallen trees. The same mile will require far less time when it is free of obstructions. It is good practice to select beforehand alternate end points for a trip, especially on an unfamiliar river.

## RIVER LEVELS IN NEW ENGLAND

The water level information given in the summary tables for individual rivers includes approximate dates, which are subject to wide variation from year to year. Some of the factors that influence water levels are discussed here.

Snow depth, temperature, rainfall, and transpiration are four seasonal factors that affect river levels. The farther south you get in New England, the less important the first two become, since snow is usually less deep and occasionally nonexistent. As the snow cover disappears, temperature becomes less important, although runoff is greater and swifter when the ground is frozen. Once the leaves are out, surface runoff decreases substantially, because plants of all sizes use a great deal of water. Conversely, the fall foliage season invariably signals a rise in water levels. Significant rainfall in autumn is also more likely than it is in the summertime.

Terrain also must be considered. A river flowing from steep-sided hills and mountains will quickly collect the runoff from rainfall and melting snow. On the other hand, lakes, swamps, and gently rolling hills buffer the spring runoff, and the result is an extended canoeing season in spite of the weather. Knowledge of New England's topography will be as helpful to you as familiarity with its weather.

You must also take into account the nature of the river itself. If a river is flat, weather matters little as far as canoeability is concerned. If the river is steep and full of rapids, then heavy snow, warm temperatures, and moderate rainfall may all be necessary to keep it runnable. Also, you must consider the size of the river. A large river will generally peak and ebb more gradually, so it will have a much longer season than will a small stream.

Many of New England's rivers have just enough quickwater and easy rapids to make high or medium water necessary for good passage. In early March, rivers all over central and southern New England become runnable. Farther north, access to the water in early spring is hindered, first by snow and later by mud. Furthermore, ice shelves along the banks are hazardous in rapids and an inconvenience elsewhere.

If you wish to run rapids in early March, Connecticut is the place. By late March the season in that state for good Class II and Class III rapids is fading, and you will probably be limited to some of the larger rivers. By May the rivers of northern New England which are fed by melting snow deposits in the high mountains are usually at optimal levels. Sometimes they are passable through Memorial Day, but there have been years when the season is over late in April.

Many of New England's rivers have gauges that have been set up by the US Geological Survey. Through a network known as the Telemark System, USGS district offices collect daily gauge readings for some of these rivers. This book contains occasional references to these gauges and other water level indicators, but comprehensive and detailed information about their use is not included.

River levels can vary tremendously from season to season, and unusually heavy rainfall can make any river passable at any time. If you do enough canoeing and kayaking, you will probably eventually meet someone who will defend winter boating and will claim that the canoeing season includes any sunny day when the temperature is above freezing.

Over a period of several years, a person who runs a lot of rivers develops a sense of river levels. Those who fish the ocean acquire an instinct for the tides, those who live off the land can almost smell the weather, and so it is with river people. After a while they get to know when a river runs and when it does not.

## WATER RELEASES

With many of New England's rivers passable for only a few weeks in the spring or after an unusually heavy rainfall, releases of water from dams can extend the canoeing season in some localities. There are many dams on large New England rivers, but unless there are rapids below them, as is the case with the examples given, effects of releases may not be too noticeable.

The first type of release comes from dams used in connection with power generation. On the Pemigewasset River (Merrimack Watershed) a dam that supplies peaking power usually provides ample water for fine Class II boating weekdays throughout the season.

The second type of release is one scheduled solely for the benefit of paddlers. These are arranged by whitewater clubs, the Appalachian Mountain Club among them. They take place on weekends during the spring, summer, and fall, and the dates can be obtained from the Appalachian Mountain Club. The West River (Upper Connecticut Watershed) is one example.

The third type of release is the annual drawdown of lakes that are used primarily for summer recreation. These releases generally take place in the middle of the fall and greatly augment the natural flow for that time of year. A drawdown often takes several weeks to complete. Rivers on which drawdowns provide ample water include the Mascoma River (Upper Connecticut Watershed), the Winnipesaukee River (Merrimack Watershed), and the Pine River and the West Branch (Saco Watershed). In New Hampshire many drawdowns are controlled by the Water Resources Board (37 Pleasant Street, Concord, NH 03301), and late in the summer you can obtain a schedule from that agency.

Water releases can also provide an augmented flow on several other rivers in the area covered by this book.

## RENTALS

There are many places to rent canoes in New England, and they are easy to find. Begin your search in the Yellow Pages under "Canoes." Grumman and Old Town dealers may be able to help you locate distant outfitters. If not, you can obtain a copy of the Rent-a-Canoe Directory by writing to Grumman Boats, Marathon, NY 13803. The Mad River Canoe Company (Box 363, Waitsfield, VT 05673) and the Old Town Canoe Company (Old Town, ME 04468) can also supply you with smaller lists of dealers who rent their canoes.

## RIVERS OMITTED FROM THIS GUIDE

Paddlers who would like to run a river that is not included in this guide and who are willing to report their findings may send a self-addressed stamped envelope to the AMC River Guide Committee (5 Joy St., Boston, MA 02108) to receive whatever information is available on that river.

## Suggested Rivers with Flatwater and Quickwater Canoeing

| chapter | page | river | state(s) | miles | portage(s) | lake | flatwater | quickwater | class I rapids | class II rapids short, easy | passage at all levels | scratchy sections in low water |
|---|---|---|---|---|---|---|---|---|---|---|---|---|
| 2 | 22 | **Lamoille River** (Morrisville–Fairfax Falls) | VT | 34¼ | 4[1] | • | • | • | • | | | • |
| 2 | 47 | **Lemon Fair River and Otter Creek** (Rte. 74–Lake Champlain) | VT | 27¾ | 1 | | • | | | | | • |
| 2 | 14 | **Missisquoi River** (Sheldon Springs–Lake Champlain) | VT | 21½ | 3 | | • | | | | | • |
| 2 | 39 | **Otter Creek** (Proctor–Threemile Bridge) | VT | 32¼ | 3 | | • | • | • | • | | |
| 2 | 26 | **Winooski River** (Montpelier–Essex Junction) | VT | 38¼ | 2 | | • | • | | • | | |
| 2 | 27 | **Winooski River** (Winooski–Lake Champlain) | VT | 9¼ | | | • | | | | | |
| 5 | 160 | **Merrimack River** (Franklin–Manchester) | NH | 42¼ | 3 | | • | • | | • | • | |
| 5 | 177 | **Baker and Pemigewasset Rivers** (West Rumney–Bristol) | NH | 31 | | • | • | • | | | • | |
| 5 | 185 | **Contoocook River** (Peterborough–Bennington) | NH | 12 | 1 | | | • | • | | | |
| 5 | 193 | **Contoocook River** (Contoocook–Penacook) | NH | 10¼ | | | • | | | • | | |
| 7 | 264 | **Saco River** (Center Conway–Cornish) | NH, ME | 49½ | 1 | | • | • | • | • | • | |

# Suggested Rivers with Easy Rapids

| chapter | page | river | state(s) | miles | portage(s) | short, intermittent rapids | several miles of continuous rapids | mostly continuous rapids | continuous rapids | flatwater | quickwater | class I | class II | class III rapids |
|---|---|---|---|---|---|---|---|---|---|---|---|---|---|---|
| 3 | 55 | **Batten Kill** (Manchester–East Greenwich) | VT, NY | 30½ | 1 | • | | | | • | • | • | • | |
| 4 | 65 | **Connecticut River** (Pittsburg–North Strafford/Bloomfield) | NH, VT | 33¼ | 1 | • | | | | • | • | | • | |
| 4 | 146 | **Ashuelot River** (Gilsum Gorge–Shaw's Corner) | NH | 4 | | | | • | | | | | • | |
| 4 | 133 | **Cold River** (South Acworth–Vilas Pool) | NH | 5¼ | | | | • | | | | | • | 1 |
| 4 | 134 | **Cold River** (Drewsville Gorge–Rte. 123) | NH | 2¾ | | | | • | | | | | • | |
| 4 | 120 | **Sugar River** (North Newport–Claremont) | NH | 9¾ | | | | • | | | • | | • | 1 |
| 4 | 100 | **Waits River** (Waits River Village–Bradford) | VT | 10½ | | | • | | | | • | | • | |
| 4 | 104 | **White River** (Granville–Bethel) | VT | 25½ | | | • | | | | • | | • | 2 |
| 5 | 184 | **Contoocook River** (Jaffrey–Peterborough) | NH | 6¾ | 2 | | | • | | | | | • | |
| 5 | 166 | **Pemigewasset River** (North Woodstock–Blair Road) | NH | 19 | | • | | | | • | | | • | |
| 6 | 238 | **Isinglass River** (Rte. 126–Country Farm Road) | NH | 11¾ | 2[2] | • | | | | • | • | | • | 1 |
| 7 | 262 | **Saco River** (Bartlett–Center Conway) | NH | 22½ | | | • | | | • | | | • | 3 |
| 7 | 272 | **Ossipee and Saco Rivers** (Kezar Falls–East Limington) | ME | 20¾ | 1 | | • | | | • | • | | • | 1 |
| 7 | 278 | **Pine River** (Pine River Road–Elm Street) | NH | 13 | | | | | • | • | • | | • | 1 |

[1]includes one Class II rapid

## Suggested Whitewater Runs of Class III Difficulty

| chapter | page | river | state | miles | portage(s) | difficult class IV rapids | water releases in summer or fall |
|---|---|---|---|---|---|---|---|
| 4 | 94 | **Ammonoosuc River** (River Bend–Pierce Bridge) | NH | 2¾ | | | |
| 4 | 94 | **Ammonoosuc River** (Pierce Bridge–above Littleton) | NH | 8¼ | 1 | 2 | |
| 4 | 115 | **Mascoma River** (Mascoma Lake–Lebanon) | NH | 5½ | 1 | 1 | • |
| 4 | 152 | **Otter Brook** (flood control dam–Keene) | NH | 4¾ | | | |
| 4 | 142 | **Winhall River** (off Route 30–West River) | VT | 7 | 1[2] | 1[1] | |
| 5 | 213 | **Souhegan River** (Greenville–side road) | NH | 3½ | | | |
| 7 | 275 | **Bearcamp River** (Bennett Corners–Whittier) | NH | 3¾ | 3[2] | 2 | |

[1]Londonderry Rapids
[2]includes two Class III–IV rapids

# Suggested Whitewater Runs of Class IV Difficulty

| chapter | page | river | state | miles | portage | covered boats only |
|---------|------|-------|-------|-------|---------|--------------------|
| 4 | 144 | **Ashuelot River**<br>(Marlow–Gilsum Gorge) | NH | 4½ | | |
| 4 | 153 | **Ashuelot River, South Branch**<br>(Troy Gap–Webb) | NH | 3 | | • |
| 4 | 98 | **Gale River**<br>(Jesseman Road–Ammonoosuc River) | NH | 4 | | • |
| 4 | 151 | **Otter Brook**<br>(East Sullivan–Otter Brook State Park) | NH | 3¼ | | |
| 4 | 143 | **Wardsboro Brook**<br>(Wardsboro–Rte. 100) | VT | 3½ | | • |
| 5 | 186 | **Contoocook River**<br>(off old Route 202–West Henniker) | NH | 3 | | •[1] |
| 5 | 173 | **Mad River**<br>(Waterville Valley–Campton) | NH | 12 | | |
| 5 | 172 | **Pemigewasset River**<br>(Kancamagus Hwy.–N. Woodstock) | NH | 6 | 1 | •[2] |
| 5 | 181 | **Smith River**<br>(Route 104–South Alexandria) | NH | 3 | | |
| 7 | 260 | **Saco River**<br>(Gorge–Sawyer's Rock) | NH | 3¾ | | |
| 7 | 267 | **Swift River**<br>(Rocky Gorge–Lower Falls) | NH | 2½ | | |
| 7 | 267 | **Swift River**<br>(Gorge–Darby Field) | NH | 4 | | • |

[1]gauge reading of 8.0 or higher
[2]gauge reading over 1 foot at Kancamagus Highway

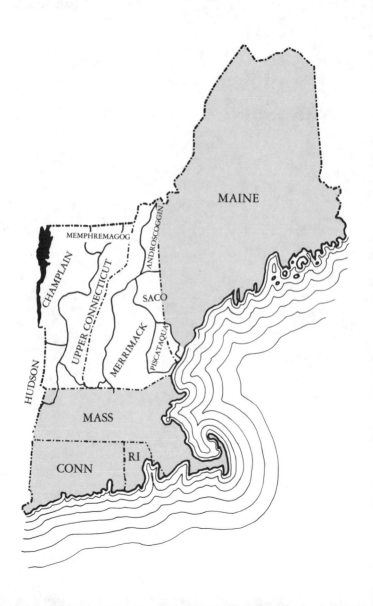

# Chapter 1

# Memphremagog Watershed

# MEMPHREMAGOG WATERSHED

*A small area in the extreme northeast central part of Vermont drains north through Lake Memphremagog and the Magog River in Quebec to the Saint Francis River and from there to the Saint Lawrence River at Lake Saint Peter. The three rivers described here flow northward through extensive sections of quickwater and easy rapids, broken intermittently by steep ledges. The rural Vermont seen from the banks is pleasant and the towns small. The quickwater parts can often be run late in the season and after summer rains.*

# BLACK RIVER                                                    VT

This more northerly of the two Black rivers in Vermont rises in Craftsbury and trickles south to meet the outlet of Eligo Pond, where it reverses course and flows north and northeast to Lake Memphremagog.

Dams, waterfalls, and ledges divide it into three distinct sections. The middle, from Irasburg to Coventry, can be run only in high water, since it is wide, with rocky rapids. The upper and lower parts can be run almost any time. Although not far from the road, the banks are forested and unsettled, and wildlife is abundant.

## Eligo Pond–Albany                                          12 mi

From the bridge a mile north of Eligo Pond, the first 1½ miles to the second bridge are very winding and overgrown. The 2 miles to the next bridge are also tortuous. From the third bridge to Albany the paddling improves, as does the size of the river, which is fed by many entering brooks. Fallen trees can be a problem. Between the two bridges in Albany there is a rocky corner blocked by a collapsing bridge.

## Albany–Irasburg                                           11½ mi

| | |
|---|---|
| Description: | Flatwater, quickwater |
| Date checked: | 1983 |
| Navigable: | Almost any time (wet summer) |
| Scenery: | Forested, rural |
| Maps: | USGS Hardwick 15, Irasburg 15 |

Put in at the northern (downstream) bridge in Albany. Bushes overhang the narrow, deep brook from both sides as it meanders, crosses under VT 14 (5½ miles), circles to the left of the valley past a log crib, and runs under three farm bridges and a number of snowmobile bridges to another VT 14/58 bridge, which is a good place to take out.

## Irasburg Portage                                    1½ mi

In ¼ mile there is another possible access on the left above the Black River Sawmill Dam. Ledges continue below the mill, as the river crosses twice under the dirt road alongside and approaches VT 58.

## Irasburg–Coventry (VT Rte. 14 Bridge)              4 mi

| | |
|---|---|
| Description: | Class I–II |
| Date checked: | 1983 |
| Navigable: | High water (early May) |
| Scenery: | Rural, forested |
| Map: | USGS Irasburg 15 |

Put in from a dirt road on the right bank below the last ledge where the river swings away from VT Rte. 58. A mile downstream is an interesting covered bridge. The Class II rapids are continuous and pleasant, and the river is wide and shallow. Take out at the next VT 14 bridge.

## VT Rte. 14 Bridge–through Coventry              3 mi

The river flows smoothly through farm country and runs under a covered bridge to an iron bridge with a 8-foot waterfall below it, which can be portaged on the right. Several minor ledges and riffles speed the river around a big loop to the north. At the base of the loop is another 8-foot waterfall in a gorge just above Coventry. Riffles continue ¼ mile as the valley opens out.

## Coventry–Lake Memphremagog                      7½ mi

| | |
|---|---|
| Description: | Flatwater, quickwater |
| Date checked: | 1983 |
| Navigable: | Spring, summer, fall |
| Scenery: | Forested |
| Map: | USGS Memphremagog 15 |

The river is shallow in low water near a small park off US 5, but it deepens rapidly. For the first few miles, the river is smaller and more obstructed by trees. An alternate start is possible at several places downstream, including the bridges at US 5 (¾ mile) or at a side road (1¼ miles). Much of the remaining distance is deadwater, as the river meanders through the Black River Wildlife Management Area. The dark-colored water shows how the river got its name. Past a final bridge (6½ miles) the river wanders through a low-lying delta and eventually emerges from a long neck of land into the South Arm of Lake Memphremagog. Deep in a cove ½ mile to the left is a launching ramp, which is accessible from a side road.

## BARTON RIVER                                       VT

The Barton River flows north into Lake Memphremagog. The valley through which it flows is one of the main routes to Canada, and it is followed all the way by a railroad and part of the way by major highways, including I-91.

### Glover–Orleans                                    9¼ mi

| | |
|---|---|
| Description: | Quickwater, Class I–II |
| Date checked: | 1983 |
| Navigable: | High water (spring) |
| Scenery: | Rural, towns |
| Maps: | USGS Lyndonville 15, Memphremagog 15 |
| Portages: | 4 mi   L   **waterfall** ¼–½ mi |
| | 8¾ mi **dam in Orleans** |

Begin on VT 16 at the first bridge north of Glover. The river there is small but navigable. The first 2¼ miles to the VT 16 bridge are Class I.

Barton is located on a broad floodplain, and the river is flat and degraded by raw sewage as it passes the town. Two and a half miles north of Barton there is a section of Class III–IV

rapids that requires scouting. Stop just before the US 5 bridge
(3¾ miles). **Caution!** Under no circumstances go under the second railroad bridge (4 miles) at the end of the rapid, because
there is an 8-foot drop. Portage part or all of this rapid on the
left along US 5 and put in at the next bridge.

Half a mile below the second US 5 bridge (4¼ miles) there is
a low, private bridge that may block the stream in high water. In
the next ½ mile to the third US 5 bridge there are several Class
II–III drops for which scouting is recommended. The last 3¾
miles of winding river to the first bridge in Orleans are Class I.

A take-out is recommended at the first bridge (8½ miles),
but if you are continuing through town, there is a dam. Additional raw sewage enters the river here. There is a bridge across
the river where the Willoughby River enters on the right (9¼
miles).

## Orleans–Newport                                        12½ mi

| | |
|---|---|
| Description: | Lake, flatwater, Class I |
| Date checked: | 1983 |
| Navigable: | Passable at most water levels |
| Scenery: | Forested |
| Map: | USGS Memphremagog 15 |

From the bridge at the confluence of the Barton and
Willoughby rivers just north of Orleans, there are no obstruc-
tions to Lake Memphremagog. The river meanders across a broad
floodplain between low hills and in 10 miles reaches South Bay.
From there it is 2½ miles to the US 5 bridge (12½ miles) in
Newport.

## CLYDE RIVER                                                VT

The Clyde River flows roughly northwest from Island Pond
to Newport on Lake Memphremagog. It offers three runnable
sections: the first two meander through farmland and small

towns, the third is a Class II run that flows away from the road between beautiful cedar-laden banks.

## Island Pond–Pensioner Pond                                    15 mi

| | |
|---|---|
| Description: | Flatwater, quickwater |
| Date checked: | 1983 |
| Navigable: | High or medium water (spring or after heavy rains) |
| Scenery: | Forested, rural, town |
| Maps: | USGS Island Pond, Memphremagog 15 |

In this first section there are lovely marshes, cedar swamps, and farmland. Trees droop their branches, and occasionally their trunks as well, into the river. Good boat control is required, and in low water this section may not be passable.

The first 2½ miles beginning at Island Pond are very obstructed with snowmobile bridges, fallen trees, rotten logs, and debris. There is a short Class II rapid.

The recommended put in (2½ miles) is near the VT 105/114 junction. A hundred yards or so northeast along VT 105/114 there are places to pull off the road, and the river is just beyond some bushes.

In ½ mile the river goes through a culvert on a side road from which there is good access downstream on the right. Soon you enter a marsh where there is little current and many side channels. There are good views of the small hills surrounding the river, but there is very little solid shoreline to the VT 105 bridge.

Past the VT 105 bridge (7½ miles) the river flows first through a cedar swamp, where there is likely to be a snowmobile bridge to lift over, and then it goes through farmland to the next bridge on a side road in East Charleston (8½ miles). There is more swamp and farmland, and another bridge, in the remaining 6 miles to Pensioner Pond (14½ miles).

It is ½ mile across Pensioner Pond to a fishing access (15 miles) at the far end on the right. It cannot be seen from a distance but is to the right of the obvious sandy beach.

## Pensioner Pond–West Charlestown                                    2½ mi

In the gorge beyond the VT 105 bridge there is an old dam.
Less than a mile further, at the far end of Lubber Lake, there
is a second dam, which diverts water to a power station. Below
the power station the river drops over ledges.

## West Charlestown–Salem Pond                                        3¼ mi

| | |
|---|---|
| Description: | Pond, **quickwater,** Class I–II |
| Date checked: | 1983 |
| Navigable: | Medium water (spring or after rain) |
| Scenery: | Forested, rural |
| Map: | USGS Memphremagog 15 |

Start at the covered bridge in West Charleston. The Class II
rapids diminish over the first ½ mile, but the river runs swiftly
all the way to Little Salem Pond. A channel on the right passes
the shallow area in the center. Access is at a bridge over the outlet from Little Salem Pond into the thoroughfare.

## Salem Pond–Clyde Pond                                              6½ mi

| | |
|---|---|
| Description: | **Pond,** Class I–II |
| Date checked: | 1983 |
| Navigable: | High to medium water (May) |
| Scenery: | Forested, wild |
| Map: | USGS Memphremagog 15 |

The thoroughfare below the bridge leads in ¹⁄₁₀ mile from Little Salem Pond into Salem Pond, with a further 1¾-mile stretch
across the pond. There is no public access at the far end.

Except for the VT 105 bridge 3 miles down the rapids, the
river stays away from the road and habitations. Its steep banks
are covered with evergreens, so the river is often in shadow. Class
II rapids start almost immediately and continue most of the way,
the most difficult section being in the vicinity of the bridge. Clyde

Pond is down another 2¾ miles of rapids. The outlet is a mile down on the northwest side, where there is a dam and a road.

## Clyde Pond–Lake Memphremagog                                    2 mi

Many paddlers will probably elect to end the trip at the Clyde Pond outlet, in view of the carries and steep running involved in the last 2 miles to Newport. With some care and finesse, however, it is possible to negotiate this section. Take out near the end of the dam. Carry past the house on the right, cross the road, and continue down a dirt road ¾ mile. If there is sufficient water, one may be able to put in at the bridge between the two powerhouses and shorten this carry. Otherwise put in again at the bridge below the lower powerhouse for the final mile to Lake Memphremagog at Newport.

# Chapter 2

# Champlain Watershed

# CHAMPLAIN WATERSHED

Hanksville
Prindle Corners
Bristol
New Haven River
Middlebury River
Vergennes
Otter Creek
Lemon Fair River
Middlebury
North Ferrisburg
Lewis Creek
Dead Creek
CHAMPLAIN
Shoreham Center
Otter Creek
Rutland
Clarendon River
Mill River
East Wallingford
North Dorset
North Rupert
Tinmouth Channel
North Pawlet
Poultney
Poultney River
Mettawee River
VT
NY

Scale in miles

0   5   10   15   20   25   30

*The rivers of the Champlain Watershed are longer and bigger than the distance of 25 miles from the main ridge of the Green Mountains would lead one to expect. Four of them have successfully pirated water from the east side of the range, making them some of the largest rivers in the area. The large watershed makes many miles of river runnable even in times of low water. Upper reaches and tributaries offer whitewater during the spring runoff.*

## MISSISQUOI RIVER                                    VT, PQ

The Missisquoi River flows westward across the top of Vermont, with a loop into Quebec, to Lake Champlain. Its course is through a beautiful valley, with views of hills and mountains. The Missisquoi was an important route to the Indians, since most of the drop is in the falls, making it easier to paddle than the Lamoille.

Many of the drops have now been harnessed for power. Roads are convenient but not unduly noticeable from the river. The entire length can be run in low water.

### North Troy–East Richford                            16 mi

| | |
|---|---|
| Description: | Flatwater, **quickwater** |
| Date checked: | 1983 |
| Navigable: | Passable at most water levels |
| Scenery: | Rural |
| Maps: | USGS Irasburg 15, Jay Peak 15 |
| | CNTS Memphremagog 31 H/1, Sutton 31 H/2 |
| Campsite: | 6 mi   R   campground |

This loop of the Missisquoi circles through Quebec as it passes through the main ridge of the Green Mountains. It is an enjoyable and popular paddle.

Report to Canadian Customs at the border on VT 105A before launching your canoe below the dam at North Troy. The river meanders leisurely and extensively to Highwater, Quebec (5¾ miles), where there is a campground on the right shore. Below that point the river is occasionally in sight of the road as it passes through farming country. Land on the left at the bridge in East Richford to report to US Customs.

## East Richford–Enosburg Falls                                    **19 mi**

| | |
|---|---|
| Description: | Flatwater, quickwater, Class I–II |
| Date checked: | 1983 |
| Navigable: | High or medium water (spring) |
| | Low water, some wading required above Richford |
| Scenery: | Forested, rural, towns |
| Map: | USGS Jay Peak 15, Enosburg Falls 15 |
| Portages: | 5¼ mi   L   **Class III rapids in Richford**— take out above factory |
| | 14 mi   L   **old dam in Samsonville** |
| | (18½ mi   L   **dam at Enosburg Falls** ½ mi) |

The river here consists mostly of pleasant riffles around islands, and much of it is close to the road. Two sections of Class II and III rapids, one in Richford and the other 2¼ miles below East Berkshire, should be avoided by inexperienced paddlers.

In the 5¼ miles to Richford there are riffles that may require some wading in low water. Below a railroad bridge (4½ miles) the river approaches Richford. Rapids begin just below a factory (5¼ miles) on the left, and just above another bridge the river becomes confined within retaining walls where it drops over ledges near an old dam site. The most difficult ledge, a Class III pitch, is below the bridge.

From Richford (6 miles) the river is mostly quickwater to the old dam at Samsonville (14 miles), which is in the process of washing out. It can be run in various places, or it can be portaged on the left. Then below it there is ¼ mile of Class II ledges.

Between Samsonville and Enosburg Falls the river is mostly smoothwater. The best way around the dam at Enosburg Falls is to take out the left under the first bridge (18½ miles). Walk up to the road along the river and follow it downstream past the second bridge about ¼ mile to a field with a gate. Go through the gate and down to the river (19 miles) to put in.

## Enosburg Falls–Highgate Falls                              18½ mi

| | |
|---|---|
| Description: | Flatwater, **quickwater, Class I–II** |
| Date checked: | 1983 |
| Navigable: | Passable at most water levels |
| Scenery: | Forested, rural |
| Maps: | USGS Enosburg Falls 15, Highgate Center |
| Portages: | 10½ mi   L   **dam at Sheldon Springs** ½ mi |
| | 17 mi   R   **ledge in Spring Rapid** |
| | (18¼ mi   L   **dam at Highgate Falls** ¼ mi) |

Although largely quickwater, this section contains several sets of rapids. Below Sheldon Springs much of it is wild and away from the road.

From below the dam at Enosburg Falls there are 5½ miles of quickwater to the North Sheldon bridge. Then there are 3 miles of Class II rapids, followed by 2 miles of quickwater and flatwater to the first dam.

At Sheldon Springs (10½ miles) take out on the left above the bridge and carry down the road past the mill on the right. Continue along the road to a crossroad and turn right. At a point 150 yards beyond a gully, leave the road, follow along the edge of the woods for 150 yards, and enter the woods at the birches below the transformer station, heading down to the river (11 miles) below the impassable cascade.

Water releases can now be made available for expert paddlers through Boise Cascade, owners of the hydropower dam. For more information, call Ray Gonda at 802-862-6164.

Below Sheldon Springs there is quickwater for 3¾ miles through woods to East Highgate (14¼ miles). Ledges start when the bridge is in sight. The abutments of an old dam are just below that bridge, and ledges of approximately Class II continue for ½ mile below it.

After East Highgate the river leaves the road again and flows through lovely woods. After a few miles there is a ledge that can be run, but just below it is another one 5 feet high (17 miles) that can be portaged on the right, but it is most easily lined on the left. This section is called Sheldon Spring Rapid because of an old mineral spring on the hill above.

In another mile the dam at Highgate Falls (18¼ miles) stands just above the old bridge. Carry on the left for ¼ mile to reach the river again (18½ miles).

### Highgate Falls–Lake Champlain                    14 mi

| | |
|---|---|
| Description: | Flatwater, quickwater |
| Date checked: | 1983 |
| Navigable: | Passable at all water levels |
| Scenery: | Forested, rural, town |
| Maps: | USGS Highgate Center, East Alburg |
| Portage: | 6½ mi   R   **dam at Swanton** |

There are no difficulties in this section except a dam at Swanton, and the river is mostly away from the road. Naturalists will enjoy the last 5¼ miles through the Missisquoi National Wildlife Refuge.

From Highgate Falls to Swanton there are 6½ miles of slow current, and in that distance you pass under I-89, US 7 (3½ miles), and an abandoned, covered railroad bridge (4¼ miles).

Below Swanton (6½ miles) the river is flat. In 2¼ miles you enter the Missisquoi National Wildlife Refuge at the entrance to Dead Creek (8¾ miles), which branches off to the right and leads in 2½ miles to Lake Champlain. The mouth of the Missisquoi has a number of islands in its delta. Once you reach Lake Champlain (14 miles), you can take out at a marina to the southwest, or you can paddle to the southeast and take out at Highgate Springs (6¼ miles).

## LAMOILLE RIVER                                    VT

The Lamoille River rises in Horse Pond north of Greensboro Bend and flows for more than 80 miles westward across northern Vermont to Lake Champlain, entering the latter north of Burlington. It was discovered by Samuel de Champlain in 1609 and put on his map as "La Mouette," the French word for gull. Either Champlain or a later engraver evidently forgot to cross his *t*'s for it eventually became "Lamoille," a meaningless but melodious name.

The river once originated a mile farther north at Long Pond, which prior to June 6, 1810, was a mile and a half long and half a mile wide. On that day about sixty people went to the pond to open an outlet to the north so that the mills on the Barton River would receive an additional supply of water. A small channel was excavated, and the water started running.

The northern barrier of the pond consisted entirely of quick-sand, except for an encrustation of clay next to the water. The quicksand was washed out, and the unsupported clay broke away. The whole pond discharged to the north within 15 minutes. The deluge advanced like a 60-foot wall of water, sweeping along livestock, barns, houses, and mills for a distance of 10 miles. A rock, estimated to weigh 100 tons, was moved half a mile. Nothing remains of the pond but its bottom, a meadow and swampy area off VT 16 called Runaway Pond, which is now in the southern headwaters of the Barton River.

## Greensboro Pond–Hardwick                                        8½

| | |
|---|---|
| Description: | Quickwater, Class **I–III** |
| Date checked: | 1988, MF |
| Navigable: | High water (April to early May) |
| Scenery: | Forested, rural, towns |
| Map: | USGS Hardwick 15 |
| Portage: | 4 mi   L   **ledges in East Hardwick** |

There is now a readable gauge under the bridge at the take-out, along Wolcott Street, VT 15. The gauge is on granite on the right and is visible from the street. It runs from 3 feet and up. Three and a half feet is runnable, 4–4½ feet is a Class III exciting run.

The town of Hardwick, after several serious ice jams, has installed two ice-retention structures to hold back the ice. These tire booms are removed as soon as the ice is gone. To find out if they have been removed, call the Hardwick Police Department at 802-472-5475. The first boom is located below the railroad bridge at approximately mile 7, just below a sharp left and ledge. The second is just above a motel at the edge of town at approximately mile 8. The lower is visible from the highway, while the upper can be seen if one walks across the field below the railroad bridge.

Begin 7 miles below the outlet of Horse Pond in Greensboro Bend at the iron bridge just off VT 16. The river at that point is about 20 feet across and quiet, but it is fast, and in the 4 miles to East Hardwick the difficulty reaches Class III. This is a nice section that has a few sharp bends to make it interesting. Close to the road about halfway down there is a pitch that must be run on the left side because of 4-foot drop. With caution it can be easily done.

Upon entering East Hardwick there is stillwater and the roar of some beautiful ledge falls that can be portaged on the left, a short carry between some houses, across a road, and down a

large path to the river. There is a bridge (4 miles) going over the
beginning of the falls.

The trip from East Hardwick is a beautiful 4½-mile Class
I–III run with some stillwater breathers. There are some
ledges and rocks in this section that make the rapids exciting.
At Hardwick, open canoes without proper flotation have to run
on the right all the way to the second bridge (8½ miles), where
the gauge is located and where there is a good parking area for
take-out.

## Hardwick–Jackson Bridge                              1½ mi

The river soon flows into Hardwick Lake, a long slim body
of water largely in the valley of Alder Creek, a tributary to the
north. The dam is at the southwest end, above the bridge. One
can start in Hardwick off VT 12B on Alder Creek at the north
end of Hardwick lake and enjoy a pleasant 2-mile paddle down
this scenic lake. Access to Hardwick Lake is also possible on
Alder Creek, 2 miles north on VT 12B.

## Jackson Bridge–Pottersville                            5 mi

| | |
|---|---|
| Description: | **Quickwater,** Class I |
| Date checked: | 1988, MF |
| Navigable: | Medium water (wet summers) |
| Scenery: | Rural, forested |
| Map: | USGS Hardwick 15 |
| Portage: | (4½ mi   L   **dam in Pottersville** 150 yd) |

The river starts again at Jackson Bridge (VT 15) at the dam at the foot of the lake. The Lamoille is still small here and flows swiftly through woods and farmland. At high water the rocks will be mostly covered, and at low water there will be more rock dodging.

The most notable landmark is the covered railroad bridge (3½ miles) with a small park to the right. This is the first ice boom location (see above). Beyond the VT 15 bridge (4 miles) there is a short rapid to the backwater from the dam. Take out the left above the dam, where a heavy-duty vehicle may be driven.

## Pottersville–Wolcott                                     1¼ mi

The ledges below the dam, which can be run by the right boat at the right water level, gradually decrease in difficulty over the next ¼ mile. Another steep drop at a washed-out dam lies above and below the VT 15 bridge (¾ mile). There is yet another ledge behind the store in Wolcott just below the bridge. All of these obstacles should be portaged individually on the left, or the whole distance can be portaged by car.

## Wolcott–Morrisville                                     10¼ mi

| | |
|---|---|
| Description: | Flatwater, **quickwater,** Class I |
| Date checked: | 1988, MF |
| Navigable: | Medium water (wet summers) |
| Scenery: | Rural, forested, towns |
| Maps: | USGS Hardwick 15, Hyde Park 15 |
| Portage: | (10¼ mi   L   **dam in Morrisville 325 yd**) |

To put in, obtain permission to cross private property in
Wolcott. A mile below town on the right bank there is a barn
with an octagonal cupola. The river flows under many small
farm bridges and some railroad bridges. The VT 15A bridge
(7¾ miles) offers good access. Below it the current gradually
slows as the river approaches the power dam below the next
bridge, VT 100. Take out as close to the red building at the
left end of the dam as safety permits. Carry down the road,
past the end of the bridge, 250 yards to the transformer station, then make a sharp reverse turn to the right. Proceed 75
yards to the river and beautiful Lake Lamoille.

## Morrisville–Johnson                                    9¾ mi

| | |
|---|---|
| Description: | Lake, **quickwater,** Class I |
| Date checked: | 1988, MF |
| Navigable: | Passable at most water levels |
| Scenery: | Forested, rural |
| Map: | USGS Hyde park 15 |
| Portages: | 1¼ mi   L   **Cady's Falls Dam** 100 yd |
| | 9¼ mi   L   **Dog's Head and Sloping Falls** 350 yd |

Put in below the dam at Morrisville at the mouth of Potash
Brook. At first there is a pleasant paddle on Lake Lamoille, the
backwater from Cady's Falls Dam (1¼ miles). Carry around the
dam on the left for 100 yards to the main road. Follow the road
across the bridge, turn left, and follow a road to an open field
where a put-in is possible. This makes for an easy carry around
the dam and ledges.

After Cady's Falls Dam (1¼ miles) there is a pleasant, 8-mile
paddle through meadows to Dog's Head Falls, a dangerous spot

that can be easily recognized by a gravel pit on the right bank. Take out on the left and carry 350 yards around both Dog's Head and Sloping Falls, two sharp drops that are separated by a pool.

One-quarter mile below the two falls you reach the Johnson bridge (9¾ miles).

## Johnson–Fairfax Falls                                                24½ mi

| | |
|---|---|
| Description: | **Quickwater,** Class I |
| Date checked: | 1988, MF |
| Navigable: | Passable at most water levels |
| Scenery: | Rural, towns |
| Maps: | USGS Hyde Park 15, Jeffersonville, Gilson Mountain |
| Portages: | 2¾ mi   L   **ledge below VT Rte. 15** (may be runnable) |
| | 3¼ mi **Ithiel Falls** (may be runnable) |
| | (24¼ mi   L   **dam at Fairfax Falls** ¼ mi) |

This is a pleasant paddle through delightful Vermont countryside. The Long Trail crosses the VT 15 bridge; just beyond there the river cuts through the Green Mountains. Farther on there are splendid views looking back to the east toward Vermont's highest mountains.

Put in ¼ mile above the Johnson bridge on the west side of the river. Immediately below it the Gihon River enters on the right. About ¼ mile below the VT 15 bridge (2½ miles) there is a ledge constriction with a 100-yard rapid going through it. This pitch can cause trouble at low water, and it can be up to Class IV in high water. About ½ mile farther is Ithiel Falls, which is also about 100 yards long and up to Class IV in high water.

Both rapids should be scouted before running for the first time.
Ithiel Falls was blasted out after the 1927 flood backed up water
into Johnson Village.

Immediately below Ithiel Falls there are huge and beautiful
granite islands, which make intricate channels that require alert
paddling. The best channel is to the left. A road follows this
whole stretch along the northern bank.

The river passes the VT 108 (11½ miles) and the VT 15
bridges (2 miles) in Jeffersonville. Then it meanders through
farmland for 12¼ miles to the bridge at Fairfax Falls (24¼
miles). Take out on the left at the bridge and portage around
the dam to the river below (24½ miles).

## Fairfax Falls–Milton                                    9¾ mi

| | |
|---|---|
| Description: | Lake, quickwater, Class I–III |
| Date checked: | 1988, MF |
| Navigable: | Passable at all water levels |
| Scenery: | Rural |
| Maps: | USGS Gilson Mountain, Milton |
| Portages: | 9¼ mi   R   **first dam in Milton** |
| | 9½ mi   L   **second dam in Milton** |

The upper part of this section is an interesting series of rapids away from the road, and the remainder is flatwater through
Arrowhead Mountain Lake.

Quickwater extends past the VT 104 bridge at Fairfax (1½
miles) to a set of rapids that begins as the river bends to the
left (3 miles). These rapids range from Class I to Class III, and
they extend nearly continuously for 2½ miles.

At the beginning of these rapids, rocks appear in the streambed
and increase in density over the next ¼ mile with a correspond-
ing increase in the velocity of the flow. The main current, which

at this section is Class I, follows the right bank about 100 yards and leads into Two Islands Rapids.

Two channels begin in another 100 yards. Very large rocks at the right bank signal a 2-foot and 3-foot drop, which are best run with care through the right channel. Two Islands Rapids are Class III in medium water, and at high water the whole set of rapids is more difficult because the rocks create big eddies.

Class I rapids continue to another 3¾-mile set of rapids that culminates at Five Chutes, a ledge that extends across the river. In another ½ mile you reach the East Georgia bridge (6 miles).

Arrowhead Mountain Lake is 3¼ miles long and shaped like a monkey wrench. Paddle west and then south to Milton (9¼ miles).

## Milton–Lake Champlain                                   8¼ mi

| | |
|---|---|
| Description: | **Flatwater, quickwater,** Class I |
| Date checked: | 1988, MF |
| Navigable: | Passable at all water levels |
| Scenery: | Forested, rural, town |
| Maps: | USGS Milton, Georgia Plains, Fort Ethan Allen |
| Portage: | 2¾ mi   L   **Peterson Dam** |

Begin at the Milton hydroelectric station. Obtain access permission on location and notify the dam operator before running below the tailrace. It is 1 mile to the I-89 bridge where the backwater of Peterson Dam begins. The remaining 1¾ miles is very isolated and scenic. Be careful in approaching the dam, and take out on the left bank past the last large ledge outcrop. It is best to portage along the power station access road to the town road unless you wish to run the 100 yards of rapids immediately below the dam.

The remaining 5¼ miles lead past West Milton (3¼ miles) and the US 2 bridge (6¼ miles), and through a wildlife refuge to Lake Champlain (8¼ miles). There is a large island at the mouth of the river, and to take out you can paddle north for 1 mile to Sand Bar State Park (9¼ miles) on US 2.

## WINOOSKI RIVER                                                      VT

The Winooski River rises in Cabot and flows westward through the Green Mountains to Lake Champlain near Burlington. Although the course circles some of the largest cities in Vermont, the banks are largely pastoral. Lovely mountain views are obtained in the middle portion. It offers 78¼ miles of paddling.

### Marshfield–Montpelier                                          24 mi

| | |
|---|---|
| Description: | Flatwater, quickwater, Class II–III |
| Date checked: | 1983 |
| Navigable: | High water (early spring) |
| Scenery: | Rural, towns |
| Maps: | USGS Plainfield 15, Barre 15 Montpelier 15 |
| Portages: | 1 mi **dam in Marshfield** |
| | 9½ mi **dam in Plainfield** |
| | 18 mi **dam below East Montpelier, three dams in Montpelier** |

The river in this section is very small, and it can be run only in high water. The 8½ miles from Marshfield to Plainfield range in difficulty from quickwater to Class II. Most of the lower part consists of short sections between dams.

The rapids below the Green Mountain Power Station above the town of Marshfield are Class II–III, and they require very high water. The US 2 bridge (1 mile) is just below the dam in Marshfield.

Access at the Twinfield Elementary School below the dam is followed by ½ mile of Class II water. Then the river meanders for several miles of mixed flatwater and small rapids to Twinfield High School, where access is available at a bridge. From the high school to the Onion River Campground, there is some Class II water. Since access is difficult near the building at the dam in Plainfield (9½ miles), take out well above it.

Below the Plainfield Dam (9½ miles) is ½ mile of Class III rapids. Then the river meanders with a good current and easy rapids past East Montpelier (16½ miles) to a dam (18 miles), which is a good place to end a trip on the upper river. Access is on the left bank off US 2.

In the next 6 miles there are three dams. Above the first one there are Class III rapids. Below it, Class II rapids diminish to flatwater above a small dam that can be portaged on either side. You reach the third dam in the center of Montpelier after passing under four bridges.

## Montpelier–Jonesville                                    22¾ mi

| Description: | Flatwater, **quickwater,** Class I–II |
|---|---|
| Date checked: | 1983 |
| Navigable: | Passable at all water levels |
| Scenery: | Rural, towns |
| Maps: | USGS Montpelier 15, Waterbury, Richmond |
| Portages: | 6 mi   L   **dam in Middlesex** 100 yd |
| | 16¼ mi   L   **Bolton Falls Dam** ½ mi |

Below Montpelier the river can be run all year. The section described here has much more quickwater with occasional rapids. The two dams are in scenic natural gorges, and the run is very attractive.

Access is at the Montpelier High School on the south bank just below the last bridge. About ¾ mile downstream from the high school, the Winooski goes under I-89 where the Dog River comes in from the left. There is another bridge 1¾ miles farther downstream. The river continues with a slow current for another 3 miles to the bridge in Middlesex. Here the river divides. Take the left channel, from which a portage can be made around the dam (6 miles).

A chute followed by a large pool lies ½ mile below the dam. With sufficient water this may cause unprepared open boats some

difficulty. There is quickwater for the next ½ mile to the mouth
of the Mad River (7 miles) on the left just above the US 2 bridge.
Below this is ½ mile of Class II rapids, where the first drop just
around a corner is the most difficult. Next the Winooski flows
through a gorge with high cliffs on both sides, and 3½ miles of
slow current bring you to the first bridge (11 miles) in Waterbury.
Just after the third Waterbury bridge, the Little River (14 miles)
enters on the right from Waterbury Reservoir.

Below the Little River in 2¼ miles is Bolton Falls Dam (6¼
miles). **Caution!** This disused dam is in a natural gorge, and it is
very dangerous to approach. Rapids start about ½ mile above
the dam where the river swings to the right. Take out on the left
at the southernmost part of the bend and carry across the field to
the railroad and the road. Take the first cart track to the right to
reach the pool below the falls.

A little way below the dam there is ¼ mile of Class II rapids above the railroad trestle (17 miles). The next 5¾ miles to
Jonesville are quickwater. The Huntington River comes in on the
left just below the bridge (22¾ miles).

## Jonesville–Essex Junction                          15½ mi

| Description: | Flatwater, **quickwater** |
| --- | --- |
| Date checked: | 1983 |
| Navigable: | Passable at all water levels |
| Scenery: | Rural |
| Maps: | USGS Richmond, Essex Junction |
| Portage: | 15½ e **dam in Essex Junction** 250 yd |

The river now leaves the mountains and follows a broad,
smooth course through farmland. It is an easy paddle.

There are 3½ miles of easy current to the bridge at Richmond
and another 2½ miles past I-89 to the US 2 bridge (6 miles).
Then you pass a railroad bridge (8 miles), the bridge at North

Williston (11 miles), another railroad bridge (13¼ miles) before reaching the power dam (15½ miles) at Essex Junction. Portage on either side. The right side, although longer, is mostly on a road.

## Essex Junction–Lake Champlain                    16 mi

| | |
|---|---|
| Description: | Flatwater, quickwater |
| Date checked: | 1983 |
| Navigable: | Passable at all water levels |
| Scenery: | Forested, urban |
| Maps: | USGS Essex Junction, Burlington, Fort Ethan Allen |
| | Colchester Point |
| Portages: | 5¾ mi   L   **dam at Winooski Gorge** |
| | 6¾ mi **dam at Winooski** |

Most of the runnable part of this run is smoothwater, but there are two difficult carries. Winooski Gorge is most easily enjoyed from the bank. In low water it is possible to visit the gorge by paddling down to it from a new access at the recreation area in Essex, then returning back upstream to take out.

After ½ mile of Class I rapids there are 4¾ miles of quickwater to Winooski Gorge, which begins behind Lime Kiln Bridge (5¼ miles). A railroad bridge ½ mile farther on preceds a dam. Take out on the left and carry up a steep bank and down the far side to the left beyond some cliffs. Below this first dam there is almost 1 mile of quickwater to the ledges above the next dam, but since there is no easy take-out above them, it is recommended the you portage both dams at one time by taking out at the launching ramp in Essex on the right bank and following the highway to Winooski. By car this portage is about 1½ miles long.

In Winooski there is access to the river below the dam. The river meanders for 6½ miles to the VT 127 bridge (13¼ miles), and in another 2¾ miles it empties into Lake Champlain (16 miles). At the mouth of the river there are cottages and a beautiful view across the lake toward the Adirondacks.

## DOG RIVER                                                    VT

This river is followed from its source in Roxbury to the Winooski River by a railroad and a main highway. Its most serious hazards are fallen trees and wire fences strung across it.

The best time to run this river is after a rainstorm in the spring before the middle of May.

### Northfield–Montpelier                                    10¼ mi

| | |
|---|---|
| Description: | Quickwater, Class I–II |
| Date checked: | 1983 |
| Navigable: | High water (April) |
| Scenery: | Rural, towns |
| Maps: | USGS Barre 15, Montpelier 15 |
| Portages: | 1¼ mi   L   **pitch by first covered bridge** 100 yd |
| | 1¾ mi **dam at Northfield Falls** |
| | 3½ mi   L   **pitch past railroad bridge** |
| | 4¼ mi **old wooden dam at Riverton** |

Put in just below the dam at Namtang Mill. There is about ½ mile of quickwater to a ledge obstruction just upstream of the concrete bridge on VT 12, from which the ledge can be seen. At the correct water level this ledge can be run with scouting.

Quickwater continues past the first covered bridge to a 6-foot pitch (1¼ miles) that requires a short carry on the left. Take out again in ¼ mile at the next covered bridge and carry along the road past the dam in Northfield Falls at the Randall Wood Products Company.

Below Northfield Falls (1¾ miles), the river is smooth for 1 mile to a high railroad bridge, past which there is a minor obstruction that can be easily run on the far left. This is closely followed by two small ledge drops that can be run at the proper water level. Scouting is recommended.

Just past the next railroad bridge (3½ miles) there is an 8-foot pitch that requires a short portage on the left. In ¼ mile there are two more ledge drops that can be run at the right water level. They too should be scouted. The remaining ¼ mile to Riverton is smooth.

The old wooden dam in Riverton (4¼ miles), which can be seen from the VT 12 bridge in Riverton, must be carried because of obstructing timbers. The next 3½ miles are smoothwater to a short Class II rapid, which begins just past the Motorcycle and Gun Shop. The first section can be run on either side, but it is best from the second section on the far right. The remaining 2½ miles to the Winooski River (10¼ miles) are smooth, with the exception of four minor ledge constrictions, each of which can be run straight through.

## MAD RIVER                                                    VT

The Mad River flows northward on the east side of the Green Mountains from Granville Notch to the Winooski River below Middlesex. It offers scenic spring whitewater runs of varying degrees of difficulty.

### Warren–Irasville                                           3¾ mi

| | |
|---|---|
| Description: | Class I–II |
| Date checked: | 1988, MF |
| Navigable: | High water (April to early May) |
| Scenery: | Forested |
| Map: | USGS Waitsfield |
| Portages: | 1½ mi   L   **ledge** 15 yd |
| | 2 mi   L   **two ledges** 100 yd |

Put in from VT 100 ⅘ mile south of the turn to the Sugarbush ski area, where the river is close to the road. Most of the distance is easy rapids, but in the first 1¼ miles to the next VT 100 bridge there are three small ledges, all of which can be run but should be scouted.

The first of the three difficult ledges is marked by a section of rock sticking up in the middle of the river, with a chute to each side. Both chutes have a sharp drop with a considerable hydraulic at the bottom; the one on the right is undercut at the bottom. The river takes a sharp right turn at this point.

The second and third ledges are immediately above and below a small bridge on a side road (2 miles). Both may be portaged by a carry of 100 yards circling the house on the left, or they can be run at the right water level.

Below the ledges the river flows easily to the next VT 100 bridge.

## Irasville–Waitsfield Picnic Area                              3¾ mi

| | |
|---|---|
| Description: | Class I–II |
| Date checked: | 1988, MF |
| Navigable: | High water (April to early May) |
| Scenery: | Forested, towns |
| Map: | USGS Waitsfield |

Begin near the VT highway garage 1¾ miles south of Waitsfield. The rapids are pleasant and easy, with no particular problems. The old dam in Waitsfield is gone; the covered bridge is passed at 1¾ miles. The picnic area 2 miles north (downstream) of town provides easy access.

## Waitsfield Picnic Area–Moretown                              4¾ mi

| | |
|---|---|
| Description: | Quickwater, Class I–II |
| Date checked: | 1988, MF |
| Navigable: | High water (April to early May) |
| Scenery: | Forested, towns |
| Maps: | USGS Waitsfield, Waterbury |
| Portage: | (4¾ mi right **gorge**) |

This section is appreciably easier than the ones above. The only difficulty is a Class II drop shortly after the start where the river abuts VT 100, then swings 90 degrees to the right and drops past a ledgy outcrop. Various routes can be taken through this pitch. It is best to scout it the first time it is run. The remaining distance is mostly quickwater.

Take out from a side road on the right ¼ mile above the VT 100B bridge. Both the landing and the carry-up at the bridge are difficult.

## Through Moretown ½ mi

The gorge directly beneath the bridge can be run in a heavy-water boat; it is Class III–IV. One should take out on the right from the pool below, since there is another gorge with a dam just below.

## Moretown–Power Dam 4¾ mi

| | |
|---|---|
| Description: | Flatwater, quickwater, Class I–II |
| Date checked: | 1988, MF |
| Navigable: | High water (April to early May) |
| Scenery: | Forested, rural |
| Map: | USGS Waterbury |
| Portages: | 2¼ mi **gauging station**—lift over |
| | (4¾ mi high dam   R   200 yd) |

Put in from a side road below the lumberyard. All the rapids are easy. The river passes the main highway again in ½ mile. The low wooden dam below the bridge on a side road can usually be run. However, in high water, when the dam is covered, a strong reversal is created and it should be avoided. Soon the river opens out into the pond, which extends nearly a mile from the dam, with several take-out options on the left.

## HUNTINGTON RIVER VT

The Huntington River is a southern tributary of the Winooski River. It flows through woods and farmland west of Camel's Hump and consists mostly of Class I–II rapids. For the first

10 miles the gradient averages 20 feet per mile, but it becomes steeper after that.

The river can be run for most of its length at high water in April. At very high water it may be run from as far south as Hanksville. At just below flood stage, it becomes a fairly big-water run with mostly large waves and a few notable holes, but without many visible rocks.

## Hanksville–Huntington Gorge                                     10½ mi

| | |
|---|---|
| Description: | Class I–II |
| Date checked: | 1988, MF |
| Navigable: | High water (April) |
| Scenery: | Forested, rural, towns |
| Map: | USGS Huntington |

Put in at the bridge that crosses the river east of the paved road in Hanksville. Just below there is a 4-foot drop that can only be run at certain water levels, and it should be scouted. Watch for fallen trees and wire fences in the 4 miles to Huntington Center. A bridge (3 miles) on the paved road south of Huntington Center also makes a good put-in.

In medium water, begin at the bridge 3½ miles farther north in Huntington (6½ miles), east from the center of town. Farther downstream the road to Richmond crosses twice (8¾ and 9¼ miles).

**Caution!** A rock wall on the right where the river bends left (10½ miles) marks the approach to Huntington Gorge, a treacherous cleft where swimmers regularly drown. There are many take-out spots on the left along the road, but be sure to obtain permission before carrying canoes or parking on the roadside strip. Although most of the road is marked NO PARKING, many of the homeowners on Dugway Road (parallel to the river above the gorge) have parking spaces and if asked may grant permission for a car or two to park for shuttle purposes. There are spectacular views from below of the falls in the gorge.

(Half a mile below this gorge is a lower gorge, which is also impassable because of a series of waterfalls. Although the river is potentially runnable for another 1½ miles below the lower gorge, it is hard to reach and first-hand reports are not available).

## LEWIS CREEK VT

Lewis Creek offers interesting paddling in attractive, rough country during the spring runoff in the latter part of March and early April. The flow varies widely with temperature, recent rain, and sunshine. If the water is right, the trip can start at the bridge on the Hinesburg–Monkton Ridge Road, or even higher up. The upper part is mostly quickwater until just before a short fall above a covered bridge south of Prindle Corners. The fall should be portaged.

### Prindle Corners–North Ferrisburg 6 mi

| | |
|---|---|
| Description: | Class I–II |
| Date checked: | 1983 |
| Navigable: | High water (April) |
| Scenery: | Forested, towns |
| Maps: | USGS Hinesburg, Mount Philo |
| Portages: | 3 mi **dam** 30 yd |
| | (6 mi   L   **waterfalls** ¼ mi) |

The usual starting point is at the covered bridge south of Prindle Corners, about 2½ miles south of Hinesburg. Easy rapids are encountered until the deadwater above the Scott Pond Dam, where a short carry must be made. This bit makes a lively Class II run through rugged country. Below the dam a ledge kicks up waves. There is a good take-out place ½ mile below, and there is another covered bridge.

After another mile there is a 4-foot ledge that should be looked over. Class I and II rapids continue on to North Ferrisburg. Shortly below a ledge by a mill site there is a waterfall. Take out on the left as soon as a house comes into view on the left bank. This point should be inspected for the best take-out before starting the trip.

## North Ferrisburg–Greenbush Road                                    2½ mi

| | |
|---|---|
| Description: | Quickwater, Class I |
| Date checked: | 1983 |
| Navigable: | Medium water |
| Scenery: | Forested, rural |
| Maps: | USGS Mount Philo, Monkton |
| Portages: | 1½ mi **ledge under bridge**—difficult |

At medium water a skillful party that wants to continue may portage the falls on the right. In this case, scout the ledge beneath the bridge in advance and make sure you can deal with it. Easy rapids continue to the US 7 bridge. Below this bridge lies an old bridge followed by another ledge. In fairly low water the ledge can be lined easily. Rapids continue halfway to the next bridge.

## Greenbush Road–Lake Champlain                                    3½ mi

| | |
|---|---|
| Description: | Flatwater |
| Date checked: | 1983 |
| Navigable: | Spring, summer, fall |
| Scenery: | Forested, rural |
| Map: | USGS Port Henry |

At high water there may still be a current, but at low water the river is slow enough to paddle upstream. Beyond the farms the marshy area widens out and is home to many birds and some beaver activity. A launching ramp provides access ¼ mile before the lake.

## OTTER CREEK                                                        VT

Otter Creek flows north from Dorset and drains a wide valley between the Green Mountains and the Taconic Range. North of Rutland it runs somewhat westward and empties into Lake

Champlain near Vergennes. At high water it provides an easy trip of just over 100 miles, but much of it can be run in medium or low water, so it is suitable for summer trips. Otter Creek is highly recommended for its pleasant paddling and its scenic views of the Green Mountains, the Taconics, and the Adirondacks in New York.

There are several dams on this river, and at many of them the current is strong right up to the edge. Take out well above all dams, especially in high water.

## North Dorset–Wallingford                                    17¾ mi

| | |
|---|---|
| Description: | **Quickwater,** Class I |
| Date checked: | 1983 |
| Navigable: | High water needed above South Wallingford (early spring) |
| | Medium water (late spring) |
| Scenery: | Forested, rural, towns |
| Map: | USGS Wallingford 15 |
| Portages: | 11½ mi   R   **Class III ledges** ½ mi |
| | 17¼ mi **Class II rapids and rock dam** |

High water is necessary in the upper part where the river is very narrow. Below South Wallingford at least medium water is necessary, and in that part the river may be obstructed by an occasional fallen tree. This whole section is mostly quickwater, except for the rapids in South Wallingford and Wallingford.

Begin in North Dorset ¾ mile north of the Emerald Lake dam by putting in from a farm road on the east side of US 7. From there to Danby it is 5¾ miles. Beaver dams and lodges are numerous. There are plenty of brushy impediments but no rapids.

Below the Mount Tabor road in Danby (5¾ miles) there are riffles over a gravel bottom. The rapids at South Wallingford (11½ miles) are Class III for ½ mile and can be easily portaged on the right along the railroad tracks.

Below South Wallingford quickwater continues to Wallingford, where there are four bridges. The first one is US 7 (16¼ miles). Class II rapids start below the second bridge, VT 140 (17¼ miles), and continue past a rock dam and under the third bridge to the fourth, where there is a ledge partially blocking the left-hand span.

## Wallingford–Rutland                                    13 mi

| | |
|---|---|
| Description: | Quickwater |
| Date checked: | 1983 |
| Navigable: | High or medium water (spring) |
| Scenery: | Rural |
| Maps: | USGS Wallingford 15, Rutland |

The winding river is still small here. There are roads on both sides of the valley, but they are hardly noticeable because of the trees that border the river.

This quickwater run has an occasional fallen tree. Begin at the fourth (last) bridge in Wallingford. In 2¾ miles the Mill River enters on the right. This is the fourth and southernmost river that cuts through the Green Mountains, and it greatly augments the flow in Otter Creek.

There is a bridge (5 miles) near Clarendon and another (9¾ miles) near North Clarendon. Take out at the River Street bridge (13 miles) in Rutland, a short distance above the first dam in that city.

## Rutland–Proctor                                    8¼ mi

| | |
|---|---|
| Description: | **Flatwater,** quickwater, Class II |
| Date checked: | 1983 |
| Navigable: | Passable at all water levels |
| Scenery: | Rural, towns |
| Maps: | USGS West Rutland, Proctor |
| Portages: | ¼ mi e **dam in Rutland** 100–400 yd |
| | 1 mi e **dam in Center Rutland**—difficult |
| | (7¾ mi   R   **dam in Proctor** ½ mi) |

The 6½ miles of flatwater in this section are set off from the rest of the river by high dams requiring long portages. Below Rutland the river is larger, and it can be run all summer.

A quarter mile below the River Street bridge, which is the first bridge in Rutland, there is a low dam that is hard to see from the river. It can be portaged on either side, and it is followed by ½ mile of Class II rapids. The current remains strong up to the dam in Center Rutland. Take out at the double bridge (1 mile). The carry up the steep bank and through the factory yards is difficult on either side.

In Center Rutland, put in at the US 4 bridge (1¼ miles) below the dam, and pass the mouth of the Clarendon River (1½ miles) on the left. From there the river flows slowly between wooded banks. Pass a railroad bridge (6¼ miles) and take out at the next bridge (7¾ miles) to portage the dam in Proctor. Carry on the right down the hill on the highway, take the first left past the sewage treatment plant, and follow the dirt tracks down to the river (8¼ miles).

## Proctor–Middlebury                                        35¾ mi

| | |
|---|---|
| Description: | Flatwater, **quickwater** |
| Date checked: | 1983 |
| Navigable: | Passable at all water levels |
| Scenery: | Rural |
| Maps: | USGS Proctor, Brandon, Sudbury, Cornwall, Middlebury |
| Portage: | (35¾ mi   L   **dam in Middlebury** ¼ mi) |

This is a beautiful paddle through farming country and under covered bridges. There are some mountain views. The river meanders through a broad valley with clear water and a sandy bottom.

In Proctor, put in at the east bank at the bottom of the hill by taking the first left past the sewage treatment plant. This trip is popular, and there are many bridges that offer access to the river. A few of them are listed here: the bridge in Florence (6¼ miles) ½ mile north of a railroad bridge; two bridges southwest of Brandon, Dean Bridge (13 miles) and Sanderson Bridge (14½ miles); the VT 73 bridge west of Brandon (18¼ miles); the bridge at Leicester Junction (21½ miles); and Threemile Bridge (32¼ miles). The latter, located next to the mouth of the Middlebury River, is the recommended take-out. It can be reached most easily from US 7 in East Middlebury by following Creek Road just to the north of the Middlebury River.

If you are continuing on to Middlebury, take out well above the VT 30/74 bridge (35¾ miles), because the dam is only about 100 feet downstream from the bridge.

## Middlebury–Weybridge                                    6 mi

| | |
|---|---|
| Description: | Flatwater, quickwater, Class II–III |
| Date checked: | 1983 |
| Navigable: | Passable at all water levels |
| Scenery: | Forested, urban |
| Map: | USGS Middlebury |
| Portages: | 1 mi   L   **second dam in Middlebury** 100 yd |
| | 3 mi   R   **Beldens Dam** ¼ mi |
| | 4¾ mi   L   **Huntington Falls Dam** ¼ mi |
| | 6 mi   L   **dam at Weybridge** 100 yd |

Three of these dams—all except Beldens Dam—are below bridges and should be portaged on the left. The banks consist of cliffs, ledges, and evergreen growth. There are rapids below the dams, and the most difficult ones are below Beldens, where there is a gorge. Below Beldens Dam after ¾ mile, the New Haven River (3¾ miles) enters on the right.

**Weybridge–Lake Champlain** 19¾ mi

| Description: | **Flatwater,** quickwater |
|---|---|
| Date checked: | 1983 |
| Navigable: | Passable at all water levels |
| Scenery: | Forested, rural |
| Maps: | USGS Middlebury, Port Henry 15 |
| Portage: | 12 mi   R   **dam in Vergennes** ½+ mi |

This section is mostly away from roads, but there are some buildings along the banks. The mouth of the river is very attractive, with views across the lake toward the Adirondacks. Below Vergennes the river is large enough for big boats, and there are many motorboats.

Put in from the end of the island below the dam at Weybridge, or ½ mile downstream on the left if you wish to avoid the faster water. The current is moderate past the mouth of the Lemon Fair River (3½ miles) to Vergennes (12 miles), where the take-out above the dam is difficult at high water. Carry on the right bank down a road.

Four miles below Vergennes, Dead Creek (16 miles) enters on the left. The best take-out is at the Fort Cassin Fishing Access, ½ mile before the mouth of the river at Lake Champlain (19¾ miles).


# MILL RIVER VT

This is a small, rural, Class II–III stream southwest of Rutland. In the spring it provides 4–6 miles of intermittent whitewater paddling beginning at East Wallingford off VT 103. See the USGS Wallingford 15 and Rutland maps.

From East Wallingford, follow the road and put in at any convenient point south of town. The best take-out is at a roadside picnic area on VT 103 north of Cuttingsville. You can paddle farther, but the road pulls away from the stream, and there are no really good places to take out. If you do continue past the picnic area take out as soon as you see the hanging bridge where the Long Trail crosses Clarendon Gorge. This gorge is definitely impassable for open boats and perhaps for closed boats as well.

## TINMOUTH CHANNEL                                        VT

South of Rutland, Tinmouth Channel flows northward through the township of Tinmouth and into Clarendon, where it becomes the Clarendon River. It empties into Otter Creek just west of Rutland. There are two runnable sections.

The first is a 5-mile section on Tinmouth Channel, which is crossed by VT 140. It can be paddled in the spring, but it is overgrown by brush.

The second section is separated from the first by a steep and unrunnable area.

### Tinmouth Channel through Tinmouth                     5¼ mi

| | |
|---|---|
| Description: | Swamp |
| Date checked: | 1983 |
| Navigable: | High to medium water |
| Scenery: | Rural |
| Map: | USGS Middletown Springs |

An athletic paddler can put in at the bridge south of VT 140 and fight through the swamp alders and beaver dams down to a bridge north of town. A less committed person can put in at the bridge north of town, paddle south as far as desired, and return. Below this bridge the river soon starts its precipitous drop.

## CLARENDON RIVER                                              VT

This is the northern (downstream) continuation of Tinmouth Channel. Most of its course is small and plunges steeply downhill, but the last few miles to Otter Creek can be paddled.

From the confluence with Ira Brook it is 4¾ miles to Otter Brook. This stretch starts as a fast Class II run. Watch for a low bridge around the first corner. Gradually the water slows down as it flows across the valley to the junction with Otter Creek just below Center Rutland. Take out at the US 4 bridge ¼ mile before the confluence, or continue down Otter Creek for 4 miles to Proctor. See USGS West Rutland.

## MIDDLEBURY RIVER                                             VT

The Middlebury River rises in Middlebury Gap and flows into Otter Creek above Middlebury.

### US 7 Bridge–Otter Creek                                    5¼ mi

| | |
|---|---|
| Description: | Flatwater, **quickwater,** Class I |
| Date checked: | 1983 |
| Navigable: | Medium water (May) |
| Scenery: | Rural |
| Maps: | USGS East Middlebury, Cornwall |

Put in at a picnic area near the US 7 bridge south of the junction with VT 125. The river winds through fields and dances over some riffles, passing under two bridges on side roads. There is good access to Otter Creek at a former bridge site, reached by following the side road that leads to the picnic area.

## NEW HAVEN RIVER                                          VT

The New Haven River rises in Lincoln Gap and flows west to Otter Creek. The upper part is scattered with unrunnable waterfalls, so the river is normally not run until just above Bristol. A frequent starting point is on Baldwin Creek.

### Baldwin Creek/Beaver Brook–Bristol                    4 mi

| | |
|---|---|
| Description: | Class I–IV |
| Date checked: | 1988, MF |
| Navigable: | High water (late April to early May) |
| Scenery: | Forested, towns |
| Map: | USGS Bristol |

Put in at the junction of Beaver Brook and Baldwin Creek. For 2 miles Baldwin Creek flows over easy rapids. The New Haven River enters from the left in the middle of a Class III rapid and soon passes under the VT 116 bridge. At the Baldwin Creek confluence, the river doubles in size.

There are steady Class II and Class II rapids for the next 1½ miles to Bristol. Here, standing above and running under a cement bridge, is a heavy, boulder-strewn Class IV or V rapid, which most paddlers will wish to portage, although a passage on the extreme right exists. This section is the hardest, with sustained technical rapids. This should always be scouted as it varies considerably with the water level. Class III–IV rapids continue through the village as the river makes a sweeping curve to the left and passes under an iron bridge.

### Bristol–New Haven Mills                               4½ mi

| | |
|---|---|
| Description: | Class I–III |
| Date checked: | 1988, MF |
| Navigable: | High water (late April) |
| | Medium water (early May) |
| Scenery: | Forested, rural |
| Map: | USGS Bristol, South Mountain |

Below the second iron bridge in Bristol the river descends in a series of rapids that decrease in difficulty. The heaviest rapids are immediately below the bridge, and you can put in a little farther down the road along the west bank. The rocks are generally small, with the river dropping over boulder bars that can generate waves in high water. Fallen trees often block the channels along the bank. After a mile the rapids moderate somewhat as they run past a bridge (2¾ miles) and nearly into Bristol Mills.

Where a white steeple becomes visible on the right, the river turns left, dropping steeply through a former mill site, which can be scouted from the bridge below. A slight pool at the bridge offers a respite before the second half of the rapids, which starts immediately below.

## New Haven Mills–Dog Team Tavern                    5¼ mi

| | |
|---|---|
| Description: | Flatwater, **quickwater,** Class I–II |
| Date checked: | 1988, MF |
| Navigable: | Medium water (mid-May or wet summers) |
| Scenery: | Rural |
| Maps: | USGS South Mountain, Middlebury |
| Portage: | (5¼ mi   L   **falls at Dog Team Tavern**) |

Below the short drop at New Haven Mills, the rapids moderate considerably; much of the distance is winding quickwater, with only an occasional rock patch or riffle. Fallen trees require more care than the rocks. A bridge is passed (4 miles), and you should take out at the next pair of bridges—look for the Dog Team Tavern's sign—since there is a small waterfall around the corner to the right.

## Dog Team Tavern–Otter Creek                    1 mi

The falls cannot be run, but the ledges below can be, at the proper water level. The ledges end around the next corner, and the gradient moderates as it approaches the confluence with

Otter Creek. There is no take-out at the confluence. Paddle down Otter Creek to the vicinity of Huntington Falls Dam for the next access.

## LEMON FAIR RIVER                                                      VT

The Lemon Fair River rises in the southeast corner of Orwell and flows north to join Otter Creek just a few miles below Weybridge. The runnable part is composed of winding channels in a flat bottomland with splendid views of nearby hills and mountains.

According to a local story, the name of the river is derived from the remark of an early traveler who had lost his horse from miring in mud or quicksand as he crossed the stream. He referred to this episode as a "lamentable affair." Another legend is that the name is an anglicized version of "Les Monts Verts."

### Richville Pond                                                       5 mi

The dam at Shoreham Center makes a pond of the Lemon Fair for 5 miles or so, offering pleasant flatwater paddling. There is a fishing access by the bridge that crosses the center of town.

### Shoreham Center–VT Rte. 74 Bridge                                    7 mi

| | |
|---|---|
| Description: | Quickwater, Class I–IV |
| Date checked: | 1983 |
| Navigable: | Medium water (late April) |
| Scenery: | Rural |
| Maps: | USGS Orwell, Bridport |

Put in ½ mile or so below the dam, where the river comes close to the road. A shallow riffle is followed by a clay rapid and finally a 3-foot rock dam. Another rapid leads into a gorge with sheer walls and over a little, washed-out dam on a 2-foot ledge. Where the gorge opens out there is a set of transverse ledges with water running in all directions, and there is another ledge above a side road bridge (4 miles). The gorge should be scouted in advance.

Rapids continue for another ¼ mile below the bridge, followed by quickwater to a rock dam a few feet high at an old abutment. The river meanders on past occasional fallen trees to the VT 74 bridge.

## VT Rte. 74–Otter Creek                                          11½ mi

| | |
|---|---|
| Description: | Flatwater, quickwater |
| Date checked: | 1983 |
| Navigable: | High to medium water (April and May) |
| Scenery: | Rural |
| Maps: | USGS Bridport, Cornwall, Middletown, Port Henry 15 |

The river flows through farmland drained by ditches along both sides. There are aquatic birds and animals in abundance. It flows under VT 125 (5¼ miles) and two bridges on back roads before reaching VT 23 (11½ miles) at the confluence with Otter Creek.

## DEAD CREEK                                                            VT

Dead Creek is a marshland stream that rises in Bridport and flows north to join Otter Creek 4 miles below Vergennes. It is as flat as a stream can be. The navigable portion extends for about 10 miles and, with adjacent land area amounting to 2,814 acres, is known as the Dead Creek Wildlife Management Area (WMA). The WMA headquarters is on VT 17, 1 mile west of Addison. It is the largest state-owned waterfowl area in Vermont and is especially recommended for all those who wish to combine bird watching and canoeing.

There are so many sloughs and potholes that it is a little difficult to follow the main channel, especially in late summer, when the weeds and rushes are at full height. There are, however, many relatively large expanses of water. The combination

makes a wonderful place for waterfowl, including ducks, bit-
terns, herons, gallinules, various shore birds, and others. Over
two hundred species of birds have been sighted here. A map and
a brochure describing the area may be obtained from the headquarters (RFD #1, Box 130, Vergennes, VT 05491).

Paddlers using the Dead Creek WMA during the spring months
(April to June) are asked to be careful not to disturb the birds
nesting along the waterways.

## Dead Creek–Otter Creek                              10 mi

| | |
|---|---|
| Description: | Flatwater, marsh |
| Date checked: | 1983 |
| Navigable: | Spring, summer, fall |
| Scenery: | Wildlife management area |
| Map: | USGS Port Henry 15 |

Dead Creek is not a flowing stream throughout the year.
The level of Lake Champlain directly influences water levels
within Dead Creek, as do periods of runoff resulting from
flooding during the remainder of the year. The main marsh
has been improved by dikes to permit flooding 1,000 acres
of cattail marsh. These dikes divide the area into three major
parts.

## South Section                                      2 mi

Access to the south section, as well as to the middle, is at the
Brilyea West and East dams, reached by a road running south
from VT 17, just west of the bridge. Access to the East Branch
is easy from the road running west from VT 22A, ¾ mile south
of Addison.

## Middle Section                                     4 mi

This section runs upstream from Stone Bridge Dam to Brilyea
West Dam 1 mile south of VT 17. The easiest approach is at
the bridge on VT 17, but approach is also possible at Stone

Bridge Dam or from the Farrell access road that leaves the country road 2¾ miles south of Panton, a few feet south of the Panton-Addison line. A permit is required to canoe this section's waterfowl refuge portion, which extends from VT 17 south to the Brilyea West Dam.

## North Section                                              4 mi

You can visit this section as a side trip from Otter Creek or you can start at the mouth of Dead Creek from the bridge on the Vergennes–Basin Harbor road. The bridge on the Vergennes-Panton road, several miles farther upstream, offers access as well. Normally one can ascend the creek only 1 mile south of this road, since the growth of reeds and rushes is very heavy in the ½ mile north of the dike (Stone Bridge Dam) that follows the line of the road running west from the East Panton School. A road has been opened to the dike from the road corner marked 125 on the USGS map. For reaching this corner, a better road is the one from the Vergennes-Panton road directly south across the Holcombe Slang.

## POULTNEY RIVER                                         VT, NY

The Poultney River rises in Tinmouth, Vermont, and flows west to Poultney, where it turns north and becomes the boundary between Vermont and New York for the rest of its circuitous route to the East Bay of Lake Champlain. The upper reaches through the Taconic Range are too rough to canoe, but from Poultney down there is much easy paddling interspersed with difficult or impossible ledges. Much of this section may be run in the summer, although the rapids may have to be carried.

## Hampton, NY–US Rte. 4 Bridge                          9½ mi

| | |
|---|---|
| Description: | **Quickwater,** Class I |
| Date checked: | 1983 |
| Navigable: | High to medium water |
| Scenery: | Forested, rural |
| Maps: | USGS Poultney, Thorn Hill |
| Difficulties: | Three low ledges |

Put in at the old slate mill, below the dam and gorge. The water is greenish and fairly clear. The stream is shallow and rocky in medium water, with the usual overhanging trees and occasional blockages. Animal tracks abound on the banks.

Below the NY 22A bridge (4 miles) there are three ledges: the first is 3 feet high, the others only half that. All can be run, lined, or lifted over. It is probably best to stay on the right.

There is a high ledge that is practically impossible to run immediately below the bridge.

## US Rte. 4 Bridge–Carver Falls Dam                    4½ mi

This is a ledge-lover's paradise, perhaps better suited to fishing and swimming than to canoeing. The ledges are of various heights, and some are difficult or impossible to run. They are interspersed with easier rapids, although jagged blocks in runnable rapids may tend to damage the boat. Before embarking be sure to inspect the ledge immediately underneath the railroad bridge that can be seen below from the US 4 bridge.

Just above the West Street bridge the Castleton River enters on the right. The Castleton adds considerably to the flow in summer months if the Lake Bomoseen hydroelectric plant is operating.

Below the West Street bridge (1 mile) the ledges become relatively more runnable, although the river runs into a deep gorge that makes portages difficult. Over the last mile the rapids moderate and run over a shallow spot, by an old abutment, to flowage from the Carver Falls dam. Take out on the far left.

The Carver Falls Cave is found by following the portage trail down the left bank into the gorge. The cave is at the head of the second little stream coming in from the left, which is a ½-mile walk.

## Carver Falls–Lake Champlain                    **12 mi**

| | |
|---|---|
| Description: | ¼ mi of Class II rapids in gorge at start, **flat-water,** quickwater |
| Date checked: | 1983 |
| Navigable: | Spring, summer, fall (dam controlled) |
| Scenery: | Rural |
| Maps: | USGS Thorn Hill, Benson, Whitehall |

During the summer this section may be difficult if the Carver Falls Station is not operating, because no water is then allowed to flow downstream. Check with the Central Vermont Public Service Company in Rutland.

Carver Falls is accessible by car only from the New York side. From Fair Haven, Vermont, take West Street 2 miles to a bridge over the Poultney River. Take the first road on the right, in ¼ mile, and another right at the sign for the dam.

The gorge below the dam is impressive, but the rapids are short. If you choose to avoid them, an old woods road goes down to the river at the lower end of the gorge. It starts between the toolsheds behind the engineer's house. It is not passable for cars, but canoes may be carried down.

The water is somewhat opaque, but the banks are high, rocky in some places, and the area is known for its wildflowers. The current slows very gradually. Below a side-road bridge (3½ miles) a four-wheel-drive road follows imperceptibly along the right bank. The bridge at the Elbow (12 miles) provides good access. You can also continue to the confluence with Wood Creek, ½ mile farther downstream, and bear right into Lake Champlain or bear left and paddle a mile up the creek to Whitehall, New York.

## METTAWEE RIVER                                          VT

The river rises on the west slope of Dorset Mountain and passes, as a small brook, under VT 30, where it might be possible to start at high water.

### North Rupert–North Pawlet                          9 mi

| | |
|---|---|
| Description: | Class I–II |
| Date checked: | 1983 |
| Navigable: | Medium water |
| Scenery: | Rural |
| Map: | USGS Pawlet 15 |
| Hazards: | Many barbed wire fences that are hard to see and barely clear a canoe at medium water |
| Portage: | (9 mi   R   **waterfall**) |

Put in at the VT 30 bridge 1 mile north of North Rupert. The stream is about 15 feet wide and runs through pastureland. Downed trees and old barbed wire fences are the worst problems; the current and rocks are easy. In Pawlet, Flower Brook joins the river and doubles its size. This section runs through attractive, high, wooded banks. After a mile the river returns to pastureland and after another 2 miles reaches a steel bridge. The bridge is on a road that is the first left off VT 30 north of Pawlet. Another 1 mile may be run to the next bridge at VT 153. **Caution!** The river drops 25 feet through a narrow cleft just beyond.

### North Pawlet–New York State barge canal          about 35 mi

Most this distance is quickwater through farmland, but there are many waterfalls and ledges. The first is Button Falls, 2 miles downstream of the previous take-out.

# Chapter 3

# Hudson
# Watershed

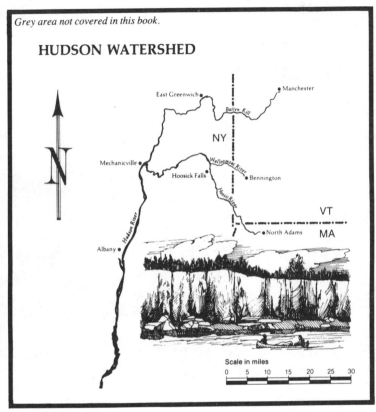

*Grey area not covered in this book.*

## HUDSON WATERSHED

Scale in miles
0    5    10    15    20    25    30

## BATTEN KILL                                          VT, NY

The Batten Kill is a beautiful, clear stream that flows west across southern Vermont, from the Green Mountains to the Hudson River. The water is also enjoyable for swimming. It has a moderate current with riffles, and there are only two places, which are fairly close together and in the first section, where a less skillful paddler might wish to line or carry.

## Manchester–Arlington 10½mi

| | |
|---|---|
| Description: | **Flatwater, quickwater,** Class I–II |
| Date checked: | 1988, FB |
| Navigable: | High or medium water (spring and normal summers) |
| Scenery: | Rural |
| Map: | USGS Equinox 15 |

To put in, take the road east of the monument on US 7 in Manchester, and follow it for ¾ mile to a bridge. At the beginning the river is small and shallow. If there is enough water to run the rapid below the bridge, the river is runnable, but some fallen trees will have to be lined or lifted over.

It is 2¾ miles to the first bridge; below that the Batten Kill is generally slower and deeper. There is flatwater, along with a few riffles. The river flows through farming country, much of which is posted. There is good access to the river on the right bank just downstream of the US 7A bridge (8 miles).

Just before the Roaring Branch, a large stream that enters the Batten Kill on the left, there is a sizable though not permanent logjam on the left. At high water levels, this might be difficult to navigate.

After a mile of flatwater, and just below the mouth of Roaring Branch, there is a strong, fast current, with Class II rapids in high water, where the river swings left and is divided into two channels by a big rock. If you wish to line or carry this spot, do so on the right.

Easy rapids continue past the VT 313 bridge (9¾ miles), which also provides good parking upstream on the left. **Caution!** Just beyond the VT 313 bridge is another bridge that has a loose tie rod hanging down into the water. The river takes a sharp turn to the right ½ mile below, where there is a pool followed by a washed-out dam that can be scouted from the right bank if desired. Shortly beyond is the Rochester bridge (10½ miles), located off VT 313 just west of Arlington.

### Arlington–East Greenwich                                    **20 mi**

| | |
|---|---|
| Description: | Quickwater, Class I |
| Date checked: | 1988, FB |
| Navigable: | Passable at most water levels |
| Scenery: | Forested, rural, towns |
| Maps: | USGS Equinox 15, Shushan, Salem, Cossayuna |

The river here is a little wider, and it runs quickly and steadily, giving a fast ride through easy riffles. Except when it is very dry, it can be run all summer, and there are occasional deep pools for swimming. The stretch is also very popular for float trips on rubber rafts, inner tubes, air mattresses, logs, and anything else that will float.

Bridges cross the river every couple of miles, from any one of which there is access to the river.

In 3 miles you pass the mouth of the Green River near West Arlington, and 4½ miles farther is the NY 313 bridge (7½ miles). To improve the fishing on the Batten Kill, the state of New York has built several rock cribs and a low, sometimes runnable weir. The latter extends across the river above the County 61 bridge (8¾ miles), which is the first NY 313 bridge, near a store called the Tackle Box.

After several miles the river swings north, passes Shushan (13¾ miles), goes under four railroad bridges and NY 22 (17¾ miles), and then heads right again. Go under another railroad bridge near East Greenwich, and take out on the right above the dam (20 miles).

### HOOSIC RIVER                                           MA, VT, NY

The Hoosic River rises in Lanesboro, Massachusetts, flows north to North Adams, where it turns west to Williamstown, and then takes off northwesterly across a corner of Vermont into New York, where it again turns north to make a big loop to meet the Hudson River near Mechanicsville. The pollution from the mills in Adams and North Adams has been reduced, but the Hoosic is still far from the beautiful stream known to the Mohawks.

The upper part of the river offers little paddling because the flood control works in Adams and North Adams have channeled the river between vertical concrete walls. Although it might look like a fun run, paddling in the flood control area is not only illegal, it is also suicidal, since several dams are confined between the high retaining walls, which allow no chance of escape.

## North Adams, MA–North Pownal, VT                                    15 mi

| | |
|---|---|
| Description: | **Quickwater,** Class I, II |
| Date checked: | 1983 |
| Navigable: | Medium water |
| Scenery: | Towns, rural, forested |
| Maps: | North Adams, Williams, Williamstown, MA; Pownal, North Pownal, VT |
| Portage: | (11¼ mi   R   **dam in North Pownal** ¼ mi) |

Put in below the last dam at the west end of North Adams, just west of the Protection Road bridge. The most convenient place is the old sewage treatment plant on the north side.

Most of the distance is smooth, with only occasional rapids of moderate difficulty and stretches of quieter water between them. Two bridges, close together, are passed in a little more than a mile; at 3 miles the bridge that carries the Appalachian Trail; at 4½ miles the US 7 bridge at Williamstown; at 6¼ miles the Massachusetts/Vermont state line; and at 9 miles the bridge at Pownal.

The dam at North Pownal is confined between cliffs and walls, so it should be scouted in advance. You can carry up the road on either side; neither is easy. By the time you can see the factory chimney from the river, you may be past the best take-out.

## North Pownal–Hoosick Falls                                    **15 mi**

This is a pleasant run through farming country, with high hills on either side of the valley. There are a few easy riffles. On approaching Hoosick Falls, take out on the left just before the railroad bridge. **Caution!** Under no circumstances go below the railroad bridge, because the steep rapid beneath it is followed by rapids confined by two concrete retaining walls, which lead into impassable cataracts below. There is no convenient place to put in below these falls, and the power dam 1 mile below involves another carry, so it is better to portage by car 2 miles to Hoosick Junction.

## WALLOOMSAC RIVER                                          **VT, NY**

The Walloomsac flows west from Bennington to the Hoosic River. It provides a delightful paddle through beautiful and historic terrain. The river riffles over gravel beds and around fallen trees, sometimes near the road or railroad, sometimes in more remote areas. It is best run in the spring, because some stretches may be too shallow in the summer.

## Bennington–Walloomsac Village                            **8¾ mi**

| | |
|---|---|
| Description: | Flatwater, Class **I** |
| Date checked: | 1988, FB |
| Navigable: | High or medium water (spring or after moderate rain) |
| Scenery: | Rural, towns |
| Maps: | USGS Bennington, Hoosick Falls |
| Portages: | 1¼ mi **dam at Paper Mill Village**—carry on island |
| | 2¼ mi   L   **dam** 30 yd |

Begin a couple of miles west of Bennington off VT 67A by following Silk Road across the covered bridge. Put in where the road comes close to the river opposite a white house.

Winding over riffles and passing under the covered bridge, the stream becomes flat as it reaches the first dam at Paper Mill Village in 1¼ miles. The dam is under the second covered bridge, which is no longer in use. The stream divides here. Take out before the iron bridge and carry on the left, crossing Murphy Road, following a path.

There is some Class II water for a short distance below the first dam (1¼ miles). The next dam, 1 mile farther, is slightly above the Henry Bridge and is not easily spotted. A white colonial house on the left across an open field is a good landmark. Carry on the left. After about 2¼ miles more of pleasant riffles, the hamlet of Sodom is reached. Here there is a tiny dam or obstruction entirely across the river. This may be readily run at high water, but it may have to be carried at lower water levels.

About 4 miles below Sodom (4½ miles), the dam at the Columbia Products factory is reached. The riffles are almost continuous in the last ½ mile, and the dam (8¾ miles) appears suddenly around a bend to the right. The tall smokestack is very conspicuous, however; observe caution as soon as it comes into view. Boats may be taken out on the left and carried uphill through a farm field to the road.

It is possible to relaunch well below the dam and rapids, but there is only about 1 mile to the next dam (10 miles) at the Flomatic Valve Company on the right (look for a tall brick chimney), where getting out is difficult. Carrying around it is even harder. There is no good take-out point below here, unless you continue down the Hoosic below the mouth of the Walloomsac (11¾ miles).

# Chapter 4

# Upper Connecticut Watershed

# UPPER CONNECTICUT WATERSHED

Canada

VT

Halls Stream

Indian Stream

Canaan

West
Stewartstown

Pittsburg

Lake Francis

East Brighton

Colebrook

Nulhegan R.

Connecticut River

Mohawk River

North
Stratford

Passumpsic River

St. Johnsbury

Moose River

Victory

Nash Stream

Groveton

Phillips Brook

Connecticut River

Moore
Reservoir

Lancaster

W. Branch

West Milan

Israel River

Ammonoosuc

River

Woodsville

Ammonoosuc

Franconia

Gale River

Jefferson

Upper Ammonoosuc R.

Ham Branch

Twin Mt.

Bretton Woods

Scale in miles

0    5    10    15    20    25    30

*The hilly and mountainous terrain of the Upper Connecticut Watershed causes rainfall and snowmelt to run off fairly fast, so quickwater and rapids dominate the rivers in this region. Most of these rivers are not very big, and they collect the drainage from a small area. There are some very nice flatwater sections, but they tend to be broken up by quickwater and rapids, so that long summer trips are generally impossible.*

*The Connecticut River always has sufficient water for passage, but much of it consists of long, thin lakes behind high dams.*

*There are water releases on a few of the rivers. Most widely known in the one on the West River which the Army Corps of Engineers schedules for a weekend early in the fall. Annual fall drawdowns of headwater lakes occur on the Mascoma and Sugar rivers.*

## CONNECTICUT RIVER                                    NH,VT

The Connecticut is New England's longest river. Like many other New England rivers it is most attractive near its source and gradually becomes more sluggish, industrialized, and polluted farther downstream. Paddling on the lower river is popular, however, and it can be done in summer.

From the upper end of First Connecticut Lake, the river offers about 400 miles of varied lake and river paddling, with few unrunnable sections but with fifteen dams that require carries of different lengths.

The Connecticut River Watershed Council, 125 Combs Rd., Easthampton, MA 01027, publishes a guidebook, *The Complete Boating Guide to the Connecticut River* ($9.95), with maps showing the fishing, sailing, boating, and water sports areas.

### The Connecticut Lakes

| Maps: | USGS Second Lake 15, Indian Stream 15 |
|---|---|

From its source at Fourth Lake, the Connecticut is a tiny trout brook to Third Lake. From Third Lake to Second Lake, it is still too small and steep to paddle, and from Second to First Lake, paddling is not advised. Some paddlers do run this stretch, but great care should be taken because there is a tremendous drop halfway down which must be carried. This drop is about ½ mile below the Second Lake dam and about 50 yards below at a left turn in the river. Although both Second and Third lakes offer pleasant paddling, fishing, swimming, and other water sports, paddlers who wish to run the river will probably start at the head of First Lake. A side road leading from US 3 to Mettaluk Point offers easy access to that end of the lake. There is a launching area at the foot of the lake near the dam. Below First Lake the stream becomes runnable for the first time, but since the level of First Lake is controlled by a dam, water is likely to be insufficient unless some is being released to generate power. Releases are posted daily at the dam. Below the dam the river is very rough and steep for 1 mile, then easier rapids follow for ½ mile to the entrance of Perry Stream to the right. These easy rapids continue another 1 mile to Lake Francis, but under some water conditions this entire stretch can offer hard rapids, and the last 150 yards should be examined in advance. Lake Francis is an artificial lake over what was formerly a less attractive stretch of river that flowed through farmland. Below the Lake Francis dam there is rapid water to the bridge and dam at Pittsburg, where you must take out. **Caution!** Take out above the dam; there is an impassable gorge for 1½ miles below to a covered bridge. It is possible to line down this gorge in low water, but if a car is available, carrying will be much easier and you *must* carry at medium or high water.

## Pittsburg–West Stewartstown/Canaan                    9¼ mi

| | |
|---|---|
| Description: | Quickwater, Class I–II |
| Date checked: | 1988, AY |
| Navigable: | Passable at most water levels |
| Scenery: | Forested, rural, towns |
| Maps: | USGS Indian Stream 15, Averill 15, Dixville 15 |
| Portage: | 9 mi   R   **Canaan Dam** ½ mi |
| | 2 mi   R   **Indian Stream** |
| Campsites: | 28½ mi   L   Countryside Campgrounds |

The upper Connecticut River will probably disappoint would-be wilderness trippers. The solitude that can be found here is all too meager when you consider the long drive from the population centers of New England and the more isolated areas that are available not much farther to the east. Nonetheless, an outing on this section can certainly be pleasant, although the river, throughout even the uppermost parts, is bucolic, not wild.

Begin at the covered bridge on Bacon Road just off US 3 and 9/10 miles south of Pittsburg. There is also a small parking area here that cannot be seen from the main highway.

Starting immediately under the bridge, there are 150 yards of Class II rapids in high water. Then in the next 2 miles the Connecticut has intermittent Class I+ rapids. The highway, US 3, follows the river, almost constantly within sight, on the right with an attractive, forested area rising on the left. Two miles beyond Indian Stream (2½ miles), which enters on the right, US 3 (4½ miles) passes over the river, and below this point there are 350 yards of Class II rips. The boundary marker between New Hampshire and Vermont is ½ mile farther and south of this point.

In another 2¼ miles, Halls Stream (7½ miles) enters on the right, and shortly after passing under a bridge with houses visible on each bank, you reach Beecher Falls (8 miles). The falls are a short Class II rapid that may be run at any point, although passage on the extreme left or right is probably drier and safer.

Canaan Dam lies 1 mile below Beecher Falls, and the easiest portage is on the Vermont side. In high water, more experienced boaters who are willing to do some scrambling over the large wooden sluice pipe on the right bank can put in again almost immediately below the dam. This river should be taken to the right of the islands after the dam, but the going is scratchy in high water and probably impassable in low. A longer portage of ½ mile on the right is the more conventional route around the dam.

After a level stretch there is a short, solid Class III drop before the NH/VT 114 bridge at West Stewartstown/Canaan (9½ miles).

## West Stewartstown/Canaan–
### North Stratford/Bloomfield                               24½ mi

| | |
|---|---|
| Description: | **Quickwater,** Class I–II |
| Date checked: | 1988, AY |
| Navigable: | Spring, summer, fall |
| Scenery: | Rural |
| Map: | USGS Averill 15 |

For the 10 miles from West Stewartstown/Canaan to Colebrook, the river is mostly smooth and relatively shallow, except for a 100-yard Class I–II rapid ½ mile below the bridge. The river meanders through level pastureland, which borders both sides. Dairy cattle graze along the banks for most of this section, reason enough to bring along fresh water if you plan to camp. At Colebrook the river passes below Mount Monadnock, which rises steeply on the Vermont side.

Below Colebrook (10¼ miles) the river is quick for 3 miles; then it develops small rips for another 2 miles. It is mostly smooth for 4 miles below the Columbia covered bridge to Countryside Campgrounds on the left (19¼ miles). The river should be taken on the right through small riffles.

Two and a half miles below Countryside Campgrounds are the remains of Lyman Falls Dam (22 miles). The river has several islands on the left, and close to the right bank there is a log crib. The dam is immediately below; the abutment is not very visible, and paddlers are often washed over this dam by mistake. Keep to the right on a wide, sweeping turn.

**Caution!** The remains of Lyman Dam should be scouted, but for moderately skilled whitewater paddlers it probably provides the most sport on the Connecticut to this point. In high water the best run over the old dam is directly below the log crib that lies 75 yards upstream. The small curler below the dam can provide some very interesting spots for paddlers to play and surf. In higher water it should be approached cautiously, but the curler should not present a problem to a strong Class II boater. Even so, it is probably best not to engage in too much play at this point unless you are prepared for a swim. The dam is in the process of washing out, and conditions change after every storm, so scout carefully.

There are riffles for the next 2¾ miles to North Stratford/ Bloomfield (24½ miles).

## North Stratford–Guildhall                              25 mi

| | |
|---|---|
| Description: | Flatwater, **quickwater** |
| Date checked: | 1988, AY |
| Navigable: | Spring, summer, fall |
| Scenery: | Forested, rural |
| Maps: | USGS Averill 15, Guildhall 15 |

The river meanders, placid and wide, from here to the dam at Guildhall. It is 5 miles to Stratford Center, opposite where Paul Stream comes in on the Vermont side, and another 6 miles to the bridge at Stratford. It is then 11 miles on a flat river plain with fine views of the mountains to the confluence with the Upper Ammonoosuc River at Groveton. Only 3 miles farther is the bridge at Guildhall.

## Guildhall–Gilman                                       23 mi

| | |
|---|---|
| Description: | Flatwater, quickwater |
| Date checked: | 1988, AY |
| Navigable: | Spring, summer, fall |
| Scenery: | Forested, rural |
| Maps: | USGS Guildhall 15, Whitefield 15 |
| Portage: | (23 mi   L   **Gilman Dam**) |

The placid water continues for the next 23 miles to the dam at Gilman. It is 10 miles to Lancaster, another 7 miles of winding river to the bridge at South Lancaster, and another 3 miles to the next bridge at South Lunenburg. About ¼ mile below the railroad bridge is a Class II rapid. From there it is only 3 miles more to the dam and bridge at Gilman. Take out on the New Hampshire side at the end of the boom above the dam.

## Gilman–East Ryegate                                          **30 mi**

| | |
|---|---|
| Description: | **Flatwater, quickwater,** Class I |
| Date checked: | 1988, AY |
| Navigable: | Spring, summer, fall |
| Scenery: | Forested, rural, towns |
| Maps: | USGS Whitefield 15, Littletown 15, St. Johnsbury 15, Woodsville 15 |
| Portages: | 11¼ mi   R   **Moore Dam** ½ mi |
| | 18¾ mi   L   **Comerford Dam** ½ mi |
| | 25½ mi   L   **McIndoe Falls Dam** 200 yd |
| | 30 mi   L   **East Ryegate Dam** 100 ft–300 yd |

The beautiful Fifteen-Mile Falls section of the river formerly began at Gilman. These fine rapids, the best on the river, are now completely inundated by the Moore Reservoir and the Comerford Reservoir, although when the former is low there is still ¼–½ mile or more of fast water with rocks and boulders. The New England Power Company, which operates these two dams and the McIndoe Falls Dam, has provided a number of boat-launching and picnic areas on the reservoirs, but no overnight camping is allowed at these points. The paddler can put in at Gilman on the Vermont side just below the bridge. From here to Moore Dam it is 12 miles. This stretch is mostly lake travel on the reservoir, although when the water level is low there may be ½ mile or more of easy rapids. Take care, however, if the water volume is great, since the waves can be high. Once you reach the reservoir the going is very pleasant, but a headwind can make progress a strenuous affair. It is therefore usually best to start this section early in the morning before the wind rises. There are three boat-launching and picnic areas on the south shore of the reservoir and one on the north bank in Waterford near the dam. The carry at the Moore Dam is on the Vermont side, about ½ mile long and well marked by signs. The bank at the put-in is somewhat unstable, so care should be taken.

Since the backwater from the Comerford Dam reaches practically to the Moore Dam, the 7 miles between the two are almost all lake paddling. This is a boat-launching and picnic area just below the VT 18 bridge on the New Hampshire side and another on the Vermont side not far from the dam. The carry at the Comerford Dam is on the New Hampshire side, about ½ mile long and marked by signs.

The 7 miles from the Comerford Dam to the McIndoe Falls Dam can be very interesting. If the Comerford Dam is discharging water, the current will be swift and paddling easy. There are, though, some large boulders about 1 mile below the dam which present a hazard to navigation. In another mile, the Passumpsic River enters on the right and the river turns to a southerly course. The next 5 miles are through a narrow, wooded valley, with high hills on either side most of the way. The portage at the McIndoe Falls Dam, on the New Hampshire side, is easy, about 200 yards long, and well marked.

The narrow, wooded valley continues for the next 4 miles to the Ryegate Paper Company's dam at East Ryegate. The 15-foot-high dam should be approached with caution, since water often spills over the top. It is just below a left bend in the river and, because the carry is on the New Hampshire side, it is best to approach it along the left bank. Several portage routes are available, varying from a few feet if the current is slow, to several hundred yards if the current is too fast to approach the dam closely. There is no car take-out above the dam, and access is poor below.

**East Ryegate–Hanover**                                              **51 mi**

| | |
|---|---|
| Description: | Flatwater, quickwater, Class I–II |
| Date checked: | 1988, AY |
| Navigable: | Spring, summer, fall |
| Scenery: | Forested, rural, settled, towns |
| Maps: | USGS Woodsville 15, Mount Cube 15, Mascoma 15, Hanover |

This is one of the more interesting and picturesque sections of the river and one on which there is a certain amount of boating, especially in the lower portion. Below the dam at East Ryegate there is some fast water, and the best channel is usually on the New Hampshire side. It is 4 miles to Wells River/Woodsville, where the Ammonoosuc River enters on the left and, ¼ mile below, the Wells River enters on the right just below the US 302 and railroad bridges. There is a short but easy rip just below these bridges, then 10 miles of shallow, winding river to the bridge at Newbury, where there is a launching ramp on the right bank. It is another mile to South Newbury. The valley has now become wider, with farmland on the level areas, and mountain views in the background. The current begins to slacken near the red barn on the right at Placey Farm as the river reaches water backed up by the Wilder Dam 37 miles below. This section is now known as Wilder Lake and is provided with boat-launching ramps and picnic areas.

There is little perceptible widening of the river for many miles. It is 6 miles to Bradford, and the entrance to the Waits River on the right bank. Bradford is easiest to visit by paddling up the Waits River. In another mile the paddler passes under the VT 25 bridge and in 10 more miles under the bridge from Fairlee to Orford. Here it was that Samuel Morey tested his steam-propelled vessel in 1792–93. At Orford, New Hampshire, there is a municipal boat-launching area where camping is possible with the permission of the selectmen. There is a campground on the New Hampshire side ¼ mile below the bridge. It is then 6 miles to a former bridge abutment still visible in the middle of

the river at North Thetford and 2 miles more to the one at East
Thetford. At this point the river is obviously becoming wider. In
5 miles you pass the mouth of the Ompompanoosuc River on the
right and in another 5 miles the bridge at Hanover, below which
only 2 miles remain to the dam in Wilder.

## Hanover–Bellows Falls                                          46 mi

| | |
|---|---|
| Description: | Flatwater, **quickwater,** Class II |
| Date checked: | 1988, AY |
| Navigable: | Spring, summer, fall |
| Scenery: | Forested, rural, towns |
| Maps: | USGS Hanover, North Hartland, Claremont |
| | 15, Bellows Falls 15 |
| Portages: | 2 mi   L   **Wilder Dam** ¼ mi |
| | 11 mi   R   **Hartland Rapids** ¼ mi |
| | (46 mi   L   **Bellows Falls** i mi) |

It is 2 miles down Wilder Lake to the dam, which should be carried on the east side, where the ¼-mile portage is well marked by
signs. New England Power runs a visitors' center (802-295-3192)
at the dam which has exhibits on the new fish ladder. Below the
dam the water level can vary quite suddenly if the generators are
started or stopped. The water is swift but shallow for 2 miles
to White River Junction and the mouth of the White River on
the right. Osprey, ducks, eagles, and beaver have been spotted
in this more isolated section, as well as the Atlantic salmon,
which is making a comeback. One mile below the White River
confluence, the Mascoma River enters on the New Hampshire
side practically at the I-89 bridge. About 4 miles below that, at
North Hartland, the Ottauquechee River comes in on the Vermont side. It is then only 2 miles to the difficult and dangerous
Sumner Falls, and the two signs that read DANGER—FALLS
AHEAD should be taken very seriously by even the most experienced boater. Also known as the Hartland Rapids, this area is
notorious for sudden changes in wind speed and, more important, water volume. Water releases occur without warning, and
this area literally washes through moments after the dam gates

have opened, and many fishermen and boaters have been caught by surprise. At the actual approach of the rapid, the river narrows, and a wooded bank on the right juts out, cutting off any view of the rapids below, although you should hear the roar of the water by this point. **Caution!** These rapids should not be attempted, at any water level. Portage on the right, on a marked path that is ¼ mile long, ending at the picnic area at the foot of the rapid. At low water expert paddlers might run these rapids, but they should check in at the Wilder Dam beforehand to check the release schedule. Below the dam are many play areas for boaters to practice surfing and other techniques; again, paddlers should be aware of changes in water level.

At this time the entire river flows through two channels. The channel nearer the west bank, about 15 feet wide, has a drop too abrupt for loaded canoes. The other channel, near the center of the river, is 30 feet wide but narrows to only 7 feet at the bottom of the initial pitch, where some large rocks must be avoided. Once through this pitch, you can ride the haystacks for 75 yards until a 180-degree right turn brings the boat into the western chute with only choppy water to the bottom of the rapid.

Below the rapids it is 8 miles to the covered bridge at Windsor and then another 5 miles to the NH 103 bridge at Ascutney. Just below the bridge the Sugar River enters on the left, and Wilgus State Park offers camping areas on the Vermont shore. This whole stretch of the river passes through fine hills, with Mount Ascutney dominating the view. Below is an 8-mile stretch of river around the Weathersfield Bow, then the Little Sugar River enters on the left at North Charlestown. There follow 4 miles more of easy paddling down to the Cheshire Toll Bridge at Charlestown, just below which the Black River enters on the right. In 7 more miles you pass the mouth of the Williams River on the right, where there is a boat-launching and picnic area. Then after 3 miles of deadwater, the dam at Bellows Falls requires a long portage, ½–¾ mile, right through the town. Either side of the river can be used, but the easier route is probably on the east bank. Be aware that ongoing major construction projects on this side continue, and portaging may be difficult. Take out on the left at a PORTAGE sign on a barn, and carry on the New Hampshire side to a put-in below the falls. A carry by car is strongly advised, because traffic is heavy and there is no shoulder.

### Bellows Falls–Vernon Dam                                    31¾ mi

| | |
|---|---|
| Description: | Flatwater, quickwater |
| Date checked: | 1988, AY |
| Navigable: | Spring, summer, fall |
| Scenery: | Forested, rural towns |
| Maps: | USGS Bellows Falls 15, Keene 15, Brattleboro 15 |
| Portage: | (31¾ mi   R   **Vernon Dam** ¼ mi) |

Below the powerhouse at Bellows Falls the paddler passes the mouth of the Saxtons River in ½ mile on the right bank, in another ¼ mile the Cold River on the left bank, and then in 2 miles more the bridge at Walpole. There are then 14 miles of unobstructed river through open farming country to the NH 9 bridge above Brattleboro. In 1 mile the river reaches the NH 119 bridge. From the island with a bridge on either side at Brattleboro, there are 7 miles of deadwater to the dam at Vernon, which requires a ¼-mile carry on the west shore from the log boom above the dam. Signs mark the portage. The Vermont Yankee Nuclear Power Plant is directly adjacent to the dam, and it has an Energy Information Center that can be visited during normal working hours (802-257-1416).

### Vernon Dam–Turners Falls                                    20 mi

| | |
|---|---|
| Description: | Flatwater, quickwater, Class I–II |
| Date checked: | 1988, AY |
| Navigable: | Spring, summer, fall |
| Scenery: | Forested, rural, settled, towns |
| Maps: | USGS Brattleboro 15, Keene 15, Northfield, Millers Falls, Greenfield |
| Portage: | (20 mi   R   **Turners Falls**) |

Below the dam the going is swift and rocky if the water is low. It is only 2 miles to the mouth of the Ashuelot River in Hinsdale, and in another 3½ miles the Connecticut crosses the Massachusetts border. All through here, and for the next 10 miles to the gorge at French King, the river flows in open farmland, which offers good camping spots.

In 1½ miles from the border the river reaches the MA 142 bridge. From there it is 8½ miles to the gorge, at the upper end of which there is a large rock, which creates turbulence even when the rest of the river is calm. A route close to either shore is preferred at this point. Here the current quickens, and the river turns right, under the French King Bridge at the confluence with the Millers River, and continues heavy to Turners Falls, 4 miles away. At high water this section of river can become extremely rough, and under these conditions some paddlers may prefer to take out at the bridge that crosses the Millers River at its mouth. At Turners Falls, take out at the steel bridge ¼ mile above the dam on the right side.

## INDIAN STREAM                                                          NH

This is the northernmost runnable stream in New Hampshire; it rises even farther north than the Connecticut River, into which it flows below Pittsburg. The river is formed by several branches joining near the former Depot Camp, an early logging headquarters so remote that it was supplied from the railroad in Malvina, Quebec.

Nearly the entire watershed is timberland owned by the Saint Regis Paper Company. The only habitations are occasional hunting camps and some farms in the valley adjacent to the Connecticut River. A gravel logging road leads up to the east bank from US 3 beyond Depot Camp, and a branch road connects to Back Lake.

The entire watershed lies within the town of Pittsburg. Although the region was claimed by both the United States and Canada, each exercised only sporadic jurisdiction. In 1836 the settlers formed the Indian Stream Republic. This led to an

immediate settlement of the boundary, and brought an end to
the dispute and to the republic.

## Depot Camp–Connecticut River                                    17 mi

| | |
|---|---|
| Description: | Flatwater, quickwater, Class I |
| Date checked: | 1983 |
| Navigable: | High water (May) |
| Scenery: | Forested, rural |
| Map: | USGS Indian Stream 15 |

Put in by carrying to the river near Depot Camp or by coming
down one of the branches if the water is high enough. There are a
few easy rapids, then a long, meandering stretch with weaker current. The road is frequently nearby. The last 2½ miles to Camp
Brook contain more rapids.

Camp Brook is about ½ mile north of the Indian Stream and
Back Lake roads. The river is close to the road, and there is an
old, unusable bridge. South of this point the road does not follow the stream. It is 2½ miles to the site of the Kim Day Dam
(10½ miles).

Below the old dam site (10½ miles) there is a ledge at the
head of an island, followed by 200 yards of Class II–III rapids, which can be portaged on an old road on the left. Then there
are about 3 miles of Class I rapids through woods. The last 3½
miles to the Connecticut River, broad and meandering through
fields, are passable in the summer. The US 3 bridge is ¼ mile
above the Connecticut (17 miles).

## HALLS STREAM                                    PQ, NH, VT

Halls Stream is one of the northernmost rivers in New Hampshire. The runnable portion of it was once the boundary between
Quebec and New Hampshire, but as a result of channel changes
the river now meanders back and forth across the border. Most
of the river is a pleasant run of easy rapids with a gravel bottom.
Fallen trees cause occasional problems.

Access to the upper river is best from the Canadian side, where
gravel roads lead close to it in two places. There is a public road

on the New Hampshire side along the lower river, and with four-wheel-drive vehicles it may be possible to reach the upper river via logging roads along Halls Stream or from Indian Stream.

The CNTS Malvina 21 E/3 map is best for the upper river since it shows the Canadian access. The USGS Indian Stream sheet is adequate for the lower river, but is shows only the US side of the border. The CNTS Coaticook 21 E/4 and Averill maps show the last mile, including the take-out.

## Malvina Stream–Tabor Notch                                          9 mi

| | |
|---|---|
| Description: | Class I–II |
| Date checked: | 1983 |
| Navigable: | High water (April and May) |
| Scenery: | Forested, rural |
| Maps: | USGS Indian Stream 15, Averill 15 |
| | CNTS Malvina 21 E/3, Coaticook 21 E/4 |

The key to Candian access is the village of Paquette (Saint Venant-de-Hereford), which is located about 10 miles north of Beecher Falls on PQ 253. Take the gravel road north out of the village up a long hill. After 5½ miles, go down a steep hill and turn right. Proceed ¾ mile to a bridge over Malvina Stream. Put in here or 1 mile downstream at a farm. If the water is too low, Halls Stream is probably too low as well.

Malvina Stream is a gravelly Class I stream about a boat-length wide. Roughly ½ mile from the farm the stream passes an old railroad embankment and enters Halls Stream. The latter is mostly Class I, but occasionally there are harder spots. One rocky drop adjacent to the old railroad embankment should be looked over. The banks are mostly wooded.

Five and a half miles from Malvina Stream a large farm on the Canadian shore provides access. It is reached by taking the road east from Paquette for 1 mile.

In another 3 miles there is a farm (9 miles) on the New Hampshire shore and a gravel road adjacent to the river. This is at the foot of Tabor Notch, a deep pass on the New Hampshire side which has no road through it.

Access is also possible elsewhere on the lower river from the Canadian side where PQ 253 comes close to the river.

## Tabor Notch–Connecticut River                        9½ mi

| | |
|---|---|
| Description: | Quickwater, Class I |
| Date checked: | 1983 |
| Navigable: | High water (spring and after moderate rains) |
| Scenery: | Rural, town |
| Maps: | USGS Indian Stream 15, Averill 15 |

To put in on the New Hampshire side, follow the road up the east bank for 7 miles to a location adajacent to the river, after which the road ascends for ½ mile and enters at a farm.

There are occasional riffles and fallen trees. From time to time there is access on the New Hampshire shore. In 9 miles the international boundary runs west from the stream, which from that point flows through Vermont. Another ½ mile brings you to the bridge at Beechers Falls and, just below, the Connecticut River (9½ miles).

## MOHAWK RIVER                                          NH

The Mohawk rises in Dixville Notch and flows west to the Connecticut River at Colebrook. It is almost continuously rapid, with a decreasing gradient.

## Kidderville–Connecticut River                          8 mi

| | |
|---|---|
| Description: | Class II–III |
| Date checked: | 1983 |
| Navigable: | High water (early May) |
| Scenery: | Forested, towns |
| Map: | USGS Dixville 15 |

Put in on the Mohawk River in Kidderville from Diamond Pond Road just below the junction of two brooks and a dam. The first mile is almost continuous Class III ledges around blind corners. All are runnable somewhere but may require scouting. Below the NH 26 bridge (1 mile) there are only a couple of additional ledges, and then it is riffly Class II going with beautiful evergreen banks all the way to Colebrook and the NH 26 and US 3 bridges (7 miles). The confluence with the Connecticut is another easy mile, and the next access if the bridge over the Connecticut ½ mile downstream.

## NULHEGAN RIVER                                              VT

The Nulhegan River and its numerous tributaries drain an extensive area of swamps, wooded hills, and mountains east of Island Pond, in the least inhabited part of Vermont. The main river rises in Brighton just east of Island Pond and flows through high but swampy country.

Although the river is close to the road and a railroad, little is seen of them. The view is mostly alders, birds, and an occasional distant mountain.

### Nulhegan Pond–VT Rte. 105 Bridge                        5 mi

| | |
|---|---|
| Description: | Quickwater, swamp |
| Date checked: | 1983 |
| Navigable: | Medium water |
| Scenery: | Wild |
| Map: | USGS Island Pond 15 |

Confirmed swamp-lovers can put in at the outlet of Nulhegan Pond, or at the inlet at the previous bridge, and paddle through the pond. The river's span is barely a canoe-width, and that is somewhat obstructed. The worst part can be avoided by putting in at a side stream about 1 mile down.

### VT Rte. 105 Bridge–Gorge                               3¼ mi

The next 3 miles are similar to those above, but the river is larger and offers easier going. A paddler who really wants to run the entire river can manage to take out on the right above the gorge to VT 105, or on either side to carry for ¼ mile (neither side is very good). It may also be possible to run or line the gorge. The railroad crosses at the top of the drop, but the rapids start above it.

## Gorge–"Stone Dam"                                    3 mi

The gorge can just be seen from the end of a private road, but access is poor. Easy rapids continue below the gorge and soon become quickwater as they approach the Stone Dam at the next VT 105 bridge.

## "Stone Dam"–East Branch                            1¾ mi

There is no dam at the bridge, but Class III–IV rapids start promptly and continue for 1 mile with one drop that is often portaged on the right. The rapids ease off to the confluence with the East Branch (no access).

## East Branch–Connecticut River                       2½ mi

This section can be run by putting in at the East Branch bridge ½ mile above the confluence or at a gate on the logging road on the right bank another mile up the East Branch. The run down the East Branch is Class II. The going is easier on the Nulhegan until the 1/2 mile of rapids that leads to the Connecticut River. Access is at the Nulhegan bridge just above the Connecticut.

## UPPER AMMONOOSUC RIVER                              NH

The Upper Ammonoosuc River drains the Kilkenny region of the White Mountains, flowing north and then west to the Connecticut River at Groveton. It has no connection with the Ammonoosuc or Wild Ammonoosuc rivers farther south.

## West Branch–York Pond Road                              2 mi

---

Take the road to the York Pond Fish Hatchery from NH 110.
Continue on the road for approximately 5 miles, take a left, and
go ½ mile to a bridge. This is the West Branch of the Upper
Ammonoosuc, a short and frisky run that can only be accom-
plished in the spring. It is a very small stream, only 20 feet wide,
and it drops 40 feet in the first ½ mile. Tight eddy turns are possible. The small size of the stream keeps the rating at Class III,
and the small size requires alertness and excellent boat control.
The first mile drops 100 feet, and a long Class III builds up to
a Class IV stretch where the river narrows and drops—watch
for rock walls on the sides—which culminates in a difficult 5-
foot drop best run right center. The river then approaches the
York Pond Road on the right bank, where you can take out for
a rest and put in to continue the run. If the West Branch is high,
the main river will be very high. This run will be up when the
Nash Stream is not.

## York Pond Road–West Milan                             6 mi

---

| | |
|---|---|
| Description: | Quickwater, **Class II** |
| Date checked: | 1983 |
| Navigable: | High water (late April and May) |
| Scenery: | Forested |
| Maps: | USGS Percy 15 |

---

Put in where the York Pond Road crosses the river. The rapids at the bridge are a good indication of what the rest of the
run is like. In high water the river is a wavy Class II; it is rocky
at lower levels.

It is 4 miles to Higgins Brook where there is a Class III rapid
that should be scouted. There is a rock ledge on the left and a
short sandbank on the right. The first drop is a ledge around a
sharp right turn, followed by a rocky rapid in a right turn.

There are more Class II rapids for 1¼ miles to a side road bridge (5¼ miles). Below this bridge there is ¾ mile of quickwater and riffles to the mouth of Pond Brook, near the bridge at West Milan (6 miles).

## West Milan–Groveton                                    17¼ mi

| | |
|---|---|
| Description: | Flatwater, quickwater, Class I–II |
| Date checked: | 1983 |
| Navigable: | High or medium water (late April and May) |
| Scenery: | Rural, towns |
| Maps: | USGS Percy 15, Guildhall 15 |

This stretch of the river begins with over 9 miles of smoothwater. The NH 100 bridge is reached in 1¼ miles and Crystal Bridge in another 2¼ miles, with the mouth of Phillips Brook a short distance below. It is 1½ miles to the Bell Hill Road bridge (5 miles) and another 2¼ miles to the bridge at Percy (7¼ miles). Then there are almost 2 miles of smoothwater, followed by a 1-mile Class II boulder patch that is often too low to run. The latter ends at a covered bridge in Stark, one of the most photographed bridges in the state.

Below Stark (10 miles) are 4½ miles of quickwater and riffles to the mouth of Nash Stream, then ¼ mile of Class II water to the bridge on Emerson Road (14¾ miles). Then it is 2½ miles to the first dam in Groveton (17¼ miles), which is the usual take-out.

## Groveton–Connecticut River                             3¾ mi

There were once four dams in the 1¼ miles through Groveton. For 2½ miles below the town, the river meanders to the Connecticut River.

## PHILLIPS BROOK                                            NH

Phillips Brook flows into the Upper Ammonoosuc River from the north, 3¾ miles downstream from West Milan. It is smaller than Nash Stream to the west.

Above Paris there are 2½ miles of winding brook, followed by 3 miles of rapids, but the only access is by a private International Paper Company road that is usually closed during the paddling season.

It is a 4-mile run from the nearby abandoned settlement of Paris to the Upper Ammonoosuc River. A 50-yard portage around a cascade in Paris is followed by ¾ mile of shallow Class II–III rapids. Then the brook meanders through swamps and fields with a good current for ¾ mile to the Bell Hill Road bridge. It is then another 1½ miles to Crystal Bridge, where you must portage around the spectacular cascade that terminates in a 6-foot-wide, undercut slit beneath the bridge. This is followed by ¾ mile of Class II–III rapids that run to the Upper Ammonoosuc. See the USGS Percy 15 map.

## NASH STREAM                                                        NH

This small mountain stream, once noted for its log drives, flows south from Nash Bog Pond in Odell to the Upper Ammonoosuc River below Stark. It drains a large, forested area that is undeveloped except around what used to be the pond. Floods in May 1969 washed out the dam at Nash Bog Pond, leaving only a large marsh.

A private Groveton Paper Company road follows the river, but it is usually closed during the paddling season. The river flows for 9 miles from the pond to the Upper Ammonoosuc, with an average gradient of 75 feet per mile. It is recommended that the river be scouted carefully before it is run.

Nash Stream has been run for 3½ miles from Benchmark 1368 to the gate near Benchmark 1061 (USGS Percy 15). There is a mile of quickwater to an old, runnable log dam, then Class IV rapids with multiple channels. Choose the ones where the water drops first. Because of the tight, rocky drops, short closed boats are recommended. Very high water is necessary, but the clarity of the water makes the water level appear lower than it actually is.

## ISRAEL RIVER                                                        NH

The Israel River originates on the slopes of Mount Jefferson in the Presidential Range. It flows northwest to the Connecticut River near Lancaster. Called Sinoogawnock by the Indians, it was renamed for Israel Glines, a hunter who frequented the area before its settlement.

The upper portion is a pleasant Class I run, while below Riverton there are Class II–III rapids. There are occasional views of the Presidential range if you look back upstream.

### Jefferson–Riverton                                             6 mi

| | |
|---|---|
| Description: | Quickwater, Class **I** |
| Date checked: | 1983 |
| Navigable: | High and medium water (May) |
| Scenery: | Forested, rural |
| Maps: | USGS Mount Washington 15, Whitefield 15 |

Put in at the NH 115A bridge 2½ miles south of Jefferson Village. The river is a small stream flowing through cultivated land with large trees along the banks. There are some Class I rapids and a few fine swimming holes. It is 2½ miles to a side road bridge and another 3½ miles to the US 2 bridge in Riverton.

### Riverton–Lancaster                                             5 mi

| | |
|---|---|
| Description: | Quickwater, Class **II**–III |
| Date checked: | 1983 |
| Navigable: | High and medium water (May) |
| Scenery: | Forested, rural, towns |
| Map: | USGS Whitefield 15 |
| Portages: | 9½ mi **ice control dam** |
| | 11 mi **dam below Lancaster** |

Class II rapids start below Riverton, followed by a mile of smooth water. Beyond the mouth of Otter Brook (3½ miles) various types of dams and ice nets have been installed to prevent flooding in Lancaster. Be alert for the net of the year. There is also an old dam that is washing out and can probably be run.

Beyond the railroad bridge the rapids become more difficult; the most difficult Class III drops lie beyond a right turn and above the covered bridge (4¾ miles). Rapids continue under the US 2 and 3 bridge, just below which is a low dam that paddlers usually run. Access is on the right below the dam.

## Lancaster–Connecticut River                                     1¾ mi

Below the dam in Lancaster the rapids slack off, and the river meanders across the flats to the Connecticut. Take-out near the confluence is difficult.

## PASSUMPSIC RIVER                                                    VT

The Passumpsic River rises from the height-of-land south of Lake Willoughby and flows south into the Connecticut River. The main river forms at the junction of the East and West branches near Lyndonville.

The Passumpsic River has suffered in the past from industrial pollution and consequent bad press in earlier canoeing guides. It does have an excess number of dams, but it is an attractive river in a rural area. You can run the Passumpsic when the water is too low to run most other rivers, and you will also find the dams easier to deal with at low water.

## Lyndonville–Connecticut River                    22¼ mi

---

Description:      Flatwater, quickwater, some rapids, Class II
Date checked:     1983
Navigable:        Anytime, but low water is best
Scenery:          Forested, rural, towns
Maps:             USGS Burke 15, Lyndonville 15, St.
                     Johnsbury
Portages:         5¼ mi   R   **dam**—lift over 10 yd
                  6 mi   R   **dam** ¼ mi
                  7¼ mi   R   **dam**—lift over 25 yd
                  8¼ mi **ledge**
                  10¼ mi **ledge**
                  13 mi **island at dam at St. Johnsbury** 50 yd
                  15 mi   L   **dam** 50 yd
                  17 mi   R   **dam at Passumpsic** 100 yd
                  21½ mi   L   **dam at Barnet** 50 yd
Note:             Portage distance given for low water; high or
                     medium water will greatly increase difficulty
                     and change take-out locations.

---

Put in near the highway garage at the VT 114 bridge north of
Lyndonville and just below the confluence of the East and West
branches. The river meanders down the valley over a sand or
gravel bed, with occasional deep pools. In a few places, old cars
have been used to stabilize the banks.

The US 5 bridge and the covered bridge immediately below it
are passed at ³/4 mile. Then comes the VT 122 bridge (2¹/2 miles)
and US 5 again (4¹/2 miles). Take out here at a side road on the
left to avoid a series of three dams in impressive gorges.

One can put in from a side road bridge adjacent to US 5 (8 miles). On the loop to the left away from the highway there is a 3-foot ledge. Below the US 5 bridge at St. Johnsbury Center, an island can be seen from the road. It had a ledge on each side (10¼ miles); the right may be easier.

When the water is medium or high, take out in the vicinity of the next US 5 bridge, above St. Johnsbury, since the Concord Avenue bridge has no access. The dam immediately below the Concord Avenue bridge can be portaged on the island when the dam is not spilling.

Pleasant Class I rapids run through town past the confluence of the Moose River on the left. The river gradually slows to the backwater of the next dam, which can be dropped on the left.

The river is quickwater to the dam at Passumpsic, which always spills. An easy portage starts under the bridge, then through the power station parking lot. In the next 2½ miles there are four ledges. The first one, under the railroad bridge within sight of the dam, is the most difficult and can be lined if desired. The others are easily run. The third is immediately below the confluence on the right where Water Andric drops over a scenic waterfall framed by the arch of a railroad bridge. This section of the river is very lovely.

The old Barnet dam is washing out and should be checked. Portage on the left over ledges. The river makes a big S through a scenic gorge with no difficult water and then fans out into the delta at the confluence with the Connecticut.

## WEST BRANCH, PASSUMPSIC RIVER                    VT

The West Branch rises in Westmore below the height-of-land at the south end of Lake Willoughby and flows south to join the East Branch northeast of Lyndonville. It offers a pleasant, easy run.

## Calendar Brook–Confluence                                    3½ mi

| | |
|---|---|
| Description: | Quickwater, Class I |
| Date checked: | 1983 |
| Navigable: | High water (early May) |
| Scenery: | Forested |
| Maps: | USGS Burke 15, Lyndonville 15 |

Put in at the bridge over Calendar Brook, which flows immediately into the West Branch. Fallen trees provide the only difficulty.

It is easier to put in at the bridge a mile farther up on Calendar Brook, if desired.

## EAST BRANCH, PASSUMPSIC RIVER                              VT

The East Branch rises in Newark and flows south to join the West Branch northeast of Lyndonville. In high water, you can probably put in farther up than the section described below. We have no description available, but the rapids appear to be Class II.

## East Burke–Confluence                                     4¹/2 mi

| | |
|---|---|
| Description: | Class II |
| Date checked: | 1983 |
| Navigable: | High water (early May) |
| Scenery: | Forested |
| Maps: | USGS Burke 15, Lyndonville 15 |

Put in immediately below the dam at East Burke to run the easy ledge below, or put in from the road below the ledge. The rapids are continuous Class II with no pools. The gradient eases as the river approaches the confluence.

Take out at the VT 114 bridge ¼ mile below the West Branch junction.

## MOOSE RIVER                                          VT

The Moose River rises in the sparsely settled area of northeastern Vermont and flows south to the Passumpsic River in St. Johnsbury. Quiet marshes alternate with exciting rapids. Although close, the roads are not obtrusive.

### Bridge on dirt road–Bog Brook                        3¾ mi

| | |
|---|---|
| Description: | Quickwater, Class I |
| Date checked: | 1988, MF |
| Navigable: | High water |
| Scenery: | Wild |
| Map: | USGS Burke 15 |

The Moose River below Gallup Mills flows through some small gorges and over ledges. The description starts at the bridge more than a mile south of Gallup Mills on the dirt road that follows the left bank.

A Class III rapid continues under the bridge. Put in wherever you desire. The intensity decrases rapidly, and the remainder is Class I nearly to the bridge over Bog Brook, which is adjacent to the river on the right.

Bog Brook offers a mile or so of padding through a marsh, but the bridge is too low to paddle under when the water is high enough to paddle the river.

### Bog Brook–snowmobile bridge                          2¼ mi

| | |
|---|---|
| Description: | Flatwater, quickwater |
| Date checked: | 1988, MF |
| Navigable: | Spring, summer, fall |
| Scenery: | Marsh |
| Map: | USGS Burke 15 |
| Portage: | (2¼ mi **water drops into Class III–IV gorge)** |

The paddle through the marsh is pleasant; the snowmobile trail is visible from the dirt road along the right bank. This is the Victory Bog Wildlife Management Area.

## Snowmobile bridge–US 2 Rte. Bridge                    5½ mi

| | |
|---|---|
| Description: | Quickwater, Class I, **II**, III, IV |
| Date checked: | 1988, MF |
| Navigable: | High water, medium water (April to early May) |
| Scenery: | Forested |
| Maps: | USGS Burke 15, Miles Pond |

There is a gauge just below the snowmobile bridge on the left. It is often missed since it lies in the middle of a rapid. The first part of the gorge can be Class IV in high water, but after ¼ mile the difficulty diminishes to and is mostly Class II. There are three difficult ledges not far above the Victory bridge. The first one is out of sight around a blind corner to the left and can be scouted from the road. The next two are more straightforward. All three may be run best to the left.

Below the bridge in Victory (3½ miles) there is a short difficult section. Then the rapids ease to Class I for a while, and finally almost to flatwater. Take out on a dirt road ¼ mile down from Victory Brook on the right.

## US Rte. 2 Bridge–East St. Johnsbury                    7 mi

| | |
|---|---|
| Description: | Quickwater, Class I–II |
| Date checked: | 1988, MF |
| Navigable: | High water |
| Scenery: | Rural, towns |
| Maps: | USGS Miles Pond, Concord, VT |
| Portages: | (7 mi **gorge**) |

Rapids start again ¼ mile below the bridge and continue on past the bridge in Concord (2¼ miles). Then another quiet section starts, almost in medium water, and continues past an abutment (5 miles). A few rapids pick up approaching the bridge on a side road in East St. Johnsbury. Take out well above the bridge to avoid a high ledge under the railroad bridge immediately downstream.

## East St. Johnsbury–The Mills                                    3¼ mi

| | |
|---|---|
| Description: | Class II |
| Date checked: | 1988, MF |
| Navigable: | High to medium water |
| Scenery: | Settled, towns |
| Maps: | USGS Concord, VT, St. Johnsbury 15 |

In East St. Johnsbury there is an impassable drop under the railroad bridge; lining is necessary. The lower section of the river is not so attractive, because the valley is settled and the railroad and highway follow the river. The river from the East St. Johnsbury railroad bridge to ½ mile above the railroad bridge in St. Johnsbury is continuous Class II rapids. The section is delightful: there are many locations for practicing eddy turns, ferrying, and other techniques.

Above the mills in St. Johnsbury, all paddlers should pull out except those with covered boats or those who are expert open boaters.

## St. Johnsbury–Passumpsic River                                  1½ mi

There are several Class IV drops that require scouting and intricate maneuvering. Strong crosscurrents and fairly large haystacks are added obstacles. **Caution!** Beyond the two bridges (railroad and highway) and after the mills, all boats must take out on the right, because there is an impassable drop hidden around the next corner.

## WELLS RIVER                                          VT

The Wells River flows into the Connecticut opposite Woodsville, New Hampshire. It is paralleled by US 302, which is occasionally visible from the river.

Above the section described here the Wells is a small, steep brook, and below it is a series of falls and ledges that most people consider a scenic attraction rather than a paddling possibility.

### Groton–snowmobile bridge                          9½ mi

| | |
|---|---|
| Description: | Flatwater, quickwater, Class II–III |
| Date checked: | 1983 |
| Navigable: | High water (April and May) |
| Scenery: | Forested, rural, towns |
| Map: | USGS Woodsville 15 |
| Portages: | 7 mi   L   **dam in Boltonville** |
| | 7¼ mi   L   **gorge below Boltonville** |

Put in from a side road ⅓ mile east of the Groton Bridge and just below an old dam. Following ½ mile of Class II rapids, the river is mostly slow current with a few riffles as it meanders through pastureland. There are old railroad pilings in South Ryegate which tend to accumulate debris.

Below South Ryegate (4 miles) Class II rapids extend for 1½ miles. After that there is a series of four ledges visible from a side road on the left bank. The last one is past an old abutment. Another drop, obstructed with old granite blocks, starts just below an old US 302 bridge. Then the current slows down, and the river meanders the remaining distance to Boltonville.

Just below the bridge in Boltonville (7 miles), there is a 50-foot dam and cascade that must be portaged on the left. Put in below the old power station, now a summer cottage. One-quarter mile of rapids leads to the head of a small gorge, where there is a 4-foot waterfall, best carried on the left. The ledges continue through the gorge, and you should scout then while you portage the falls.

Below the high I-91 bridge (7¾ miles) the river becomes slow and meandering, with a sandy bottom, for 1¾ miles. Take out on the right where the river first approaches US 302 (9½ miles) at the major snowmobile bridge in the area.

## Snowmobile bridge–Connecticut River                    2½ mi

Below the first access to US 302 the Wells River drops over a series of ledges ranging from 3 to 15 feet high. Most are unrunnable. After the ledges the river reaches a small millpond with a dam. There is another mile of ledges to the Connecticut River.

## AMMONOOSUC RIVER                                          NH

The Ammonoosuc River, one of the largest rivers in New Hampshire north of the White Mountains, flows from the western slopes of Mount Washington to the Connecticut River in Woodsville. It offers some of the finest whitewater paddling in New England. This river is famous for a strong upstream wind, and even in rapids it may be necessary to paddle hard to progress downstream.

## Bretton Woods–Twin Mountain                            7 mi

Scouted only:   See the USGS Mount Washington 15 and
                Littleton maps.

Begin at the junction with Clinton Brook near the Bretton Woods church. The water is smooth but fast for 3½ miles to Lower Ammonoosuc Falls, a 30-foot cascade.

The next 3 miles after the falls contain several rapids that are normally impassable. The last is ½ mile east of Twin Mountain. Then there are moderate Class III rapids to Twin Mountain where there is an especially rocky drop above the US 3 bridge (7 miles).

## Twin Mountain–Littleton                                    16 mi

| | |
|---|---|
| Description: | Quickwater, Class **II–IV** |
| Date checked: | 1988, BL |
| Navigable: | High water (late April to end of May) |
| Scenery: | Forested, rural, towns |
| Map: | USGS Whitefield 15 |
| Portages: | 7½ mi e **Maplewood Dam** 100 yd |
| | (16 mi **dam at Littleton**) |

Put in at the US 3 bridge (or ½ mile above town off US 302). Below the bridge there are Class II rapids with small waves at high levels and lots of rocks to dodge at low water levels. It is 3 miles to the River Bend Motel, where the road leaves the river and the difficulty of the rapids increases to Class III. At high water levels the boater should hug the shore to avoid the large waves in the center, and when the water is lower, fast maneuvering is required.

It is 2¾ miles from the motel to the steel truss Pierce Bridge on US 302 (5¾ miles), which is preceded by a rocky patch that gives trouble at lower water levels. Most of this run is away from the road, but one of the more difficult sets of rapids called Boatbreaker can be inspected by driving east along the road on the south bank and looking upstream from the gauging station. This is a Class III rapid that should be scouted from the bank. Run left of center.

The first 1½ miles from Pierce Bridge to Maplewood Dam contain easier Class II rapids that lead to the Maplewood Dam backwater. It is possible to take out on the right at this point to avoid the dam and the gorge. Otherwise, paddle ¼ mile of deadwater to the abandoned 15-foot dam and portage on either side for 100 yards. The gorge below contains Class IV rapids, the most difficult usually run on this river. The hardest rapid begins

100 yards below the dam, and there is another difficult one adjacent to the old powerhouse. It is ¾ mile from the dam to the NH·142 bridge in Maplewood.

Below Maplewood (8¼ miles) the rapids begin as Class III and gradually get easier. It is 1¾ miles to the Wing Road bridge, followed by 2¼ miles of Class II rapids to Hatch Brook (12¼ miles), where you can see a small, pink house on the right bank and hear some rapids ahead. **Caution!** A short distance below is the Class IV Alderbrook Rapid. At high water those who wish to avoid large waves can run down among the rocks on the right, while at lower levels the best channel starts near the left bank and moves in an S shape to the center. Scouting either route is advisable.

It is ½ mile from the end of Alderbrook Rapid to the significant rapid, a series of rocky Class III drops adjacent to the railroad tracks which is best run near the right bank. Then there is 1 mile of easier rapids past a railroad bridge to a convenient take-out on the old road on the right bank (14 miles). Then there are 2 miles of quickwater to the 40-foot Littleton dam (16 miles), which spills water over the top.

## Littleton–Lisbon                                                    13 mi

| | |
|---|---|
| Description: | Class I–II |
| Date checked: | 1988, BL |
| Navigable: | High water (late April to end of May) |
| Scenery: | Rural, towns |
| Maps: | USGS Whitefield 15, Littleton, Sugar Hill, Lisbon |
| Portages: | 1¾ mi  L  **unrunnable ledges** |
| | (13 mi  R  **dam in Lisbon** ¼ mi) |

Put in below the dam or at the Redington Road bridge ¼ mile beyond. There are 1½ miles of Class II rapids to the center of town, where there is a girder bridge on US 302. Below it there is a series of granite ledges that are normally unrunnable and can be most easily lined or carried on the left. Below the ledges there is a short Class III rapid, followed by ½ mile of Class II rapids to Bridge Street (2½ miles), which is an alternate put-in for those who wish to avoid the ledges.

The remainder of the run to Lisbon is unusual in that different routes in a rapid vary from Class I to Class III in difficulty, and skilled paddlers can choose between thrills and a dry boat. It is 4½ miles to a bridge on a side road and then another ¼ mile to the Gale River, which enters on the left under a railroad bridge.

The mouth of the Gale River (7¼ miles) marks the beginning of a particularly heavy rapid that is ½ mile long. In another ½ mile a yellow house on the right bank marks a ledge that extends across the river at an island, but this ledge can be run in several places. In another 2 miles you reach a US 302 bridge (10¼ miles). The last major rapid is just below it; then there are 2¾ miles of Class I rapids to Lisbon (13 miles). Take out well above the bridge on the right, because there is a dam just before it.

## Lisbon–Woodsville                                    11½ mi

| | |
|---|---|
| Description: | **Quickwater,** Class I |
| Date checked: | 1988, BL |
| Navigable: | High or medium water (April and May) |
| Scenery: | Rural, towns |
| Maps: | USGS Lisbon, Woodsville 15 |
| Portages: | 6¾ mi   R   **dam at Bath** 200 yd |
| | (11½ mi **dam at Woodsville**) |

Put in on the right at a ballfield ¼ mile below the bridge. There is a fast current with occasional standing-wave rapids for 6½ miles to Bath. Take out above the covered bridge on the right and carry 200 yards to a cove below the dam. There is a mile of fast current with one rapid to the mouth of the Wild

Ammonoosuc River (7¾ miles), which is followed in ¼ mile by a railroad bridge.

Below the railroad bridge (8 miles), keep to the right bank to avoid a large wave adjacent to the gauging station. There are another 2½ miles of fast water to where a road on the right bank offers a potential take-out. Then a mile of smoothwater leads to the covered bridge (11½ miles) in Woodsville. Just below it there is a dam, and at the foot of the dam is the Connecticut River.

## GALE RIVER                                                    NH

The Gale River drains the northern side of Franconia Notch and the surrounding mountains. Because the stream is confined in a narrow valley and the drainage area includes the steep slopes of Mount Garfield and Mount Lafayette, a summer rain sometimes raises the river to a runnable level. The stream's flow generally peaks twelve to twenty-four hours after a rain.

### Off NH Rte. 18–Jesseman Road                              4 mi

| | |
|---|---|
| Description: | Class II |
| Date checked: | 1983 |
| Navigable: | High to medium water (late April to end of May and after heavy rains) |
| Scenery: | Forested, town |
| Maps: | USGS Franconia, Sugar Hill |

Put in about 1 mile above NH 18 from a side road reached by taking Coal Hill Road up the south side of the river and following the leftmost road at a three-way fork.

The first mile to the NH 18 bridge is rocky, with occasional fallen trees, so much boat handling is required. Just below the bridge the river doubles in size as Lafayette Brook enters from the left at a heavy rapid. For the next 2 miles the river flows through Franconia Village, with NH 18 on the bank. The rapids are easy Class II.

The Ham Branch enters from the left just above the NH 117 bridge (2½ miles). A concrete water gate on the right bank

marks the point at which NH 18/116 leaves the river, although
a side road continues on the right bank. Another mile of similar
going brings you to the truss bridge on Jesseman Road (4 miles),
the last take-out before the difficult rapids below.

## Jesseman Road–Ammonoosuc River                          4 mi

| Description: | Quickwater, Class **III–IV** |
| --- | --- |
| Date checked: | 1983 |
| Navigable: | High to medium water (late April to end of May and after heavy rains) |
| Scenery: | Wild, rural |
| Maps: | USGS Sugar Hill, Littleon 15 |

Below Franconia Village the Gale River drops through a winding valley to its confluence with the Ammonoosuc. The banks are
uninhabited woods; the whole run is one of the more scenic and
unspoiled in the White Mountains.

This run is for closed boats only. There is a hand-painted gauge
on the rocks underneath the NH 116 bridge in Franconia. A reading of 0.5 constitutes a low but runnable level.

To reach the put-in, travel north on NH 18 through Franconia.
One mile past the center, go left onto Streeter Pond Road to
Jesseman Road. Streeter Pond Road continues downstream to
the take-out, but it does not follow the river.

The first ½ mile is quickwater through open fields. The rapids begin at a power line crossing. They are Class III, with many
large boulders in the streambed.

The rapids get a little harder. After 2 miles a sharp left turn
brings you to the entrance of a gorge (2½ miles), recognizable
by rock walls on both sides below a pool. Take out on the right
well above the beginning of the gorge and scout. The gorge contains four drops, each followed by a short pool.

Below the gorge there is a short drop. The chute is on the far
left, with a total drop of about 6 feet. A final drop must then be
negotiated to a railroad bridge where the Gale River joins the
Ammonoosuc (4 miles).

## HAM BRANCH, GALE RIVER                                    **NH**

This scenic tributary of the Gale River drains the western slopes of Kinsman Ridge. The highway, NH 116, runs parallel to the river, but it is not close.

### NH Rte. 116–Franconia                                    **7 mi**

| | |
|---|---|
| Description: | Class I–II |
| Date checked: | 1983 |
| Navigable: | High water (May) |
| Scenery: | Forested, rural |
| Map: | USGS Sugar Hill |

Put in at the northernmost NH 116 bridge, since the stream above reportedly contains impassable drops. The trip is initially a twisting, rocky Class II run with some small, fallen trees, so take care on blind corners. After 2¼ miles the river splits around an island that has two barbed wire fences at the end. In another ½ mile you reach a truss bridge on a road to a farm.

Below the truss bridge (2¾ miles) the river has easier Class I–II rapids. There are good views of the Kinsman Ridge across the fields. Just above the third side bridge, Bickford Hill Road (5¾ miles), there is a washed-out dam that is easily runnable. A short distance below, where the river approaches NH 116 on the right, there is a ledge that is best run on the left. In another 1¼ miles the Ham Branch enters the Gale River (7 miles) just above the NH 117 bridge in Franconia.

## WAITS RIVER                                              **VT**

This is a sporty run in high water. The valley is narrow, and consequently the river rises quickly when there is moderate runoff. The scenery consists of wooded hills and some pastureland; the water is clear. The stream is followed by VT 25 its entire length. Although the river is runnable from West Topsham, the usual trip is from Waits River to the VT 25B bridge. There is a painted gauge on the downstream side of the right pier of this bridge. A level of 1.6 is medium, a level above 2 is high.

## Waits River–Bradford                                    11½ mi

| | |
|---|---|
| Description: | Quickwater, Class II |
| Date checked: | 1988, NC |
| Navigable: | High and medium water (late April to early May) |
| Scenery: | Rural, settled |
| Maps: | USGS East Barre 15, Woodsville 15, East Corinth, Mount Cube |

Put in from a bridge on a side road opposite a very pretty church in the village of Waits River. The river is narrow, steep, and rocky, dropping 50 feet per mile. Watch out for barbed wire, both along the banks and in the river. Below the first VT 25 bridge (2 miles) there are three ledges. The first one is around a sharp bend to the left, and it is usually run in the center. Below, the river widens, and the other two are recognizable from above. Look them over first, because the best channel changes with the water level. The third ledge is the most difficult, and the best route is usually near the right bank, which is difficult to scout because of the barbed wire and a side stream. The pace slows below.

Just past the junction with the South Branch of the Waits River (just below the next VT 25 bridge) the current picks up. A large ledge creates a hole at some water levels that can best be avoided on the right. Strong rapids continue for half a mile before easier rapids continue, with a gentle surprise or two to Bradford.

Take out under the VT 25B bridge. In Bradford, ½ mile below, is a high, dangerous power-generating dam, below which the river meanders another ½ mile to the Connecticut.

## OMPOMPANOOSUC RIVER                                          VT

The main branch of the Ompompanoosuc rises in Vershire and flows generally south to meet the West Branch above Union Village. Below the confluence is a large flood control dam. The section of the main river above the dam contains many rapids; below, the going is easier. The mile or two just above the dam is frequently very overgrown and therefore difficult to navigate. Portaging the flood control dam on foot is quite difficult. A dirt road, only sometimes accessible, runs along the east side of the river through much of the flood plain. Drive right up over the dam to get to it. Below the dam, the river riffles for a while before reaching the impounded Connecticut.

## West Fairlee–Union Village Dam                    12 mi

| | |
|---|---|
| Description: | Quickwater, Class I–II |
| Date checked: | 1988, NC |
| Navigable: | High to medium water (late April to early May) |
| Scenery: | Forested, rural |
| Maps: | USGS Strafford 15, Mount Cube 15 |
| Portages: | 2 mi   R   **waterfall** 50 yd |
| | 8 mi   L   **waterfall** 100 yd |

There are two bridges in West Fairless providing access to the river. Neither is particularly satisfactory. From here to Post Mills is mostly smooth. Just above the VT 133 bridge in Post Mills is a 12-foot waterfall, which should be carried to the right. From here there are 4 miles of easy Class II rapids that lead to a high bridge on Sawnee Bean Road near Thetford Center (6 miles). There are three or four more difficult Class III drops in this section, the hardest being ½ mile above this bridge.

The two miles to the covered bridge in Thetford Center (8 miles) meander among fallen trees. **Caution!** The river goes over a 40-foot cascade just below this covered bridge. The portage is not easy. Below here, quickwater alternates with ledges that should be looked over carefully. Now away from any roads, at some water levels, these ledges should be carried around. The river gradually flattens out. Below where the

West Branch enters, assuming there is no pool behind the flood control dam, the river meanders below steep overgrown banks. Taking out below here, though it is another mile to the dam, becomes increasingly difficult.


## Union Village–Connecticut River                    3¼ mi

This part can be run anytime. The rapids and riffles continue for a way, with the river gradually becoming wider and slower as it reaches the Connecticut. The VT 132 bridge is passed (2¼ miles) and then I-91 before you reach the wide mouth into the Connecticut.


## WEST BRANCH, OMPOMPANOOSUC RIVER          VT

The West Branch rises in Strafford and flows southeast to join the main river 1 mile above the flood control dam. The river rises to runnable levels only rarely, with the level frequently becoming too low before the rain stops. Below Rices Mills, access becomes increasingly difficult, and the quality of the river and the view deteriorate as the flood control dam impoundment area is reached.


## Strafford–Rices Mills                              7¾ mi

| | |
|---|---|
| Description: | Class II, III |
| Date checked: | 1988, NC |
| Navigable: | High water |
| Scenery: | Forested |
| Map: | Strafford 15 |

Although it is possible to put in along the quickwater section between Strafford and South Strafford, the usual put-in is in, or just downstream from, South Strafford. From South Strafford, for the next 3 miles, Class II rapids are reasonably continuous. Look over very carefully the small gorge in Rices Mills. The river here goes over a ledge and around a right turn before narrowing to 10 feet or so. The currents bouncing off the rock walls make balance precarious. There is a nice pool below. The pool can serve as a take-out, or you can continue 100 yards or so to the VT 132 bridge.

## Rices Mills–Ompompanoosuc River                            2½ mi

Easy rapids continue under the VT 132 ridge and dwindle to quickwater. At the end of a left-turn loop is a drop over a ledge, and farther on is a waterfall that must be portaged. The river flows through pastureland, and the road visible along the bank is private and gated.

## WHITE RIVER                                                    VT

There are more than 100 miles of good canoeing on this river system, with nearly every kind of water, some of which can be run even in summer. The valleys are highly cultivated, and much of the river may not be attractive to those in search of wild surroundings. However, in the tributary valleys especially one can see rural Vermont at its very best; the First Branch is perhaps the prettiest.

The main river rises north of Granville, flows south, then east, then southeast, finally emptying into the Connecticut River at White River Junction. At or near flood stage, some of the faster parts become Class III, but when the gauge at West Hartford reads 4.2 to 5.8 it is Class II.

There is another gauge under the bridge in Gaysville. When the gauge reads 0 the river would be mostly large waves and Class III.

The river is the first in Vermont to witness the return of the Atlantic salmon. A vigorous program is in effect to restore the salmon to the Connecticut River Watershed. Remain alert for fishermen in the river, and respect the multiple uses that coexist on this large river system.

## Granville–Stockbridge                                        14½ mi

| | |
|---|---|
| Description: | **Quickwater,** Class I–II |
| Date checked: | 1983 |
| Navigable: | High water (early April) |
| | Medium water (late April to mid-May) |
| Scenery: | Rural, towns |
| Maps: | USGS Hancock, Rochester |

Begin on VT 100 at a bridge 1 mile north of the VT 100/125 junction in Hancock. The river above this point is small, but in high water it can be run for an additional 2 miles if you put in at another VT 100 bridge about ¾ mile south of Granville.

For almost the entire distance from the bridge near the Granville-Hancock town line to Stockbridge, this shallow stream winds past farms at the bottom of a narrow valley. There are only a limited number of short Class II rapids, and the first is just below a bridge in Hancock (2½ miles). After the VT 73 bridge (7¼ miles) it is ½ mile to the second and most difficult rapid at a bridge beside VT 100. There is one more pitch in the remaining 6¾ miles to Stockbridge (14½ miles).

## Stockbridge–Bethel                                    **11 mi**

| | |
|---|---|
| Description: | Quickwater, Class II |
| Date checked: | 1988, MF |
| Navigable: | High water (early April) |
| | Medium water (late April to end of May) |
| Scenery: | Forested, settled |
| Maps: | USGS Rochester, Randolph 15 |

There are intermittent Class II rapids that extend over much of the distance to Bethel. Some of them can be scouted from VT 107, which is occasionally close on the right bank. In medium water this is not a difficult run, but in high water the current can be strong.

The most difficult section is 4½ miles below Stockbridge at an S-turn just above Gaysville. The river swings to the left away from the highway and passes through a narrow cut. There are heavy waves, a submerged rock near the center that often cannot be detected as you approach, and a strong whirlpool at the bottom just before the river turns right. Under the high bridge at Gaysville (5 miles) there is another strong current where a rock ledge on the right deflects the river to the left.

## Bethel–Sharon                                    **11¾ mi**

| | |
|---|---|
| Description: | Flatwater, **quickwater,** Class I–II |
| Date checked: | 1983 |
| Navigable: | Passable in all but dry summers |
| Scenery: | Rural, towns, forested |
| Maps: | USGS Randolph, Strafford 15 |

The river gets bigger in Bethel after the Third Branch enters and becomes a much larger stream suitable to summer running if the season is not too dry. Put in at the VT 107 bridge. The river is less rapid and is wider, and the valley is more open. However, for a long way there are numerous traverse ledges that create sharp drops with fair current between. In 4 miles, North Royalton, where the Second Branch enters from the left, is reached. It is 2 miles more to Royalton and another 2 miles to South Royalton, where the First Branch enters. About halfway between these two towns there are ledges and a sharp drop. Just below the bridge at South Royalton there is a rapid, followed by 5 miles of easy river to Sharon.

## Sharon–Connecticut River                              13½ mi

| | |
|---|---|
| Description: | Quickwater, Class I, **II** |
| Date checked: | 1983 |
| Navigable: | Passable in all but dry seasons |
| Scenery: | Rural, towns |
| Maps: | USGS Strafford 15, Quechee, Hanover |

This section of the White River is similar to the section above, but the river is larger and the ledges closer together and more difficult. Below Sharon after 1¼ miles there is an old dam that can be recognized by its abutments. It can be run, but scout carefully from the right, or from the left if you plan to line or carry.

Below Sharon the 5½ miles to West Hartford are characterized by numerous ledges with rather sharp pitches, but the river between is smooth. These ledges begin at a gravel pit below Sharon, and there are usually only one or two passable notches at each drop. The most difficult place is 1½ miles below the gravel pit at a part known as Quartermile Rapids, which should be scouted. After approaching near the right bank, cross to the left of a large rock in the middle and to the left of haystacks below it. About 4 miles below Sharon there are several ledges;

the first is open in the middle, the second on the far left. At the island below, the right channel is better, and the last rapid above West Hartford (6 miles) is best run near the right bank.

For the 6 miles to Hartford the river is wide, and there is a lot of picking around ledges at low water. An old dam/ledge is above the Hartford bridge. Then it is 1½ miles to the bridges at White River Junction and the Connecticut River.

## THIRD BRANCH, WHITE RIVER                                    VT

The Third Branch is the westernmost branch of the White River. It rises in Roxbury and flows south to the main river at Bethel. The Third has a more uniform gradient than the other branches, more like the main river, with only two small dams to break the continuity in the upper part. It provides a pleasant, easy run for its entire length.

### Roxbury–Riford Park                                        9½ mi

| | |
|---|---|
| Description: | **Quickwater,** Class I–II |
| Date checked: | 1983 |
| Navigable: | High water |
| Scenery: | Forested, rural |
| Maps: | USGS Barre 15, Warren, Randolph 15 |
| Portage: | (9½ mi **ledge**—may be run) |

Put in at a bridge adjacent to a railroad underpass ½ mile north of the Roxbury/Granville town line. The Third Branch here is very small and fast, with overhanging alders and leaning and fallen trees. Class II rapids extend for ¼ mile above and below a small bridge in East Granville. Quickwater, shallow rapids, and a few trees make the trip interesting. The river passes under a bridge (4½ miles) above West Braintree and the VT 12A bridge (6¾ miles). Just above the small bridge near Riford

Brook a rocky ledge should be scouted, but it can be run (Class III).

## Riford Brook–Randolph                                              3¾ mi

| | |
|---|---|
| Description: | Quickwater |
| Date checked: | 1983 |
| Navigable: | High water |
| Scenery: | Rural, towns |
| Maps: | USGS Randolph 15 |
| Portages: | 3¼ mi **dam at recreation area** 15 yd |
| | (3¾ mi e **dam at Randolph**—lift over) |
| | 3¾+ mi   R   **ledges below dam** 100 yd) |

Below the bridge at Riford Brook, which is the usual put-in for the upper segment, the river is still obstructed by trees, but not by rapids. A sharp turn under a railroad bridge 2 miles down may collect debris.

At the recreation area west of Randolph (3¼ miles) there is a dam that may open when the river can be paddled. Do not attempt to run or line the rip-rap below, because the rocks are extremely jagged.

The high VT 12 bridge at Randolph is just around a bend. The low dam below can be lined or run under favorable conditions. A series of Class II–III ledges is below, within sight of the bridge. Put in or take out at the dam from a side road on the right, or do so below the ledges behind the Vermont Castings Company on the right.

## Randolph–Bethel                                                  10¾ mi

| | |
|---|---|
| Description: | **Quickwater,** Class I |
| Date checked: | 1983 |
| Navigable: | Medium or low water |
| Scenery: | Rural, forested |
| Map: | USGS Randolph 15 |
| Portage: | (10¾ mi   L   **dam at Bethel**) |

From the road on the right bank, put in below the VT 12 bridge in Randolph before or after the rapids, at your choice. The river is attractive, with clear water riffling over a sandy bottom, and it is generally out of sight of roads. Fallen trees are less of a problem, since the river is wider. Sandbars project here and there.

The railroad crosses the river ½ mile above a bridge on a side road (8¼ miles). Just below, a small rapid forms at the mouth of a side stream coming in from the right, and there are more easy rapids below.

The best take-out is on the right ¼ mile above the bridge at the ballfield in Bethel (10½ miles), which can be reached from VT 12. The dam in Bethel is immediately below the bridge. It is only another ½ mile to the confluence with the main river.

## SECOND BRANCH, WHITE RIVER                                    VT

The Second Branch rises in Williamstown and flows through the scenic Williamstown Gulf, although it cannot be paddled until farther downstream. The valley is well cultivated, and VT 14 and many small roads follow the stream and cross it frequently. Covered bridges are the main attraction of this run.

### East Brookfield–East Randolph                              8¾ mi

| | |
|---|---|
| Description: | **Quickwater**, Class I–II |
| Date checked: | 1983 |
| Navigable: | Medium–high to medium water |
| Scenery: | Rural |
| Maps: | USGS Barre 15, Randolph 15 |
| Portages: | near beginning **many low farm bridges** |
| | 5¼ mi **old dam** |
| | 6¾ mi **old dam** |
| | (8¾ mi   L   **dam at East Randolph**) |

At the start, the Second Branch is still only a meadow brook wandering through farms. Besides the many alders and fallen trees, low farm bridges must be portaged. The remains of two old dams in North Randolph must also be scouted and probably carried. The first, just east of town (5¼ miles), is the steepest, and the other (6¾ miles) is west of the highway between the two VT 14 bridges. After the second dam, Class I–II rapids continue most of the way to the dam below the VT 14 bridge in East Randolph.

## East Randolph–White River                                       14 mi

| | |
|---|---|
| Description: | **Quickwater,** Class I |
| Date checked: | 1983 |
| Navigable: | Medium-high to medium water |
| Scenery: | Rural |
| Map: | USGS Randolph 15 |
| Portages: | 8¾ mi   L   **dam at East Bethel** 100 yd |
| | 11¼ mi   R   **waterfall** 100 yd |
| | 12 mi **ledge**–can be lined |

Put in below the dam in East Randolph. The river is somewhat larger here, and although the trees still obstruct the channel, few block it completely. The stream often wanders well away from the highway past scenic high banks and through serpentine turns. Covered bridges cross the river at 1 mile, 2¼ miles, and 7¾ miles, while VT 14 crosses at 2 miles and at 6¼ miles. There are also more farm bridges, although all are high enough to paddle under.

At East Bethel check the dam below the second side road bridge in advance to determine the best portage. The old mill downstream on the right is being restored. It may be best to take out on the left, cross the bridge, and carry down past the mill.

The Second Branch crosses under VT 14 again at 11¼ miles. Take out on the right well above the bridge to carry a steep ledge at an old dam site. After the next VT 14 bridge, a low ledge can probably be run. The hight VT 107 bridge (13¾ miles) comes shortly above the confluence with the main river. A bridge ½ mile down the White River offers access.

## FIRST BRANCH, WHITE RIVER                              **VT**

The First Branch of the White River, coming in from the north,
is the easternmost of the three branches and has the steepest drop.
Rising north of the town of Chelsea, it drops precipitously over
ledges and empties into the main river at South Royalton. The
valley is a lovely, although highly cultivated, part of rural Vermont. The covered bridges are an added attraction.

### Chelsea–Sawmill                                       **3 mi**

| | |
|---|---|
| Description: | Ledges, Class III–IV |
| Date checked: | 1983 |
| Navigable: | High water only |
| Scenery: | Rural |
| Map: | USGS Strafford 15 |

Although the run is popular with expert ledge enthusiasts,
water level is critical, so it is difficult to schedule trips: too
much water is dangerous and too little is hopeless.

Put in below the lower VT 110 bridge in Chelsea from a side
road by a creamery (with permission). Rocky rapids alternate
with steep ledges, all of which can be run by the right boat at
the right water level. They should be scouted in advance from
shore. The road follows the river closely for much of the way,
so prior scouting is easy.

Take out where the river is near the road, well before the old
sawmill dam.

### Sawmill–Tunbridge                                     **3¾ mi**

The river continues rapid, but the ledges diminish in frequen-
cy, if not in ferocity. Beside the dam at the sawmill, there is a dam
at North Tunbridge (1¾ miles) and two dams at Tunbridge, one
above and one below the VT 110 bridge. Two covered bridges
add to the scenic run.

## Tunbridge–South Royalton                    7½ mi

| Description: | Class I |
| --- | --- |
| Date checked: | 1983 |
| Navigable: | High water (early April) |
| | Medium water (late April to end of May) |
| Scenery: | Rural |
| Maps: | USGS Strafford 15, Randolph 15 |
| Portages: | 3¾ mi **broken dam** |
| | 6¼ mi **dam** |
| | 6¼ mi **dam** |

A possible put-in is on the right side of the river just below Mill Bridge, the covered bridge just below the two dams in Tunbridge. The ledges and rocks that follow make this a walk and drag at low water levels, but more water can make this stretch a short but sporty, possibly Class II, rapid.

Just around the right corner is the Tunbridge Fairgrounds, and put-in is much easier here. Opposite the post office and next to the fire station an unmarked road leads down into the fairground. At the bottom take the first right, between some buildings, to the river. Park elsewhere, though, taking care not to block the fire station. Also, take time to notice the high-water markings on the fair buildings from the 1978 flood.

From here the river meanders with good current some 7 miles to the White River. Numerous ledges can provide some excitement, but this can be dampended by numerous downed trees that on occasion completely block the river. In 1 mile the river passes under the Cilley Bridge (another easy put-in if the fairground is closed) and in 1¾ miles under a concrete bridge, which is VT 110. Be especially careful of downed trees in this area. In 2¾ miles, the Howe bridge in South Tunbridge is reached. This bridge, the third and last of the covered bridges in this stretch, was built in 1879.

Following one another in short order, there are some ledges, another concrete VT 110 bridge, and a broken dam. It is an easy lift over the right side of the dam. At some water levels, a chute in the middle can be run solo, but check it carefully.

One mile after the second of two steel bridges and under another concrete bridge (6¼ miles), there is the first pair of dams. Without too much difficulty, boats can be lifted over the left side of the spillway. **Caution!** A breach in the middle of the dam may look runnable to some, but several steel rods extend downstream at various angles from the dam, and one of them dangles in this chute. Rather than lifting over the spillway, you can do a difficult but short carry on the right, around the dam and the bridge.

The second dam is 100 yards downstream. It also can be portaged on the right, but it is probably easier to lift over the spillway on the right and carry down the ledge. Stop on the right before the dam to scout this.

After entering the White River ¾ mile farther on, paddle across and take out on the right just under the bridge at South Royalton.

## MASCOMA RIVER                                        NH

The Mascoma River basin drains a large area west of Mount Cardigan and flows into the Connecticut River in Lebanon. The river is more removed from highways than road maps appear to indicate.

The upper section of the river is small, until it is joined by the Indian River, which flows from Mount Cardigan along US 4 from Canaan. Scenery is a mixture of alder swamps, meadows, fields, and the town of Enfield.

For those who enjoy Class II and III rapids in attractive settings, the 4 miles between Mascoma Lake and the dam upstream from the Lebanon water treatment plant are highly recommended. One of the oldest slalom and wildwater races in the country occurs on this river each April.

The annual fall drawdown of Goose Pond frequently provides medium water for the upper section. Check with the Water Resources Board (603-271-1110) for dates.

## Canaan Center–Mascoma Lake                                    **12 mi**

| | |
|---|---|
| Description: | Quickwater, Class II |
| Date checked: | 1988, NC |
| Navigable: | High and medium water |
| Scenery: | Forested, rural, town |
| Map: | USGS Mascoma 15 |
| Portage: | 2 mi   L   **dam** 25 yd |

While it is possible, depending on water levels, to put in farther upstream, the bridge in Canaan Center is a convenient spot.
Two washed-out dams here are evidence that a village once
existed here. Meanders, downed trees, and deadfalls are common until the US 4 bridge (3½ miles) is reached. The Indian
River enters on the left shortly (4 miles), and the river increases
in size to about 50 feet in width. Past the first railroad bridge 1-
mile section of Class II water begins at a broken dam (the old
sluiceway on the right now takes the overflow in high water); the
best route depends on water level. The next drop runs best on
the left but requires tight maneuvering. The next rapid, another
broken dam, generally runs best on the right. After easier rapids, the second railroad bridge is passed. Here is an old gauging
station that must have been reached by railroad, since there hav-
en't been roads in here for many years. The river slackens as it
passes under two more railroad bridges, then US 4 is reached in
West Canaan (6¼ miles).

Quickwater runs by the entry of Goose Pond Brook (7¾
miles) and the next US bridge (9 miles). This is a convenient
spot to end or begin a trip. Twenty or 30 yards separate the US
4 bridge, a railroad bridge, and Blackwater Road bridge. Quickwater rapids lead under several bridges in Enfield (where one can
take out) and eventually bring one to Mascoma Lake (12 miles).
If continuing downriver, keep to the right shore and pass under
the bridge over the lake. Cross the lake where convenient on a
Northwest course. The dam at the outlet of the lake can be most
easily carried on the left.

## Mascoma Lake–Lebanon                                          5½ mi

| | |
|---|---|
| Description: | Class **II–III** |
| Date checked: | 1988, NC |
| Navigable: | High and medium water |
| Scenery: | Forested, urban |
| Maps: | USGS Mascoma 15, Hanover |
| Portage: | (4 mi e **dam**) |

This is the classic whitewater section of the river. The scenery is quite good, but a requirement to maneuver will allow little viewing. If paddling across the lake, you will find the carry easier on the left shore. There is a nice parking lot there for those putting in. A large eddy under the dam on this side allows a comfortable put-in. Class II rapids begin immediately; around the first left turn is the USGS gauge. A reading of 2.3–2.8 is the medium water level; over 3.0 is high water, and over 3.5 is flood stage. Class II rapids pick up speed under the high US 4 bridge. An island is sighted; the right channel is frequently blocked by trees. The left channel is too, below the right turn, so stop in the eddy on the left first. The next ½ mile is frequently used for a slalom course. Please don't disturb the wires or gates if they are up. The river quickly passes under two more railroad bridges before slowing a bit. Along a straight section of river, one often sees the right bank breached and the river beginning to divert into a field. After the main course turns right, another section with many downed trees witnesses the wandering courses returning. Just past the high I-89 bridge (3 miles) the river turns right; watch for congestion and a hole at higher levels on the outside.

After the river leaves I-89, it narrows to pass under a small stone and metal bridge. The drop under this bridge is the beginning of the second race course. Many take out at this bridge on the right. The river bends left under a low railroad bridge. A sandy beach on the left is a good rest spot before an S-turn that immediately follows. Because of ledgy pourovers, these turns cannot be taken on the inside, so a middle course is the most conservative. Below this turn a 100-yard straight stretch leads

to a right turn under a railroad bridge. There is an eddy under
the bridge on the right which allows scouting of the next section.
Excelsior Rapids follows, named for the defunct mill at the end
of the drop. Excelsior is Class III rapid at most levels, and it
borders on Class IV as the water level rises. It is best scouted
by climbing the right bank from the eddy, crossing the railroad
bridge, and walking down the path on the left. The rapid contains no unusual features, but a variety of rocks, waves, and
holes lead to some larger waves toward the bottom which are
difficult to navigate in boats that have taken on water above.
**Caution!** It is important, especially in high water, to observe
the runout of Excelsior to the dam below (4 miles). The dam
in medium water and higher is only 3 or 4 feet high, but is is
very dangerous. In low water, it is easy to lift over on the right.
In higher water, there is a path on the left that works best to
portage.

Below the dam is a 100-yard stretch of Class II water that leads
to an eddy by the city pool and water treatment plant. This is the
usual take-out for this section. The river continues another mile
with quickwater and a few Class II drops to the city of Lebanon.
**Caution!** Be sure to take out to a parking lot on the left before
reaching the NH 120 bridge. The river through Lebanon is not
recommended.

### Lebanon–Connecticut River                                    4 mi

| | |
|---|---|
| Description: | Quickwater, Class II |
| Date checked: | 1988, NC |
| Navigable: | High and medium water |
| Scenery: | Rural, urban |
| Maps: | USGS Hanover |
| Portage: | (4 mi e **dam**) |

Look over the rapid through the city of Lebanon. This has
been run, but because of the dam partway down and the rough-
cut rocks in the streambed, it is not recommended. Quickwater
follows to a renovated power dam by an old mill building. One
hundred feet downstream is another dam.

The best put-in is below this third dam behind Dulac's Hardware store (ask permission) of ¼ mile below, where US 4 crosses the river. The river, with some easy Class II rapids, wanders through some rural, almost attractive sections of Lebanon. A difficult but runnable broken dam is reached around a left turn (2 miles), and just below, under a railroad bridge and the high US 4 bridge, is a low 1-foot weir that should be run with care of carried on the left—at high water it is very dangerous. Class II rapids continue alongside I-89. Below the next railroad bridge, around a left turn, is the next dam (3 miles). During 1988 this dam was being rebuilt to generate electricity. Scout carefully along Glen Road, which follows this section of the river. Much of the river is diverted to a generating plant ½ mile below at the NH 12A bridge. When there is sufficient flow, this half mile is pleasant Class II paddling. Below this bridge, the river flattens out and meanders to the Connecticut. It is possible to take out behind the shopping center just beyond the NH 12A bridge or at the mouth of the Connecticut River, reachable by some dirt roads behind the shopping center.

## OTTAUQUECHEE RIVER                                    VT

The Ottauquechee River drains the east side of Sherburne Pass and flows east to the Connecticut River at North Hartland. The upper part offers a long run for novice paddlers. The middle section is broken by dams and the spectacular Quechee Gorge. The lower part is within the impoundment of a large flood control dam.

Although the valley is one of the major east-west routes across Vermont, the river itself is a lovely wooded aisle through its gorges large and small.

## West Bridgewater–Woodstock                              13½ mi

| | |
|---|---|
| Description: | Class I–II |
| Date checked: | 1983 |
| Navigable: | High water (late April to early May) |
| Scenery: | Forested, rural, towns |
| Maps: | USGS Killington Peak, Plymouth, Woodstock South |

Put in at the VT 100 bridge in West Bridgewater. The rapids are continuous and easy Class I and II. The river is crossed by bridges of both US 4 and side roads. However, as the river swings from one side of the valley to the other, the outside is a steep wooded bank or a shaley cliff. None of the rapids is especially notable, although you should, as always, watch for fallen trees.

The rapid immediately above Bridgewater is Class II. The dam is mostly gone, especially on the left side, and can be run. Below Bridgewater the valley widens and also the river, although tributaries keep the water level up.

For an easy trip, take out where the river comes close to the road upstream of the US 4 bridge a mile west of Woodstock.

## Woodstock–Taftsville                                    4½ mi

| | |
|---|---|
| Description: | Flatwater, **quickwater,** Class I–II |
| Date checked: | 1983 |
| Navigable: | Medium-high water, medium water |
| Scenery: | Towns, forested |
| Maps: | USGS Woodstock South, Woodstock North, Quechee |
| Difficulty: | ½ mi **pipe at US 4 bridge**–get out on   R to scout |
| Portages: | 1 mi e **2-foot waterfall** under VT 12 bridge |
| | (4½ mi   L   **dam at Taftsville**) |

The rapid immediately above the first bridge in Woodstock is a difficult Class II, harder than those above. Just at the bridge, a pipe crosses but can be run. The river flows through town and under a covered bridge to the VT 12 bridge (1 mile) where there is a 2-foot drop with some rocks below.

The rapids gradually diminish to the backwater of the dam at Taftsville. A road on the left bank makes the take-out possible at various points. A covered bridge crosses the river at the dam.

## Taftsville–Connecticut River                    12 mi

Maps:               USGS Quechee, Hartland, North Hartland

Below the Taftsville dam 4 miles of mixed rapids and smoothwater bring you to the dam and covered bridge at Quechee. An interesting terrain model of the lower river can be seen at the offices of the Quechee Lakes Corporation on the left bank. It is 1 mile to the dam and cascade at Deweys Mills. The next mile is the spectacular Quechee Gorge, best viewed from the US 4 bridge midway down.

A dirt road on the left bank leads to the foot of the gorge. The formerly Class II–III lower gorge has been flooded out, and there are 4$^1/2$ miles of riffles and sandbanks to the North Hartland flood control dam. At maximum pool Quechee Gorge will be filled nearly to the brim, and the dams at Deweys Mills and Quechee will be under water. There is a boat ramp above, but access below is blocked by a chain link force. About ¼ mile below the flood control dam there are unrunnable falls above the US 5 bridge. It is 1 mile to a side road crossing a rock island with a dam on each side. One of the bridges is a covered bridge. It is then ¼ mile to the Connecticut River.

## SUGAR RIVER                                                        NH

This river drains Lake Sunapee. It begins with several dams and an unrunnable section, so the best part of the river starts at North Newport.

The river can often be run late in the season, because the drainage area is large and the flow is dam controlled. A good indication of the water level can be obtained from the NH 11 bridge at Kelleyville because the rapids there are typical of the rest of the river.

The Water Resources Board (603-271-1110) draws down the level of Lake Sunapee every fall. The exact dates vary from year to year.

### North Newport–Kelleyville                                    2½ mi

| | |
|---|---|
| Description: | Class II–III |
| Date checked: | 1988, CK |
| Navigable: | High water (April) |
| | Medium water–scratchy (May to end of June and wet falls) |
| | Dam controlled (annual fall drawdown to Lake Sunapee) |
| Scenery: | Rural, towns |
| Maps: | USGS Sunapee 15, Claremont 15 |

Put in at the bridge in North Newport. If the water is high, there will be standing waves and turbulence, with relatively few rocks visible. At lower levels you must dodge many moderate-sized rocks.

About 1 mile below the start, around the second right turn, there is a difficult Class III drop among boulders. It should be scouted from the right bank. The next corner is also more difficult than the first part, but the rapids ease off closer to Kelleyville.

## Kelleyville–training tower                                    5 mi

| | |
|---|---|
| Description: | Class I–II |
| Date checked: | 1988, CK |
| Navigable: | High water |
| Scenery: | Forested, settled |
| Map: | USGS Claremont 15 |

Below the NH 11/103 bridge in Kelleyville the rocks are smaller and the run tends to involve a lot of picking around them at lower water levels. At higher water levels this section is likely to wash out into big waves. The outside corners tend to generate waves at all water levels.

The rapids gradually diminish, and access is possible at the fire department training tower, which is reached by a rough dirt side road along the left bank. A unique feature of this section is two covered railroad bridges, now used as part of the path.

## Training tower–Claremont                    2¼ mi

Although there are no noteworthy rapids, the current is still swift and the run into Claremont is pleasant. Take out well above the NH 11 bridge on the right because the first dam is above it and the river is confined there between retaining walls. You must park on the road, since parking is no longer available in the fire department training field.

## Claremont–Connecticut River                    5 mi

Gorges and more dams highlight the river through Claremont. Resist the temptation to put in again, because there is still another dam in a gorge in West Claremont.

## CROYDON BROOK (NORTH BRANCH SUGAR RIVER)                                        NH

This branch of the Sugar provides a taste of virtually everything. In 10 miles, one experiences lake paddling, quickwater, and whitewater up to Class III. The river rises north of Newport and Lake Sunapee and south of the Mascoma drainage basin. Longer stretches of relatively flat water, home to many beaver, are interrupted by bursts of whitewater, one section of which merits a trip by itself. It is important to emphasize that downed trees and low-hanging branches are a hazard the entire length of this river.

## Grantham–Sugar River                                          10½ mi

| | |
|---|---|
| Description: | Lake, quickwater, Class II |
| Date checked: | 1988, NC |
| Navigable: | High water |
| Scenery: | Forested, rural, towns |
| Map: | USGS Sunapee 15 |

The best put-in is on NH 10 just off Exit 13 on I-89 anywhere between the post office and the Grantham fire station. There is quickwater until Stocker Brook enters on the left, where Class II rapids start, continuing under NH 10 and past the foundation of an old mill on the left. Shortly, the river flattens out. Going over a beaver dam or two, quickwater continues under Dunbar Hill Road (1½ miles, which, if the water is quite high, you may not be able to pass under (carry on the right). The river then moves under a wooden footbridge (2½ miles), which may also have to be lifted over. At the next NH 10 bridge (3½ miles), just north of Croydon village, Class II rapids start. They parallel the road a short distance and then turn left. Obstructions in the middle force the paddler to one side or the other. Below the next bridge (4 miles) the rapids diminish. Continue to and through Spectacle Pond (4½ miles), which is aptly named for the view of the surrounding hills, especially craggy Grantham Mountain. The pond is really two ponds with a connecting stream on the far left. It is ½ mile long and may be covered with ice when the river at its best.

Quickwater continues to where a decrepit bridge crosses the river (5¾ miles). This is 1½ miles south of the Croydon fire station on NH 10. The bridge is on a side road off and visible from the paved highway. For those interested only in the white-water stretch that follows, this spot is an excellent put-in. The rapids start almost immediately, are generally Class II, and continue uninterrupted to Croydon Flat, where NH 10 again crosses the river (7½ miles). Keep particularly in mind that if the river is high (which it frequently is when best run), much of this section may warrant a Class III rating. Suddenly there is a sharp right turn and a Class III drop that is actually two drops, with holes and obstructions on each side dictating a center route. It is helpful to approach from the right. This drop is easily scouted during the car shuttle; it is located where the road approaches the river ¼ mile above the bridge in Croydon Flat.

Below this bridge the rapids diminish, and one can take out on the left where, after changing to quickwater, the river nears NH 10 on the left (8¼ miles). Quickwater continues to the main branch of the Sugar River. One can take out on the left under the covered bridge on the north Newport Road at the mouth of the Croydon Branch, or continue down the Sugar River toward Claremont.

## BLACK RIVER                                            VT

The southern of the two Black rivers in Vermont starts from a series of lakes and runs southeast to the Connecticut River. Although sectioned by dams, it provides good runs on easy to moderate rapids. Below Cavendish the water level is controlled by release from the power dam.

### Black River Lakes                                    6 mi

These lakes, situated near Tyson, begin about 6 miles south of the source of the river near Plymouth Union. Set deep among the hills, they offer attractive paddling in all seasons. VT 100 passes along the west side of all four lakes. The paddler can put in directly from the main highway at the northern end of Lake Amherst. Lift over a low dam 1 mile below into the short river leading to Echo Lake, which is 1 mile long. At the southern end of the lake a mile-long river, which is rocky and presents problems except at high water, leads through Tyson to Rescue Lake. Rescue Lake provides another two-mile trip to Reservoir Pond, which is also 1 mile long. A low, 2-foot-high dam at the southern end is easily crossed into the river, or you can take out at VT 100.

## Lakes–Cavendish                                          9¾ mi

| | |
|---|---|
| Description: | Quickwater, Class I–II |
| Date checked: | 1987, GE |
| Navigable: | High to medium water (April to early May) |
| Scenery: | Forested, settled, rural, towns |
| Map: | USGS Ludlow 15 |
| Portage: | 5¾ mi e **5-foot dam** |

Put in at the dam at the south end of Reservoir Pond close to VT 100. The first ½ mile is Class II, but the rapids become easier and mix with quickwater to provide a run very reminiscent of the South Branch of the Piscataquog. The river become smoother and slower above Ludlow (4 miles), where the dam is gone. A ledge under a small bridge east of town gives no trouble. Beyond the bridge near the sewage treatment plant watch for a small dam. The river riffles on past Proctorsville where the remains of a washed-out dam are still present. Approaching Cavendish, there is another small dam in the process of washing out which can be run; this one is visible from VT 131. Take out at the bridge on a side road in Cavendish.

## Cavendish–Whitesville                                     1½ mi

The take-out above the dam is difficult, and a carry of ¼ mile is necessary. Access below the gorge would be a problem.

## Whitesville–Perkinsville                                  7¾ mi

| | |
|---|---|
| Description: | Class II–III |
| Date checked: | 1987, GE, JR |
| Navigable: | High to medium water (late March to mid-May) |
| Scenery: | Forested, rural |
| Map: | USGS Ludlow 15 |
| Portage: | (7¾ mi **dam in Perkinsville**) |

The customary put-in for the run is at a side road bridge in Whitesville. You can put in on the right below the ledge, but at favorable water levels, the river can be run through the extreme left channel.

The rapids are moderate Class II for 2½ miles to an iron bridge. In another ½ mile, at the second pullover, with a big pine tree on the right, rapids start. The best whitewater is to be had along the 5 miles between Cavendish and Downers. From Exit 8 on I-91, drive 13 miles west on VT 131, then turn left on Carleton Road, which crosses the Black River in about 50 yards. Scout the ledges below the Carleton Road bridge. These can be run on the left, or avoided by putting in just downstream of the drop.

All the rapids can be run in moderate water, but they can be dangerous in high water. Rock formations along the shore are of interest.

The major excitement is over by the covered bridge at Downers (5¾ miles). The best take-out is at the covered bridge, reached by turning south on a dirt road ½ mile west of where VT 131 crosses VT 106. The gauge is painted on the upstream concrete bridge abutment on the left. Readings of 0.8–1.5 produce a Class II run. Good Class III water can be had in readings between 1.7 and 2.8.

## Perkinsville–North Springfield Flood Control Dam    3¾ mi

The going is difficult below the dam in Perkinsville for a way, until the river comes into the ponding of an old power dam that is less than 1 mile downstream. The gorge is attractive, with high cliffs.

Past the confluence with the North Branch (1¼ miles), with its earthen dam visible upstream, the river flows through grassy fields in the flood control dam's recreation area. Since the permanent pond is less than 1 mile away, the paddle is pleasant but not exciting.

## North Springfield–Springfield    3½ mi

Below the flood control dam, starting at a put-in reached from North Springfield, the river runs swiftly over a few rocks, gradually becoming quickwater as it approaches Springfield. This section can be run during much of the year. Take out at the first bridge in Springfield.

## Springfield–Connecticut River    5 mi

The Black River through Springfield is a series of dams and cascades. Below town a few rapids alternate with ledges before flattening out into the Connecticut. The lower part could be paddled as a side trip from the Connecticut. All of the lower part of the river is followed by VT 11.

## WILLIAMS RIVER                                        VT

The Williams River rises in Andover and flows to the
Connecticut. Most of the rapids are easy to moderate, and
there is also a terrific scenic gorge to admire. In high water,
the river can be paddled from above Proctor and the Middle
Branch can be paddled as well.

### Gassetts–Chester                                     3½ m

One can put in somewhere in the vicinity of the junction of VT
103 and 10 in very high water. The rapids are mostly Class II, and
the river follows the road fairly closely, so it can be inspected in
advance. In North Chester a dam at an old gristmill is adjacent
to the VT 103 bridge and is a short and easy carry.

### Chester–Brockways Mills                              7½ mi

| | |
|---|---|
| Description: | Quickwater, Class **I, II,** III |
| Date checked: | 1983 |
| Navigable: | High to medium water (early May) |
| Scenery: | Forested, rural |
| Maps: | USGS Ludlow 15, Saxtons River 15, Bellows Falls 15 |
| Portages: | 4 mi   L   **ledge**–lift over |
| | (7½ mi   L   **waterfall 1 mi**) |

The Williams is suitable for beginners if they are protected
and supported by a strong lead boat that can recognize ledges
and fallen trees in sufficient time and can deal with them appropriately.

Put in from the VT 103 bridge in Chester. The river is small and shallow in medium water, with easy rapids. High water washes the rapids out to fast current. Watch for barbed wire and cows in the first mile to the VT 11 bridge. Only ¼ mile below the bridge the middle branch enters on the right, greatly increasing the flow. Ferry across this junction in high water. After 1 mile more the railroad crosses. After lazing along for another 1½ miles, the river wakes up as it passes under two bridges in quick succession, makes a sharp right turn, and roars over a rocky ledges that is perhaps Class II in high water.

The difficulty then decreases, with a few Class II spots, until the big ledge (4 miles). This ledge is difficult to recognize in advance and is hard to land above. Hug the left bank as you approach. It can be run, but most parties will wish to lift over at least the upper drop, even if they run or line the lower part.

Two more distinct Class II–III ledges interrupt the slightly more difficult rapids that run to the first covered bridge (5 miles).

The major rapids are past, but the river is still pretty, with high, wooded banks and gravel bars. There is another covered bridge at 6¼ miles, and the third railroad bridge is shortly below it. The best take-out is at the fourth railroad bridge on a road on the left bank that can be reached from Brockways Mills. A confident party can paddle another ¼ mile and hope they can manage to take out above the next bridge. Immediately below, the river drops over a 30-foot falls into a gorge. A gauging station is on the left.

## Brockways Mills–Connecticut River                              3½ mi

Most of the next mile is in a deep gorge, with rapids that are only marginally navigable. It is possible to carry ¾ mile on either side and relaunch down a steep bank into a swimming hole. In

high water the Connecticut River ponds upstream for an inde-
terminate distance.

Another bridge is reached at 2¼ miles and I-91 at 3½ miles.
The Connecticut River is just below, with an access upstream on
the left at the confluence.


## MIDDLE BRANCH, WILLIAMS RIVER          VT

The Middle Branch of the Williams River rises in Londonderry
and Andover and flows into the Williams just below the VT 11
bridge in Chester.

In high water it can be paddled for 3 or 4 miles, with rapids
that are mostly Class II. Since VT 11 closely follows and crosses
the river, the paddler can scout easily to select a put-in. Unless
you plan to continue down the Williams, take out at one of the
three bridges in Chester.


## SAXTONS RIVER          VT

The Saxtons River rises in the hills of Windham, Vermont, and
flows generally eastward to join the Connecticut River just below
Bellows Falls. Both the South Branch and the main river above
Grafton look as if they might offer interesting paddling at high
water, but no description is available. The run from Grafton to
the village of Saxtons River is a popular intermediate whitewater
trip, but frequent dams discourage use of the rest of the river.
Since there are no sizable swamps or lakes in the headwaters,
spring runoff is shorter than on several nearby rivers.


### Grafton–Saxtons River Village          8½ mi

| | |
|---|---|
| Description: | Class II–III |
| Date checked: | 1983 |
| Navigable: | High water (April) |
| Scenery: | Rural, towns |
| Map: | USGS Saxton River 15 |
| Portage: | (8½ mi **ledge under bridge**) |

This run has about the same gradient as the nearby Cold River South Acworth, New Hampshire, but is considered more difficult because of several steep drops spaced among easier rapids. VT 121 is usually nearby, although often out of sight. There is a USGS gauging station near the covered bridge off VT 121, 1¼ mile east of Saxtons River village; at a reading of 4.5, a double open canoe will probably scrape, while at 5.5, waves will be a serious problem.

Start at the VT 121 bridge about ¾ northwest of the intersection with VT 35 in Grafton. In about 1 mile, the South Branch enters, doubling the size of the river; in low water it may be necessary to start below this point. The river reaches Cambridgeport 5 miles and four VT 121 bridges from the start. The next 3½ miles to the village of Saxtons River have less gradient and are generally easier, although there are still some steep drops. Under the side road bridge in the center of the village there is a dangerous drop that has allegedly been run by a kayak, but it is easy to take out well upstream. There is a road to the river behind the fire station, but no parking is allowed, and a shallow rapid makes it difficult to reach by boat. Some parties choose to take out ½ mile west of town, where the VT 121 is near the river.

## Saxtons River Village–Connecticut River                       5¼ mi

**Scouted only**
Maps:                          USGS Saxtons River 15, Bellows Falls 15

Put in below the ledge in the center of town. It is less than ½ mile to the next dam, which it is best to carry on the right. The rapids in the next section are easier than those above. It is 1¼ miles to the start to the covered bridge and gauging station, then

1¾ miles to the VT 121 bridge. In another ½ mile comes the side road bridge at North Westminster with a dam just below, which is best to carry on the right. In another ½ mile there is a 60-foot cascade with a difficult portage. Next is 1 mile of easy running to the US 5 bridge, where there is another dam (carry left), followed by a short rapid to the Connecticut River.

## COLD RIVER                                                     NH

There are many Cold rivers in New Hampshire. This one originates in Acworth and flows west into the Connecticut below Bellows Falls. It offers a fine set of fairly continuous rapids that are broken into short segments by impassable obstructions.

At high water most of the rocks are buried and standing waves appear. At lower levels there will be a considerable amount of rock dodging. There are many blind corners and fallen trees.

### East Acworth–South Acworth                                4 mi

| | |
|---|---|
| Description: | Class **II**–III |
| Date checked: | 1988, GT |
| Navigable: | High water (early April) |
| | Medium water (late April) |
| Scenery: | Rural, towns |
| Map: | USGS Lovewell Mountain 15 |
| Portages: | (4 mi   R   **dam and gorge at South Acworth** ½ mi) |

In the first mile below East Acworth, the river drops 100 feet; all of it is visible from the road. Put in at the first bridge 1¼ miles south of East Acworth where the rapids become very small and the gradient even, making a pleasant and exciting run. In medium water, this portion starts out scratchy, but the water level increases downstream as several side streams enter. This entire run is virtually continuous Class II rapids that require frequent rock dodging. Within the first 100 yards, there is a runnable rock dam. There are a few Class III rapids. A mile

above South Acworth NH 123A crosses. Take out on the right
above the dam in the town. Portage the dam and the gorge ½
mile along NH 123A.

### South Acworth–Vilas Pool                                    5½ mi

| | |
|---|---|
| Description: | Class II |
| Date checked: | 1988, GT |
| Navigable: | High water (early April) |
| | Medium water (late April) |
| Scenery: | Forested |
| Maps: | USGS Lovewell Mountain 15, Bellows Falls 15 |
| Portages: | (5½ mi   L   **dam at Alstead** 100 yd) |

The put-in for the usual Cold River run is below the gorge,
where the river comes close to NH 123A ½ mile west (downstream) of South Acworth. This portion of the Cold starts with
quick current and easy Class II rapids that gradually increase in
difficulty to hard, long, Class II rapids toward the end.

The first 1½ miles to the first bridge consists of quick current and up to easy Class II rapids, but watch for fallen trees.
This bridge is on a side road and only 10 feet from NH 123A.
An alternate put-in is in the field on the left bank upstream of
this bridge. In another ¾ mile NH 123A crosses. The next 1¾
miles to a covered bridge and a new adjacent bridge consist of
frequent rapids with blind corners and fallen trees. NH 123A
is often visible from the river, and many sugar maples line the
banks.

Below this pair of bridges the rapids increase in difficulty. In
½ mile there is a particularly difficult spot with several channels and many fallen trees. Where a small slide appears on the
left bank and the river turns right, get out to scout. In another
¾ mile the river reaches the small pond and dam at Vilas Pool
(9¾ miles), which is located on NH 123A just east of its junction near Alstead with NH 12A. Take out at the large pullover
area overlooking the pond.

## Vilas Pool–Drewsville Gorge                                    3¼ mi

| | |
|---|---|
| Description: | Class **II**–III |
| Date checked: | 1983 |
| Navigable: | Medium water (late April) |
| Scenery: | Rural |
| Map: | USGS Bellows Falls 15 |
| Portages: | 0–³/4 mi **frequent obstructions** |
| | (3¹/4 mi   R   **Drewsville Gorge** 1/4 mi) |

The first ½ mile consists of Class III rapids, a triple ledge, called Krstyna's Staircase, a very sharp right turn called Cave Sluice, and following a left turn, a Class IV at a broken dam called Glen Drop In. If you prefer not to begin in rapids, put in directly below them. The remainder of the run is followed by NH 123. This section and the following one can be run when the previous section is too low. The paddling is easier, but the take-out is tricky. Directly under a NH 123 bridge the river flows rapidly over 30-foot falls into Drewsville Gorge. Be sure to spot a landing in advance that you know your party is capable of making.

## Drewsville Gorge–Connecticut River                          3½ mi

| | |
|---|---|
| Description: | Class **II**–III |
| Date checked: | 1983 |
| Navigable: | Medium water (late April) |
| Scenery: | Settled |
| Map: | USGS Bellows Falls 15 |

Portage around the gorge is physically difficult, and it is also hard to get permission. It is relatively easy to put in from NH 123A on the right bank at a pull-off less than ½ mile downstream of the bridge.

The rapids below are Class II–III at the start, and the river here is a steep, rocky gorge. The rapids soon diminish to Class

II, except for one Class III pitch 1½ miles below near a gravel pit where the quarrying equipment is visible from the river. Three miles below the falls you reach the third NH 123 bridge at Cold River (3 miles). This is a good take-out for those who don't want to paddle the remaining ½ mile of quickwater past the NH 12 and railroad bridges to the Connecticut River (3½ miles).

It is often possible to run the portion of the river below the waterfall when the water above it is too low.

## ROCK RIVER                                              VT

This small stream enters the West River just above the Maple Valley Ski Area. The upper part is a fine Class III run, while the lower section contains several Class IV drops which require scouting.

### South Newfane–West River                        3¾ mi

| | |
|---|---|
| Description: | Class III–IV |
| Date checked: | 1987, ST |
| Navigable: | High water only (late March to early April) |
| Scenery: | Town, forest |
| Map: | USGS Brattleboro 15 |
| Portage: | 1½ mi   L   **dam in Williamsville** 50 yd— approach carefully |

Put in at the green iron bridge just below the village of South Newfane. The first mile, ending at a covered bridge, is continuous rapid, up to Class III in difficulty. Below the covered bridge, watch for a sharp left turn and a slide area on the right. **Caution!** This turn should be scouted, since the Class II rapid in turn leads immediately into a short pool above a 15-foot dam. Portage left. Below the dam, the rapids get tougher (Class IV). Take out on the right after the first corner to scout the first long rapid, which has a rock ledge in the center that must be avoided.

A high concrete bridge is passed, followed shortly be a double ledge that should be scouted. Watch for houses on the left bank, which mark the hardest rapid on the river (tough Class IV). Take out on the left to scout. Four ledges mark this run. Eddy right below the first ledge and ferry to the left eddy below three large rocks. Run the second ledge right center, angling right. The third ledge, which follows immediately, must be punched through. Avoid getting surfed into the undercut rock on the left. The fourth ledge can be run either far right into an eddy, or just right of the undercut and then left around a hole. A series of Class III rapids leads to a pool above the last big drop at an island. A sneak route exists left of the island, or run to the right through the drop. The take-out is at the VT 30 bridge (difficult) after another 1/4 mile of Class III rapids, or farther down the West River.

## WEST RIVER                                                    VT

The West River, known to the Indians and the early settlers as the Wantastigeset, rises in Weston and flows southeast to the Connecticut. It is almost continuous canoeable rapids except where three dams block the flow. Although the river follows VT 100, the river's clear rocky bottom, fine banks, and wooded hillsides create the predominant scenery for the paddler.

### Weston–Londonderry                                        6¾ mi

| | |
|---|---|
| Description: | Class **II** |
| Date checked: | 1988, ST |
| Navigable: | High water |
| Scenery: | Forested, rural |
| Maps: | USGS Wallingford 15, Londonderry 15 |
| Portage: | (6¾ mi   L   **dam at Londonderry**) |

Put in at the bridge in Weston. Although the river is channeled, it gives some indication of water level farther downstream. The rapids are nearly continuous for the first 2 miles. The S-turn rapids should be scouted because of the possibility of strainers in a blind corner. Take out on the right to scout just before a sharp right turn with a high bank on the left. The rapids soon moderate into quickwater. There is a good take-out just past a small bridge (6 miles) where VT 100 is close to the right bank. For gauge location, see the next section. It is estimated that a reading of 0.5 is necessary for a smooth run.

## Londonderry–South Londonderry Ledges                            5¼ mi

| | |
|---|---|
| Description: | Class I, II, **III,** IV |
| Date checked: | 1988, ST |
| Navigable: | High to medium water (April, May, after fall rains) |
| Scenery: | Settled |
| Map: | USGS Londonderry |

This is the famous Londonderry Ledges section. Most of the rapids are Class III at the usual level, with connecting sections of Class II and I. Put in at the dam or from a roadside turnoff on the VT 100 bridge south of Londonderry. The river gradually builds in difficulty to the first ledge section in the vicinity of the VT 100 bridge. Competent paddlers will find endless eddying and surfing opportunities in this section. A short pool under the bridge leads to a steep rapid with a strong eddy (Larry's Eddy) on the left halfway down. Easier going leads to the second VT 100 bridge. Dead Cow Rapids lies immediately under the bridge and provides good surfing opportunities. The ledge section starts shortly below, with a friendly hole on the right at the entrance and numerous ledges, waves, and holes throughout its length. Take out below the ledges from a dirt road on the right. The gauge is on the left just downstream of the first VT 100 bridge. It is estimated that a reading of 0.0 will provide a low but runnable level. with 2.0 considered high. This section often has water when the Winhall, the Rock, and the Wardsboro do not.

## Below South Londonderry Ledges–
## Ball Mountain Dam                                        6½ mi

| | |
|---|---|
| Description: | Class II–III |
| Date checked: | 1988, ST |
| Navigable: | High water, medium water (May or after fall rains) |
| Scenery: | Wild |
| Map: | USGS Londonderry 15 |
| Portage: | 6¼ mi **Ball Mountain flood control dam**— extremely difficult |

This section is easier than the one above. The gradient is constant, with waves in high water and rocks in low. The mouth of the Winhall (1¾ miles) is a possible take-out, although it is not accessible in mud season.

The gradient steepens for the next 2 miles, ending suddenly at the backwater of Ball Mountain Dam. At low pond there are another 2 miles of gradually diminishing current and rapids to the portage trail on the right above the dam. Ice floes may block the river in the spring. The carry up is exceedingly strenuous: 250 vertical feet in ½ mile to the road. When continuing the run, you should scout the portage trail before putting in. There are better river sections in the area to paddle, considering the effort required in portaging.

## Ball Mountain Dam–Salmon Hole                          2¾ mi

| | |
|---|---|
| Description: | Class III–IV |
| Date checked: | 1988 |
| Navigable: | Controlled release |
| Scenery: | Wild |
| Map: | USGS Londonderry 15 |

This is the famous West River run, which has greatly increased in popularity with the water releases from Ball Mountain Dam.

Access to the upper river is a problem. Kayakers sometimes carry across the dam and put in on the left below it, which is a long, steep carry. A dirt road on the old railroad bed along the left bank can be reached from Salmon Hole. Although narrow and muddy, it is the usual route. Access may be regulated.

A difficult drop lies just below the put-in, then the rapids moderate somewhat, with waves in high water and rock dodging at medium stage. The entire river can be seen from the access road.

The most difficult part is the Dumplings shortly above Salmon Hole. The river drops and swirls around huge boulders, to the delight of boaters and spectators alike. On water-release weekends even the bank is standing room only. The large pool below is Salmon Hole, the take-out.

This area is now a state park; admission is charged and entrance regulated.

## Salmon Hole–Townshend Dam                                    5½ mi

| | |
|---|---|
| Description: | Class II–III |
| Date checked: | 1988, ST |
| Navigable: | Controlled release |
| Scenery: | Forested, rural |
| Maps: | USGS Londonderry 15, Saxtons River 15 |
| Portage: | (5½ mi   R   **Townshend Dam** ½ mi by car) |

This section is somewhat easier to paddle than the one above and is more accessible.

Put in at Salmon Hole or at the bridge ¼ mile below. At high water the waves are heavy; open boaters are especially advised to have proper flotation. Almost immediately the river divides around an island, with most of the water flowing left. In high water the right channel feels more like a small river, for those who prefer rocks to waves.

The most difficult spot is at the foot of the island, where the left channel drives toward the right shore around some large rocks. The spot is visible from VT 30.

The waves are heavy to the VT 30 bridge (2½ miles) but moderate slightly to the VT 100 bridge (3¾ miles). Below here is the nicest part of the run, where the river is not near the road and the waves are very large.

## Townshend Dam–West Dummerston                          12½ mi

| | |
|---|---|
| Description: | Class I–II |
| Date checked: | 1988, ST |
| Navigable: | Spring, fall, wet summers; controlled release |
| Scenery: | Forested, rural |
| Map: | USGS Brattleboro 15 |

This section offers easy running for the less experienced paddler. The water is regulated by the flood control dam upstream, but natural water is usually allowed to flow through. The water releases above Jamaica raise this section to very high water.

Put in on the left from the dirt road between the road across the dam and the covered bridge. The first part is narrow, curving, and mostly away from the road. In low and medium water easy rapids alternate with long, smooth sections. Very high water washes out all the smaller rapids and ledges, leaving only really big rocks as obstacles, but the current is very fast.

Below the VT 30 bridge (3¾ miles) the river becomes wider, straighter, and less difficult. Below a bridge on a side road (6¼ miles) the river again approaches VT 30 and passes the site of the West Dummerston dam, of which little trace remains. Above the covered bridge and within sight of it is a series of ledges best run to the right at most water levels.

## West Dummerston–Connecticut River                                    6½ mi

| | |
|---|---|
| Description: | Class I–II |
| Date checked: | 1988, ST |
| Navigable: | Spring, summer, fall; controlled release |
| Scenery: | Forested, settled |
| Map: | USGS Brattleboro 15 |

The most difficult rapids in this section lie below the West Dummerston covered bridge. A ledge around the next corner can be dangerous in high water. Under any conditions but low water, hug the right bank. If the right channel can be run, the ledge will generate hydraulics. In low water the river funnels through a selection of channels with various obstructions, and some paddlers may want to try them all to practice technique. Farther on, many large rocks are scattered about the river.

If the water is low, it is well to take out at the next iron bridge (1½ miles); below it the water is only spread thinly over the rocks. With sufficient water this section offers excellent practice in water reading and a pleasant run with riffles, fast corners, and islands. All of it is within sight of VT 30, which provides good access but destroys the aura of remoteness of the river above West Dummerston. A convenient take-out is directly below the high I-91 bridge (5½ miles, no access).

The mouth of the West River is ponded from the Vernon Dam 7 miles down the Connecticut River, and it is filled with low islands that are interesting to explore. The US 5 bridge and a railroad bridge cross a rocky cut at the mouth.

## WINHALL RIVER                                                    VT

The Winhall River is a small stream that rises on the north slope of Stratton Mountain and flows east to join the West River. With sufficient water it provides one of the longest advanced whitewater runs in Vermont. There is rarely enough water to paddle. All the rapids can be run by skilled open boaters, although most will portage Londonderry Rapids.

### Off VT Rte. 30–West River                                     7 mi

| | |
|---|---|
| Description: | Class III–IV |
| Date checked: | 1987, ST |
| Navigable: | High or medium water (April) |
| Scenery: | Forested |
| Map: | USGS Londonderry 15 |

A dirt road leads up the north bank from Grahamville School, which is a mile west of Bondville on VT 30. From one put-in at a large field on this road, there are continuous Class II–III rapids for a mile to the bridge at Grahamville School. The next mile to the VT 30 bridge (2 miles) is about the same, with a more difficult section around a big rock in the middle just above the bridge.

From Bondville to the VT 100 bridge in Rawsonville, 2 miles of Class III–IV rapids keep the paddler very alert. Another mile of similar rapids brings you to a bridge on the unpaved Londonderry Road (5 miles). **Caution!** Pull out at this bridge and scout the difficult Londonderry Rapids in the next left turn. These rapids, at an old dam site, can be portaged on either side. For the more skillful paddler, routes exist on both the extreme left and the extreme right.

Below Londonderry Rapids (5 miles) there are 2 miles of easier Class II–III rapids to the confluence with the West River, but the waves can be heavy. Take out either just above or just below the confluence on the right, where there is a campground that is accessible from VT 100 to the north of Rawsonville.

## WARDSBORO BROOK                                    VT

This small stream enters the West River below Ball Mountain Dam, and it is paralleled by VT 100. It is a demanding Class IV run that requires high water. Since runoff here occurs rapidly, Wardsboro Brook is recommended for only a few weeks of the year.

### Wardsboro–West River                              4½ mi

| | |
|---|---|
| Description: | Class III–IV |
| Date checked: | 1988, ST |
| Navigable: | High water only (early April) |
| Scenery: | Forested |
| Map: | USGS Londonderry 15, Saxtons River 15 |

A put-in can be made below the bridge and the waterfall in the town of Wardsboro. Class III rapids make up the first mile of this run. Wardsboro Brook then passes under VT 100 and turns right with the first of many difficult Class IV rapids. This right turn should be scouted, as the channel changes with water levels and may not exist at low water. The next 2½ miles are continuous difficult rapids to the next VT 100 bridge, where they get even harder.

A take-out may be made at a dirt road on the left just below the bridge. If you choose to run the last mile, take out at the bridge just above the confluence (4½ miles). If you had difficulty up above, don't run the last mile.

## ASHUELOT RIVER                                                        NH

The Ashuelot River is a beautiful tributary of the Connecticut, entering from the east only a short distance above the Massachusetts state line. The river offers such a variety of paddling that short trips can be arranged to suit just about anyone's taste.

The upper stretches are rapid and rough. The middle reaches are largely winding and placid, and the last few miles provide some of the wildest paddling in NH. The upper part must be done in the spring; the lower section can sometimes be run in the summer or fall. The middle section can be paddled during most of the year.

### Power line–Lower Stillwater                                       5¾ mi

| | |
|---|---|
| Description: | Flatwater, quickwater, Class I–III |
| Date checked: | 1983 |
| Navigable: | High water (April) |
| Scenery: | Forested, towns |
| Map: | USGS Lovewell Mountain 15 |
| Portage: | 2½ mi   R   **dam in Marlow** 25 yd |

Put in at a power dam 1½ miles north of Marlow on the road to Ashuelot Lake. From here the river is mostly Class I, with a ledge ¼ mile below the start, to the flowage from the dam in Marlow.

Below the dam a little fast water runs to the next pond, which is about a mile below. After the pond there are some interesting Class III rapids. The first ones run under a footbridge and pass around a corner by an abutment. The rapids are followed by more ledges, which might have to be lined, and the river comes out in a pond-like section, known as Lower Stillwater. Take out at the white bridge by a pull-off.

**Lower Stillwater–Gilsum Gorge** **4½ mi**

| | |
|---|---|
| Description: | Class III–IV |
| Date checked: | 1983 |
| Navigable: | High to medium water (April) |
| Scenery: | Forested, town |
| Map: | USGS Lovewell Mountain 15, Bellows Falls 15 |
| Portage: | (4½ mi  L  **Gilsum Gorge** [cross river in 200 yd] ¾ mi) |

A gauge near the beginning of Gilsum Gorge is located on the right retaining wall a bit upstream of an old stone bridge just off NH 10. This section is scratchy but passable at a reading of 3.5; at 5.5 the river is Class IV. The gorge has been run at levels around 3.5 and 4.1.

This section, known as the Upper Ashuelot, makes a good whitewater run for intermediate or expert paddlers. The scenery is somewhat marred by NH 10, which is almost always present on the bank, but this makes put-ins and take-outs easier.

Just below Lower Stillwater, there is a small bridge over the river which offers a possible put-in. This spot is recommended only for those who like to start with a bang: the most difficult regularly run pitch in the river is about 200 yards below the put-in. Called Surprise Rapids, this stretch can be examined from NH 10, and it should definitely be scouted.

Surprise Rapids is followed by much easier Class II–III rapids. The river bends to the right and is followed by an old elbow of NH 10 (1/2 mile), while the newer road continues straight ahead. This old loop is the usual put-in, since most groups do not want to start off with Surprise Rapids. The rapids here are easy Class II. The river passes another small bridge, and the easy rapids flatten out to smoothwater (1 mile).

Below a short pool the current speeds up considerably, marking the beginning of 2 miles of continuous rapids. The river is narrowed by the road embankment to the left. The 2 miles contain many difficult Class III and IV rapids and require a great deal of maneuvering, even at high water levels. Fortunately, NH 10 and its older loops are also nearby for an emergency take-out.

At the end of this 2-mile stretch, the river becomes relatively calm and splits around an island. The right side should be taken to get into position for a small broken dam below. The broken dam is about 1½ feet in height, and it is best to run it from the far right. One hundred yards below, near the NH 10 bridge in Gilsum (3½ miles), the sawmill on the left provides a possible take-out.

Rapids continue through Gilsum, with the road or houses fairly close on the right. The rapids in this section are less difficult than those above, but they can have heavy waves, particularly near the end. Take out just below the NH 10 bridge (4½ miles) at a picnic area on the left. Plan and execute this landing with caution because the current is strong and the gorge begins about 200 yards below.

An old stone bridge just off NH 10 marks the actual entrance to the gorge. From the bridge, the gorge and its first drop are very impressive. The main current undercuts and deflects off an enomous rock in the center. Gilsum Gorge has been run in relatively low water, but the run is a difficult stunt.

## Gilsum Gorge–Shaw's Corner                                    4 mi

| | |
|---|---|
| Description: | Class **II–III** |
| Date checked: | 1983 |
| Navigable: | High to medium water (April) |
| Scenery: | Forested |
| Map: | USGS Bellows Falls 15 |

This is a popular intermediate trip, with continuous rapids, but it is closely followed by a road.

Water levels required for this section are about the same as for the stretch above Gilsum Gorge. If the gauge above the stone bridge at the head of the gorge reads 3.5, the river is low but runnable; at 5.5 or higher you can expect a number of Class III rapids.

A put-in can be made where the river first approaches the road below Gilsum Gorge. The small May Brook enters the river at this point, and there is a short island in the stream.

Class II rapids continue to a small bridge (¼ mile). Just below this bridge is a shallow rapid: if this spot is passable, then so is the rest of the run. The Ashuelot bends away from the road. The next stretch contains many Class II rapids and some tight turns. The river then returns to the road (1¾ miles). The rapids become slightly more difficult, approaching Class III at water levels of 5.0 and higher.

About 2½ miles from May Brook there is one spot where the river rounds a right bend with large boulders blocking the left side. The channel then empties back into the left. This is the most difficult spot except for Shaw's Corner Rapids, farther downstream.

For a long distance above Shaw's Corner, the road remains close beside the river. The river turns left (3½ miles) and passes a long straight stretch with a field on the right. Then the stone remains of a bridge abutment come into view on the right bank, marking the beginning of Shaw's Corner Rapids. The river turns sharply left with a ledge on the left. A short, rocky section is followed by three ledges, with waves or hydraulics, depending on the water level. Novice and intermediate paddlers should scout this area.

A suspension bridge (4 miles) just below Shaw's Corner Rapids is the usual take-out.

## Shaw's Corner–flood control dam                    5¼ mi

The Class II rapids continue for about a mile to an old abutment, after which they gradually change to fastwater, undercutting the banks. In the spring, when the water is high, there is a little pond above the dam, but what little water there is may be frozen. Also, there is a gate on the road. Therefore it might be best to run this section after a fall rain.

## Flood control dam–Keene                                6¾ mi

| | |
|---|---|
| Description: | Flatwater, **quickwater** |
| Date checked: | 1983 |
| Navigable: | Medium-high for upper part |
| Scenery: | Rural, towns, forested |
| Maps: | USGS Bellow Falls 15, Keene 15 |
| Portage: | (6¾ mi   R   **dam in Keene** 10 yd) |

Put in at a bridge below the dam. The Ashuelot River here is a winding brook with a sandy bottom. It runs swiftly through a golf course and then gradually slows down approaching the dam in Keene, which is above the first bridge to the north of town. There is a large island just above the dam. It is easy to take out on the left, but the shorter carry is to the right.

## Keene–West Swanzey                                8¾ mi

| | |
|---|---|
| Description: | Flatwater, quickwater |
| Date checked: | 1983 |
| Navigable: | Passable in all but dry weather |
| Scenery: | Forested, rural, towns |
| Map: | USGS Keene 15 |
| Portage: | (8¾ mi   L   **dam in West Swanzey**) |

The river flows around rather than through Keene; even so, it is less clear and enjoyable. There is an old stone arch bridge above the new bridge in the middle of town. There are several bridges in town, and at least two of them have gauges.

Otter Brook comes in on the left shortly below the last bridge, near where sewage once flowed into the river from a huge conduit. One covered bridge is passed at Swanzey, and there is a dam near the next one, Carleton covered bridge, in West Swanzey.

## West Swanzey–Ashuelot                                    13¼ mi

Map:                    USGS Keene 15

Below the dam at West Swanzey the river continues placidly for 3 miles to a point ½ mile below the Westport bridge, where there is a broken dam. This is easy to run at ordinary water levels. The next 8 miles to Winchester are all flatwater. The dam there can be carried to the left. Stillwater continues for another 3 miles to Ashuelot. This section has been very polluted in the past but should make a nice run when it has been cleaned up.

## Ashuelot–Connecticut River                              5 mi

| | |
|---|---|
| Description: | Quickwater, Class **III–IV** |
| Date checked: | 1983 |
| Navigable: | Medium water (spring and after heavy rains) |
| Scenery: | Forested, urban |
| Map: | USGS Keene 15 |
| Portages: | ¼ mi e **first dam** 30 yd |
| | ¾ mi   R   **second dam** 50 yd—after dam |
| | 1½ mi   R   **third dam**—difficult 50 yd— after dam |
| | 2¼ mi   R   **fourth dam**—approach cautiously 30 yd |
| | 3 mi **fifth dam** 30 yd |

This section of the Ashuelot has distinct advantages and disadvantages. On the positive side, the rapids are heavy and challenging, and the water level is often high enough for summertime paddling. As drawbacks, frequent dams necessitate short and difficult portages, the water is polluted, and many factories back right on the river.

There is a telemark system gauge a short way up the left bank from the NH 63 bridge in Hinsdale. A reading around 4.5 corresponds to medium water and 5.0 to high water. At any runnable level the lower Ashuelot is one of the larger and more forceful whitewater runs in New England. Often the waves are too large and the dams too close together for safe sport in open boats.

Put in at the covered bridge in Ashuelot. Here the river is wide, with a good current but no real rapids. The first dam (¼ mile) has washed out and can be run in the center. Mostly smooth river continues to the second dam (¾ mile). There are several long, wavy Class III rapids to the next dam (1½ miles), which requires a short but tough portage on the right. The rapids here are typical of the Lower Ashuelot—turbulent and powerful in high water.

Below the third dam (1½ miles) the Ashuelot passes under a bridge to the Ashuelot River Company. In the next right turn lies the heaviest rapid of the trip, Class III–IV even at lower water levels. This rapid should be looked over from the side road on the right bank. More rapids continue to the fourth dam (2¼ miles), which lies on a diagonal across the river, from upstream left to downriver right. It can be run safely after scouting, but for those who prefer not to try, use the right side for portage. Approach with caution because of the strong current above the dam and because there is a diversion canal on the right.

More large rapids in several stretches bring you to the backwater from the fifth dam. This last dam (3 miles) is just below a steel bridge in Hinsdale. Below it there is a sharp drop, then some easier rapids to the NH 63 bridge (3½ miles) in the town. Rapids diminish to smoothwater, and the river flows through a gap into the broad Connecticut River (5 miles).

## OTTER BROOK                                              NH

Otter Brook is a small tributary of the Ashuelot and is sometimes called the East Branch, or just the Branch. The water is often clear, particularly above the Otter Brook flood control dam, making the stream very appealing. The upper part of Otter Brook is an excellent advanced whitewater run when it has water. The lower portion also holds intermediate rapids before giving way to quickwater in Keene.

## East Sullivan–Otter Brook State Park 3¼ mi

| | |
|---|---|
| Description: | Class III–IV |
| Date checked: | 1983 |
| Navigable: | High water only (early April) |
| Scenery: | Forested |
| Map: | USGS Monadnock 15 |

For one or two weeks in the year this section of Otter Brook is runnable. It is definitely a small stream, averaging 10–15 yards in width. Expert boaters who catch it will find Otter Brook an enjoyable but not intimidating Class IV run.

There is a hand-painted gauge on the upstream side of the NH 9 bridge abutment, but unfortunately the water piles up against it, so accurate readings are hard to get. From East Sullivan to Otter Brook State Park, NH 9 is next to the brook.

Put in just below the NH 9 bridge in East Sullivan. The rapids are Class II for the first 100 yards, and then the difficulty increases to Class III. The rapids are continuous. A long stretch of easy Class IV rapids follows, with no pools in which to rest.

The most difficult drop in the river comes when it bears slightly left away from the road and plunges 1 foot and then 3 feet over an angled ledge (1 mile). There is another class IV drop shortly below, where the river turns right and returns to the road. Rapids continue past an old iron bridge (1¾ miles) to the bridge at Pinnacle Ski Area.

Below the ski area (2½ miles) the rapids diminish in intensity, but they remain continuous. Here, as above in Otter Brook, a capsized boat can be swept a long way downstream.

The suggested take-out is at the next bridge (3¼ miles), which is the access road to Otter Brook State Park. Picnic tables on the left here provide a pleasant lunch spot. Because the gate at the NH 9 entrance to the park is usually locked when the river is runnable, boats must be carried 200 yards or so from the river to NH 9.

The rapids flatten out quickly below Otter Brook State Park, with mostly quickwater to the pool behind the flood control dam. A ½-mile flatwater paddle brings you to the dam itself (5 miles), which is a long steep carry.

## Flood control dam–Ashuelot River                                    5 mi

| | |
|---|---|
| Description: | Quickwater, Class **II–III** |
| Date checked: | 1988, JVZ |
| Navigable: | High to medium water (April) |
| | Dam controlled |
| Scenery: | Forested |
| Maps: | USGS Monadnock 15, Keene 15 |

Below the dam Otter Brook contains continuous intermediate rapids. The amount of water for the run is controlled completely by the dam, which is managed by the Corps of Engineers.

Put in right below the spillway from the dam. The put-in can be found by following signs to the Otter Brook dam from NH 101 just east of Keene. Rapids begin immediately, with a wavy Class III drop in a right turn. Otter Brook passes the stone abutments that remain of an old bridge and continues south-ward with Class II–III rapids. After 2 miles NH 101 is visible ahead. The most difficult drop of the trip begins just before Otter Brook reaches NH 101. The river turns right and is joined by Minnewawa Brook on the left. A green house appears straight in front. Just at this point there is a ledge that should (and at times must) be run on the right.

After the NH 101 bridge (3 miles) the rapids diminish quickly as the river flows to a high railroad bridge, followed by a dam (3½ miles). This dam has cement flanges that extend upstream on either side, and the stream has cut a new channel above the right flange. Before entering, scout this passage for overhanging brush or fallen trees. To avoid this potentially blocked section of the brook, take out on the left just past the bridge.

After the dam the brook is mostly quickwater, with a good current and a sandy bottom. Take out on the right just before the NH 12 bridge in Keene (4¾ miles) or continue to join the Ashuelot River (5 miles).

## SOUTH BRANCH, ASHUELOT RIVER                                          NH

The South Branch of the Ashuelot River is a small stream that rises in Troy, rushes steeply northward to Webb, and then flows more smoothly westward to a junction with the Ashuelot River in Keene. The rapid, upper part is only runnable for a few days of the year.

### Troy Gap–Webb                                                       3 mi

| | |
|---|---|
| Description: | Class IV |
| Date checked: | 1983 |
| Navigable: | High water (April) |
| Scenery: | Forested |
| Map: | USGS Monadnock 15 |

This portion of the stream is hemmed by very steep banks, and it contains many difficult rapids. The river drops 300 feet in these 3 miles. The railroad and NH 12 follow the river closely, although they are not always visible. When runnable, the South Branch is so narrow that paddlers find it a challenge to avoid running on top of one another. This problem is accentuated by the possibility of fallen trees, which can be a real hazard.

The South Branch is a difficult run. It should not be attempted by inexperienced paddlers or open boats.

Put in from NH 12 about 1½ miles north of the center of Troy. Here there are two bridges close together where the South Branch loops under a road. The stream passes immediately under a railroad bridge, with flatwater for the first 100 yards.

The rapids begin, become continuous, and increase to Class IV in the next ½ mile. The river then turns left under a railroad bridge and crosses twice under NH 12 (¾ mile). These bridges mark the most difficult rapids in the river. Paddlers must first contend with a large crosswave off the railroad bridge abutment, then a very steep drop, followed by extremely rocky going between the two road bridges. Because this stretch has steep, rocky walls, it should be scouted from the road bridges before you put in. Highway construction may alter this area.

The next 1¼ miles to a small pool and dam (2 miles) contain many more Class IV rapids. The dam, easily visible from NH 12, has a notch in the center that makes it runnable. Rapids moderate in the next mile to a culvert that is on a construction company road in Webb. This spot is reached by leaving NH 12 and following the road toward East Swanzey for a few hundred yards to a side road on the left, which leads in 100 yards to the river.

## Webb–Ashuelot River                                          9 mi

| Maps: | USGS Monadnock 15, Keene 15 |
|-------|------------------------------|

Put in where the stream turns south away from NH 12 and follows the road to East Swanzey. It is about 2 miles to the millpond above the dam just below East Swanzey, with rapids for much of the way. Below here the South Branch has good current and few rapids, winding through pastureland until it joins the main Ashuelot near Swanzey, some 7 miles down.

## GREEN RIVER                                          VT, MA

The Green River is a crystal mountain stream that descends a narrow valley through the hills north of Greenfield, Massachusetts, and empties into the Deerfield River near that city. Rising to the west of Governors Mountain in Guilford, Vermont, it is large enough to paddle during the spring by the time it reaches the Green River Post Office. There are excellent swimming holes and plenty of opportunities for trout fishing. It is an unusually beautiful stream and a delight to the nature lover.

**Green River–West Leyden**                                              **8 mi**

| Description: | Class III |
|---|---|
| Date checked: | 1983 |
| Navigable: | High water (early April) |
| Scenery: | Forested |
| Maps: | USGS Brattleboro, Colrain |
| Portage: | 8 mi  L  **dam** |

The access and car shuttle are as difficult as the canoeing on the Green River because the best water level for canoeing coincides with the last part of mud season in the dirt access roads. Although a dirt road follows immediately along the right bank, it is often impassable for all except four-wheel-drive vehicles. Even the long way around is not particularly easy.

A boat can be launched a short distance below the mill dam at Green River from the dirt road on the right bank. All the pitches can be run at oridinary high water levels. The river is small, steep, and full of ledges, particularly in the uppermost part where it rounds Pulpit Mountain. It is best to proceed cautiously, inspecting each bad chute before you run it.

The Massachusetts state line is passed at 3¼ miles. At Stewartsville the dam at the sawmill is best carried on the left.

# Chapter 5

# Merrimack Watershed

# MERRIMACK WATERSHED

North Woodstock

East Branch

Wentworth

Pemigewasset River

Baker River

Plymouth

Campton

Mad River

Cockermouth River

Bristol

Newfound River

Fowler River

Smith River

Grafton Center

Lake Winnipesaukee

Winnipesaukee River

Franklin

Merrimack River

Pearls Corner

Suncook River

Suncook River

Pittsfield

Little Suncook R.

Scale in miles

0    5    10    15    20    25    30

Grey area not covered in this book.

*The Merrimack Watershed dominates central New Hampshire. It encompasses and borders large population centers, so the Merrimack and its tributaries are local rivers to many people and are frequently paddled. In the past the larger rivers suitable for summer paddling have been badly polluted, but they are now being cleaned up and are available for recreational use.*

*The divides are low to the east and west, so the tributaries have many miles of quickwater and easy rapids, as well as difficult drops to challenge experts. Many of the rivers provide easy paddling throughout the summer.*

## MERRIMACK RIVER                                          NH

The Merrimack River begins in Franklin, New Hampshire, at the confluence of the Pemigewasset and Winnipesaukee rivers. It flows south into Massachusetts and then turns east and runs into the sea at Newburyport.

Except in the large cities, the banks are still rather nice from a distance. Suburban sprawl usually does not reach the river's edge. From Franklin to Concord, the river has a sandy bottom. The closer you get to the sea, the muddier and more polluted the river becomes.

Almost all of the river is runnable throughout the paddling season. However, it should be avoided at high water when the current is fast, since the landings are difficult, and the approaches to the dams are dangerous.

Most of the big drops have been harvested for power. When the river's natural flow is low, the water level is affected by the demand for electricity. Low water has the biggest impact on the paddler below Franklin and below Amoskeag Dam in Manchester. Information on daily flows can be obtained by calling the dispatcher at the Public Service Company of New Hampshire (603-225-6182).

The Merrimack is close to many large population centers, and launching ramps provide access to all sections of the river.

In Penacook, at the mouth of the Contoocook River, sits Hannah Duston Island. It was there that Hannah Duston, who was captured by Indians in a raid on Haverhill, Massachusetts, on March 15, 1697, a week after the delivery of her eighth child, escaped her captors. On the morning of March 31, with the help of Mary Neff, who had been taken prisoner at the same time, and a youth who had been captured in a raid in Worcester, Massachusetts, she killed and scalped ten of the twelve Indians guarding her. The other two Indians fled, and three prisoners went downriver by canoe to reach Nashua that night. Hannah later received a bounty of twenty-five pounds per scalp from the Massachusetts General Court.

## Franklin–Concord                                                    24 mi

| | |
|---|---|
| Description: | Flatwater, quickwater, Class I |
| Date checked: | 1988, WF |
| Navigable: | Passable at all water levels |
| | Dam controlled, peak power generation on Pemigewasset River |
| Scenery: | Forested, settled |
| Maps: | USGS Penacook 15, Concord |

Put in on the Pemigewasset River below Eastman Falls Dam, if you want to begin with 1 mile of Class II rapids, or on the Winnepesaukee River behind the high school in Franklin, if you prefer ½ mile of quickwater.

From the confluence of the Pemigewasset and Winnipeasukee rivers, there are Class I rapids for the first ½ mile. Then there is a moderate current to Boscawen (10½ miles), where the first bridge (closed) is located. Another 4½ miles of meandering river brings you to Penacook, the US 4 bridge off Exit 17 of I-93 (poor access), and the mouth of the Contoocook River on the right.

In the mouth of the Contoocook River (15 miles) there is an island, joined to the mainland by two railroad bridges, a monument to Hannah Duston. In 2 miles there is another bridge with a launching ramp downstream on the right. From that point it is 1 mile to Sewall Falls Dam, which has been breached and no longer needs to be portaged. Beware of assorted debris and a new set of standing waves now rated as Class III. Scouting of the run should be considered. A nice sand beach on the right shore just above the dam offers a fine landing place. The dam itself is old, and care should be used when using it as a vantage point.

Below Sewall Falls Dam (18 miles) there is a Class III rapid that is 1/4 mile long and rocky in low water. In another 3 1/2 miles there is a railroad bridge and an I-93 bridge, just upstream from which there is a launching ramp that can be reached from Exit 16. The remaining distance to the Bridge Street bridge (24 miles) was shortened in 1976 when a new channel was cut across a meander. A new launching ramp is on the right bank near the cloverleaf of I-393, 1 mile above Bridge Street.

## Concord–Manchester                                    18 1/4 mi

| | |
|---|---|
| Description: | Flatwater, quickwater |
| Date checked: | 1988, WO |
| Navigable: | Passable at all water levels |
| | Dam controlled, good flow all year |
| Scenery: | Forested, settled |
| Maps: | USGS Concord 15, Suncook, Manchester North |
| Portages: | 5 mi   L   **Garvin's Falls Dam** 100 yd |
| | 10 1/2 mi   L   **dam at Hooksett** 1/4 mi |
| | (18 1/4 mi   R   **Amoskeag Dam** 200 yd) |

There are boat-launching ramps just above the Bridge Street bridge and the US 3 bridge (1 1/2 miles) on the left. After 2 1/4 miles of meandering, you pass under a railroad bridge, below which there is some turbulence. Then Garvin's Falls Dam (5 miles) comes in sight. Portage on the left. There is a short Class II rapid below it.

In the next 5 1/2 miles to the dam at Hooksett, you pass the mouth of the Soucook River (5 3/4 miles) and the Suncook River

(8¾ miles). About ¼ mile above Hooksett Dam there are two nice boat-launching ramps on the left, but experienced paddlers who are carrying by hand can continue in low water as far as the abutment on the left (10½ miles). Carry past the parking area to another launching ramp below the dam.

There is some turbulence around the bridge abutments below the Hooksett dam, then 7¼ miles of smoothwater to Manchester. Amoskeag Bridge and the Manchester skyline can be seen from a long distance upstream. Take out at the bridge on the right to portage Amoskeag Dam. Look for concrete "steps" by the river and the Holiday Inn.

## Manchester–Nashua                                              17¾ mi

| | |
|---|---|
| Description: | Flatwater, quickwater, Class II–III |
| Date checked: | 1988, GE |
| Navigable: | Passable at most water levels |
| | Dam controlled, peak power generation |
| Scenery: | Forested, settled, urban |
| Maps: | USGS Manchester North, Manchester South, Nashua North |

Gauge readings at Amoskeag Dam in Manchester can be obtained by calling the Public Service Company dispatcher at 603-225-6182, x 2281. Flood stage is anything over 20,000 cubic feet per second (cfs). Spring runoff typically produces 12,000–15,000 cfs. Early summer levels run around 5,000 cfs, and dry summers bottom out at 1,200–1,300 cfs. At 5,000–12,000 cfs, the two most difficult rapids, Goffs Falls and Griffins Falls, are easy to moderate Class III; at high water, they wash out. The Merrimack moves a lot of water, but it does so with a constant current of strong quickwater, rather than through rocky drops.

There is a mile of Class II rapids through Manchester. On the left bank the walls of old factories rise straight up from the river, and on the right there is a limited access highway. In high water, keep to the right.

Past two highway bridges and shortly below the rapids, the Piscataquog River (2 miles) enters on the right in South Manchester. A cascade of sewage, attested by a crowd of herring gulls, comes in on the left just above the Queen City Bridge, which is the third highway bridge below Amoskeag Dam. In 1½ miles there is a riffle, and soon the I-293 bridges come into sight.

Land under the I-293 bridges (4¼ miles) to scout the Class III drops, Griffins Falls and Goffs Falls, which can be run on either side but not in the middle. This spot can be reached on the right via a dirt road. In another ¾ mile there is a railroad bridge with a ledge starting just above it. It too can be run on either side but not in the middle, where there is an island. This ledge can be inspected in advance from dirt roads on either side.

Below the railroad bridge (5 miles) there is smoothwater for 1¼ miles to a short Class II drop, and then more smoothwater for another 2 miles to a longer Class II rapid just below a big power line. After 2¼ miles of smoothwater the Souhegan River (10½ miles) enters on the right. Almost 3 miles downstream of the confluence with the Souhegan, on the right, are the best preserved remains of the old lock and canal system. In another mile there is a Class II rapid, followed by 3¼ miles of easy paddling to the NH 111 bridge (17¾ miles) in Nashua just below the mouth of the Nashua River on the right.

## Nashua–Lowell                                          14 mi

| | |
|---|---|
| Description: | Flatwater, quickwater |
| Date checked: | 1988, GE |
| Navigable: | Passable at all water levels |
| Scenery: | Forested, settled, towns |
| Maps: | USGS Nashua South, Lowell |

From the NH 111 bridge in Nashua, it is only 1 mile to the south end of town, where Salmon Brook enters on the right.

The river now is all smoothwater. It passes between tilled fields and meadows for some distance, finally entering a section with wooded banks before it reaches the next bridge, MA 113, at Tyngsboro, Massachusetts, 5 miles below. There are more signs of human habitation in the next 4 miles to North Chelmsford, where Stony Brook enters on the right. In another 3 miles one arrives at Lowell. Take out at the public launching ramp above the dam.

The river is followed by the railroad. Watch for interesting old stone bridges and culverts spanning small tributaries.

## PEMIGEWASSET RIVER                                    NH

The Pemi is a born-again river. In the midtwentieth century, much of it was fetid and frowzy. Today it is clean and clear.

Analysis of the river water in the mid-1960s yielded results typical of severe pollution. Some tests in 1966–67 showed less than 10 percent saturation of oxygen. But completion of several wastewater treatment facilities resulted in a significant improvement in water quality. The Pemigewasset is now a Class B river, which means it is suitable for swimming and fishing.

The Weeks Act of 1911 authorized the federal government to purchase land in the White Mountains to protect watersheds. By that time many of the steep slopes in the Pemigewasset watershed had been denuded by logging, which in some cases was followed by forest fires. Thus, there existed the possibility of severe flooding caused by rapid runoff into the Pemigewasset River. This potential threat to the many communities downstream along the Pemigewasset and Merrimack rivers helped lead to the establishment of the White Mountain National Forest.

During and after a heavy rain the water level can change very quickly, sometimes by several feet in a couple of hours. Be conscious of this if you are camping along the river, for there is plenty of evidence that the islands are flooded each year.

Most of this river consists of swift current over a gravel bottom, but there are two stretches with challenging rapids. The popular one begins at North Woodstock. It is usually a good

Class II run, but in very high water there are large waves and usually a few fallen trees sticking hazardously out into the main current. Above Livermore Falls in Campton there are more fine rapids, but high water produces high waves that must be handled carefully in open boats. The danger is that the pools of calm water, which are present at medium water, cease to exist when the water is high, so that the heavy rapids and fast-moving water continue right up to the lip of the falls.

The river is attractive and seemingly remote, which is surprising considering that there are three highways, a railroad, and transmission lines following the narrow valley. All of these are occasionally obvious, but on the whole the trip is a scenic one. In many respects this section is similar to the Saco River from Bartlett to North Conway.

## North Woodstock–third NH Rte. 175 bridge                4½ mi

| | |
|---|---|
| Description: | Class I–II |
| Date checked: | 1988, CR |
| Navigable: | Medium to high water (May) |
| Scenery: | Forested |
| Map: | USGS Lincoln |

This section of the Pemigewasset is most responsive to rainfall and melting snow. The gradient is not so steep that it requires a heavy runoff, as is the case with the East Branch, yet it is just enough to require a good flow for easy passage. A soaking summer rain usually raises the river to medium levels and provides a day or two of pleasant boating. Most of the river below Woodstock remains passable at moderately low water, although travel may be slow because some walking down will be necessary. Between Plymouth and Woodstock, I-93 crosses the river four times, so you have a good opportunity to check the water level as you drive along.

Put in just below the stone bridge on NH 112 just east of NH 3, and park your car out of the way. At the start of the run the river is shallow and rocky, but it is immediately joined by the

East Branch, which forces the water against a cliff on the right, creating large waves that may sink the unwary. The ensuing ¼ mile of Class II rapids (III in high water) ends just before a NH 175 bridge, which serves as an alternate put-in for less experienced boaters.

For the next 4 miles the river flows through intermittent Class II rapids and around islands where the channel changes frequently. Frequent sharp corners with many fallen trees pose the only special danger for competent whitewater paddlers.

Below the second NH 175 bridge (4 miles), where I-93 comes in sight on the left, the river makes a sweeping S-curve. Pull in below at the old abutment to scout the ledges above the third NH 175 bridge. These ledges constitute the most difficult rapids in this section. They may be carried on either side or run in various places, depending on water level. The easiest route is an obscure channel on the left. The banking on the right also provides take-outs above and below the ledges. There is a small parking lot on the right below the bridge.

## Third NH Rte. 175 bridge–Blair Road                    14½ mi

| Description: | **Quickwater,** Class I–II |
|---|---|
| Date checked: | 1988, CR |
| Navigable: | Medium water |
| Scenery: | Forested, rural |
| Map: | USGS Lincoln |

The rapids in this section are not as difficult as the ones above. Class I rapids and riffles are interspersed with more and more quickwater the farther you go downstream. The banks are still largely wild, although bridges cross more frequently. As in the previous section countless bends with inconveniently located downed trees are a hazard.

Access to the West Thornton NH 175 bridge (5 miles) is via a side road off NH 3 just north of the bridge. This leads to a launching ramp under the bridge, which is an excellent site for rainy day picnicking or for loading boats in foul weather.

There is more of the same past the second railroad bridge (10¼ miles), the second crossing of I-93, a bridge in West Campton near a gravel mill (12¾ miles), the mouth of the Mad River (13¾ miles), the third crossing of I-93, and finally the Blair Road covered bridge (off Exit 27, I-93).

## Blair–Plymouth                                                    4 mi

| | |
|---|---|
| Description: | Quickwater, Class I–III |
| Date checked: | 1988, CR |
| Navigable: | Medium water, dangerous in high water |
| Scenery: | Forested, towns |
| Maps: | USGS Lincoln, Plymouth 15 |
| Portage: | 2 mi  R  **Livermore Falls**—dangerous landing above |

Class II–III rapids begin a mile below the covered bridge at Blair and continue to the top of the falls. Be sure to scout this stretch in advance from a side road to the old power station off US 3. This must be done by foot, however, as vehicle access and parking in the area of the falls are restricted. These restrictions also eliminate this spot as a convenient take-out.

The falls are dangerous. Paddlers should take out well above them on the right and line their boats to the beach opposite the lip of the falls. Portaging is difficult but not impossible. It involves carrying along the railroad tracks next to the right bank, with steep ascents and descents to the river, or, in low water periods, carrying along the ledges next to the falls.

The water runs smoothly through a sheer gorge below the falls, then separates around an island where the Class II rapids to the left are easier than those to the right. Shortly below the I-93 bridge the Baker River enters on the right. Access to the river at the bridge in Plymouth is poor. A municipal parking lot behind the Plymouth business district lies next to the river, however, and a short dirt road from it to the river provides a good take-out in ¼ mile below the bridge on the right.

## Plymouth–Bristol                                        15¾ mi

| | |
|---|---|
| Description: | Flatwater, quickwater |
| Date checked: | 1988, CR, GT |
| Navigable: | Passable at most water levels |
| Scenery: | Forested, rural |
| Maps: | USGS Plymouth 15, Holderness 15 |
| Portage: | (15¾ mi   R   **Ayres Island Dam** ½ mi) |

This section is attractive and easy. The section above Squam River is mostly shallow, with sandy banks and bottom, offering very pleasant swimming throughout the summer. There are only a few houses along the banks, and roads are only occasionally visible. For much of the distance, however, I-93 lies close enough to the left bank so that traffic is frequently heard, even though it is seldom seen.

For two-thirds of the distance there is a good current, but after that you are in deadwater behind Ayres Island Dam above Bristol. On very rare occasions in the fall, the water level behind the dam is drawn down, exposing wide mud and sand banks that are visible from the interstate highway. The effect is noticeable as far back as the Squam River, where a ledge just above a small island becomes exposed and is difficult to pass.

The best put-in for this section is reached from a municipal parking lot behind Main Street buildings in Plymouth, an area mentioned earlier as a take-out for the Blair–Plymouth section.

From the bridge in Plymouth the river has a fast current for many miles. Good current continues past the US 3 bridge in Ashland (4¼ miles) to the mouth of the Squam River (6¼ miles), where there is a small ledgy island. Low water at this point exposes some more ledges that are not normally noticeable. The current weakens in the next 3 miles as you approach the deadwater behind Ayres Island Dam.

There is public access to the river on the west bank beside the NH 104 bridge in New Hampton (12¾ miles). Portage the dam (15¾ miles) on the right. There is also access on the west bank at the Sawhegenet Falls Park Recreation Area, Bridgewater, New Hampshire, on River Road.

## Bristol–Franklin                                                   15 mi

| | |
|---|---|
| Description: | Flatwater, quickwater, Class II–III |
| Date checked: | 1988, CR |
| Navigable: | High water, heavy waves (spring runoff) |
| | Medium water (1,500 cfs) |
| | Low water, scratchy (550 cfs) |
| | Dam controlled, peak load hydroelectric stations |
| Scenery: | Forested, rural |
| Maps: | USGS Holderness 15, Penacook 15 |
| Portages: | 12½ mi   L   **Franklin Falls flood control dam** ½ mi |
| | 14 mi   R   **Eastman Falls Dam** 200 yd |
| Restriction: | No camping |

Below Ayres Island Dam in Bristol, there are 1½ miles of heavy rapids that vary in difficulty with the water level. Usually they are Class II–III, but during periods of heavy runoff the current is powerful and the waves are large.

This dam supplies peaking power, so when the flow in the river is low, you must time your trip with the demand for electricity. During the week there is usually a medium water flow of 1,500 cubic feet per second (cfs) from 9:00 A.M. to 12:00 noon and from 1:00 to 3:00 P.M. On Sundays there is often a low water flow of 500 cfs from 9:00 A.M. to 3:00 P.M. A call to the dispatcher at the Public Service Company of New Hampshire (603-225-6182) can give you current information.

Eastman Falls Dam at Franklin is also operated by the Public Service Company. The generating schedule is about the same as that at Ayres Island Dam in Bristol.

The best run on this portion of the river is the 7½-mile section from the Bristol dam to Hill. There are rapids and quickwater most of the way. It is a scenic trip, with secluded shorelines altered somewhat by the effects of periodic flooding.

Hill has a ghostly atmosphere. Back from the river a short distance, the main street, somewhat dilapidated but complete with a sidewalk, is lined with maples and elms that are aged and in poor health. The driveways are lined with old trees, and lone apple trees dot the farmyards. But there are no houses, no telephone poles, no people, only cows and corn; the town is gone. It was moved when the Franklin Falls flood control dam was built downstream. Today, standing in the still fertile fields, you can almost feel a part of the past.

The trip below Hill is not so attractive. The effects of flooding are more noticeable, and the flood control dam necessitates an uninteresting and somewhat difficult portage. Shortly beyond there is another portage around Eastman Falls dam. The rapids at Franklin, easier than those in Bristol, would be a more logical part of a trip down the Merrimack River.

One mile east of the center of Bristol on NH 104 a road to the right leads past some highway department buildings and down the hill. Turn left near a water treatment facility and follow the dirt road to the river just below the dam.

In the first 1½ miles there are several nice Class II rapids that have heavy Class II waves at high water levels. The last important drop is ½ mile below the Bristol bridge at a right turn. This rapid may be run on the inside of the bend to avoid the waves. If you wish to run only the rapids, there is a road along the left bank, or you can put in at this road for an easier run.

Quickwater continues for the next 3½ miles past the mouth of the Smith River (3½ miles) and around a large island. One mile after the flatwater begins, the valley widens and there are fields on the right. This is Hill. At the other end of the town there are some old bridge abutments (7½ miles). The river at this point can be reached from NH 3A.

Flatwater continues to the Franklin Falls flood control dam (12¼ miles). Road access to this dam is off NH 127 at a sign north of Franklin. If you are continuing down the river, portage on the left, from the log boom, up over the dam, and down either of two bays of deadwater below. After this dam there is more deadwater above the power dam at Franklin (14 miles). Portage on the right. There is a 1-mile Class II rapid in the remaining distance to the confluence with the Winnipesaukee River (15 miles).

## EAST BRANCH, PEMIGEWASSET RIVER                    NH

This large, clear river drains the Pemigewasset Wilderness. There are several miles of difficult whitewater above the Kancamagus Highway bridge, but you must carry your boat. The rapids are continuous below the bridge.

### Kancamagus Highway–North Woodstock                6 mi

| | |
|---|---|
| Description: | Class IV |
| Date checked: | 1988, ST |
| Navigable: | High water, difficult (April) |
| | Medium water (May) |
| Scenery: | Forested, settled |
| Maps: | USGS Mount Osceola, Lincoln |
| Portage: | 4½ mi   L   **dam at Lincoln** |

There is a fairly even gradient of over 70 feet per mile in this section, but the large drainage basin gives the East Branch a long season. There is a painted gauge on the center abutment of the Kancamagus Highway bridge: 0.3 is the minimal level, 1.0 is high, and 2.0 is Class V. Because of the clarity of the water and the size of the riverbed, the river always looks lower than it really is.

For the first 2 miles from the put-in, the river is fairly continuous Class III–IV, with a good rapid in every corner. Upper Condo marks the end of this section, with the heaviest waves of this section. The next rapid, First Island, finds you blasting down a chute at the end of the island heading toward a large boulder. Go right. Second Island should be scouted. The right channel has three large boulders, with various routes around them, and the remains of metal culvert.

Upper Loon Mountain Rapid is extremely technical. Take out just above the Loon Mountain bridge on the left to scout Lower Loon Mountain Rapid. Recent floods have channeled the river down a deep chute to the right of the abutment, which is slightly easier than it looks. The runout of Lower Loon is on the right into an extremely small pool above a boulder sieve. The boulder sieve can be run right or portaged on either side. The next 1½ miles are harder than those above and are vastly different since the flood.

There's no decision to Decision Rapids anymore, since the channel goes right with a series of steep, tight turns. Condominiums on the right bank mark two very technical rapids: Ethel's Back Yard and Lower Ethel, which are separated by a nice pool. The current continues to the dam, which is an easy portage on the left. It is sometimes possible to scrape down on the left. Watch out for the next island. Closed boaters should go left, and open boaters right. There is a bridge halfway down the island. Take out just past the bridge to scout Lower Condo, a staircase with a sharp turn left if you go left, a technical run with bow pinning possibilities if you go right. Class III rapids continue to North Woodstock.

## MAD RIVER                                                    NH

The Mad River, a tributary of the Pemigewasset River north of Plymouth, provides paddlers with many miles of continuous rapids. The steepness of the terrain around it means that runoff occurs very quickly.

### Waterville Valley–Campton                              12 mi

| | |
|---|---|
| Description: | Lake, Class III–IV |
| Date checked: | 1988, DS |
| Navigable: | High to medium water (mid-April to early May) |
| Scenery: | Forested |
| Map: | USGS Plymouth 15 |
| Portage: | (12 mi   L   **dam at Campton** 30 yd) |

This portion of the river flows through Waterville Valley, one of the most beautiful in the White Mountains. It does not often have enough water for boating, but on a few days of the year it provides a long and continuously interesting whitewater run. The season for flexible boats is somewhat extended. The river contains a multitude of small and medium-sized rocks that force paddlers to dodge rocks constantly.

At Six-Mile Bridge there is a hand-painted gauge on a rock just upstream of the left abutment. It is estimated that a reading of 1.0 may be passable but very low, that 1.75 is a medium level, and that 2.5 is a high water level.

Begin near the town of Waterville Valley. Follow NH 49 through the town, and shortly after passing the tennis courts make a sharp left turn by the library. This road soon crosses the river and continues on to join the Tripoli Road to North Woodstock. The Tripoli Road is not plowed in winter, so NH 49 from the south is usually the only route into the Mad River basin in the spring.

The West Branch of the Mad River, which enters shortly below, is visible from the put-in. Rapids begin almost immediately, with the difficulty reaching Class III. A mile and a half of rapids brings you to the Mount Tecumseh Ski Area bridge, which can also be used as a put-in, but access there is more difficult.

Below the ski area bridge (1½ miles) there are 3 miles of continuous Class III–IV rapids with a couple of drops that are slightly harder than the rest. The hardest rapid is in a right turn about 1½ miles below the bridge. It is actually a little easier than it looks: a fairly straight course in the center is the best route in medium to high water. A turn-off makes it easy to scout this drop from the road.

There is a nice view of Welch Mountain on the right bank (4½ miles), after which the rapids become a tough Class IV. The river narrows, and resting or rescue places are even hard to find. The rapids are continuous for 2 miles to Six-Mile Bridge, where take-out access can be found.

From Six-Mile Bridge (6½ miles) there are 2 miles of Class III–IV rapids with larger waves but fewer rocks. At Goose Hollow (8½ miles) there is a single bridge. The best take-out is at an unmarked rest area just below Goose Hollow at a White Mountain National Forest campground.

In the next 3 miles to Campton Pond, the rapids ease steadily from Class III to Class I. Take out at NH 49, which follows along the western shoreline.

If you are continuing downstream, portage the dam (12 miles) on the left.

## Campton–Pemigewasset River 2½ mi

| | |
|---|---|
| Description: | **Quickwater,** Class III–IV |
| Date checked: | 1983 |
| Navigable: | High to medium water (mid-April to mid-May) |
| Scenery: | Forested |
| Map: | USGS Plymouth 15 |

In Campton there is a steep gorge that used to be the site of whitewater slalom races. The rapids there are created by steep drops over and around ledges as well as by boulders. Campton Pond tends to make the flow in this section steadier and more dependable.

Just below the bridge there is a partially washed-out dam that should be scouted and probably lifted over. Past an old factory on the left, the river swings right and enters Campton Gorge, where there is 1/2 mile of Class III–IV rapids. They can be run by skilled paddlers but should be scouted first.

Below Campton Gorge there are 2 miles of quickwater to the Pemigewasset River (2½ miles). The first take-out is 1½ miles downstream on US 3 (4 miles), a short distance above the I-93 bridges.

## BAKER RIVER NH

This river was named for Thomas Baker, a lieutenant from Northampton, Massachusetts, who traveled along it in 1712 on a raid against the Indians. It rises on the south slopes of

Mount Moosilauke in Benton and runs south, then east to the Pemigewasset in Plymouth.

The scenery is rural and very attractive. A main highway follows up the valley, but it usually cannot be seen from the river. An abandoned railroad grade is scarcely noticeable.

## NH Rte. 118–Wentworth                                    6 mi

| | |
|---|---|
| Description: | **Quickwater,** Class II–III |
| Date checked: | 1983 |
| Navigable: | High water (April) |
| | Medium water, scratchy above Warren (early May) |
| Scenery: | Forested, rural, towns |
| Map: | USGS Rumney 15 |
| Portage: | (6 mi   L   **ledge at Wentworth** 100–200 yd) |

The river has been channeled from NH 118 through the town of Warren, an indication that runoffs are often fast and furious. The watershed is mountainous, and the gradient is initially steep, making boating for the first 2 miles very dependent on the weather. If the spring is early or dry, the water needed for good Class III rapids above Warren will already be in the Merrimack by mid-April.

Put in at the NH 118 bridge north of Warren. The gradient is steepest in the first ¾ mile, where there are Class III rapids as the river drops steadily over small boulders. The river widens, and the rapids become easier as the town of Warren comes into view.

The first bridge in Warren, Studio Road (1¼ miles), can be used as a starting point if the rapids above are too shallow. The current through Warren to the NH 25 bridge is swift. Much of the remaining distance is quickwater, with wide turns where overhanging trees are an occasional hazard. Below the second NH 25 bridge (3½ miles) there is a short Class II rapid. In Wentworth (6 miles) take out above the old truss bridge, because underneath it is a very turbulent Class IV drop. It can be carried on the left under the bridge, unless the water is very high.

## Wentworth–Plymouth                                    **21 mi**

| | |
|---|---|
| Description: | **Flatwater, quickwater,** Class I–II |
| Date checked: | 1988, CR |
| Navigable: | High or medium water (April to end of May and after moderate rains) |
| | Low water, passable below West Rumney |
| Scenery: | Forested, rural, town |
| Maps: | USGS Rumney 15, Plymouth 15 |

The farther you start downstream on the Baker River, the more it becomes a leisurely float trip, with less and less water required to keep you off the bottom. The river is clean, and the riverbed is sandy in many locations. With a little helpful rain, the part below West Rumney makes a nice summer trip.

The river winds through a rural valley hemmed in by wooded hillsides. It frequently undercuts banks, dumping trees into the current. These obstacles are hazardous, but you can almost always paddle around them. Noise from the highway is most noticeable as you near the end.

Put in at the ballfield below the NH 25 bridge on the north bank. There are short Class I–II rapids and quickwater 6 miles past two bridges to the girder bridge on a side road in West Rumney. Below here the river is generally wider with less current. In 1¼ miles there is a highway rest area on the right, followed in ½ mile by an overhead cable at a gauging station which precedes a short Class II rapid at the site of an old dam. More quickwater continues for 6¾ miles past the rusty Stinson Lake Road bridge (10 miles) to an old bridge site in an S-turn by Polar Caves (14 miles). Stinson Mountain is occasionally visible. The river is more sluggish for the next 2¼ miles to the Smith Road covered bridge (16¾ miles).

There are 4 more miles of flatwater to the truss bridge on US 3 (20¾ miles) in Plymouth. Access is not good here, however. It is easier to continue to Plymouth. The half mile of river between the US 3 bridge and the confluence of the Baker and Pemigewasset rivers tends to be shallow in summer and may require some wading. It is less than a half mile from the confluence to the bridge in Plymouth and less than a quarter mile to a good take-out on the right bank, which is reached via a dirt road from a municipal parking lot next to the river in downtown Plymouth.

## NEWFOUND RIVER                                    NH

This river drains Newfound Lake and flows into the Pemigewasset River at Bristol. It is a short, narrow river, with continuous and difficult rapids. In one section the drop is 50 feet in ½ mile, a challenging run in high water for covered boats. In medium water, this is an ideal section for a small inflatable canoe, which, being flexible, can easily slither past the rounded boulders.

The annual fall drawdown of Newfound Lake does not provide sufficient water for this run.

### Newfound Lake–Bristol                                    1¾ mi

| | |
|---|---|
| Description: | Class II–IV |
| Date checked: | 1983 |
| Navigable: | High water (early April) |
| | Medium water (late April) |
| Scenery: | Forested, settled |
| Map: | USGS Cardigan 15 |
| Portage: | 1¼ mi   L   **hydroelectric dam** 20 yd |

Begin on the left bank below the dam at the south end of Newfound Lake. The rapids that follow are Class II–III for 1 mile to the first millpond. The most difficult drop in this section is just above the first bridge. Portage the dam on the left.

Below the first small hydroelectric dam (1¼ miles), the rapids soon become Class IV. **Caution!** Just 50 yards below the first US 3A bridge, there are two large, nasty spikes sticking straight up from a shoal in the middle of the river. Fortunately for the inflatables, the spikes are exposed at medium water. The Class

IV rapids extend for ½ mile on the east side of the highway, from which the whole section can be scouted. The most difficult pitch is behind a restaurant near the end. Take out at the second millpond beside the lower bridge (1¾ miles).

The remainder of the river is tame by comparison. If curiosity impels you to run it, carry the second hydroelectric dam on the left and begin again in the millrace, which is deeper and more accessible than the main channel. The Class I rapids soon end, and they are followed by quickwater. Take out at the NH 104 bridge (2¾ miles), the second in this section. Do not continue, because the river is not easily accessible from the Main Street bridge, and below that there is a steep, unrunnable cascade that continues the rest of the way to the Pemigewasset River.

## COCKERMOUTH RIVER                                        NH

This small river empties into the northwest end of Newfound Lake. Its water is clear, and the valley through which it flows typifies rural New England at its best. It takes about two hours to run.

### Groton–Newfound Lake                                   3½ mi

| | |
|---|---|
| Description: | Flatwater, **quickwater** |
| Date checked: | 1983 |
| Navigable: | High to medium water (early spring, after heavy rains) |
| Scenery: | Rural |
| Map: | USGS Cardigan 15 |

Start in Groton where the road to North Groton crosses the river, which at this point is about a canoe-length wide. The current is fast as the stream winds along the edges of fields. Just above the second bridge (2 miles) there is a short and easy Class II rapid. In the last ¾ mile the river is flat and wide. It flows under a road along the northern end of Newfound Lake ½ mile before it empties into Hebron Bay (3½ miles).

## FOWLER RIVER                                    NH

The Fowler River rises on Mount Cardigan and flows to Newfound Lake. Welton Falls is on the upper reaches. For most of its length it is too steep for canoeing, but the lower part is navigable at high water, or it can make a short side trip from the lake. Refer to the USGS Cardigan quandrangle.

### Crawford School–Newfound Lake                 2¼ mi

The first few rapids might be Class II, but the gradient decreases rapidly, and the river meanders along most of the way, becoming flatwater by the time it reaches the bridge ½ mile above the lake.

## SMITH RIVER                                     NH

The Smith River rises near Grafton as a small stream and flows east to the Pemigewasset River near Bristol. The upper part is a pleasant quickwater trip, and the lower part contains difficult rapids. There is a scenic waterfall below the part that is normally run. The banks are wooded, and there are frequent road and railroad crossings, so trips of varying lengths can be planned.

### Grafton Center–NH Rte. 104                     13 mi

| | |
|---|---|
| Description: | Flatwater, **quickwater,** Class I |
| Date checked: | 1983 |
| Navigable: | High water (April) |
| Scenery: | Forested, rural |
| Map: | USGS Cardigan 15 |

Put in from the road to the Ruggles Mine just west of Grafton Center. In the next 6½ miles to Fords Crossing, where there are adjacent railroad and road bridges (the first of two such pairs), the river is a winding meadow brook, with overhanging bushes and occasional fallen trees. There is often quickwater under bridges. The next 6½ miles are more open and less obstructed, and they lead you past the US 4 bridge (9¼ miles) to the girder bridge on NH 104.

Just above the NH 104 bridge (13 miles) there is a short Class II rapid, which can be avoided by taking out just above it at the Eastern District Road bridge.

## NH 104–Profile Gorge                                    8 mi

| | |
|---|---|
| Description: | Flatwater, Class **III–IV** |
| Date checked: | 1983 |
| Navigable: | High to medium water (April to mid-May) |
| Scenery: | Forested, town |
| Maps: | USGS Cardigan 15, Holderness 15 |

The river in this section offers some very fine whitewater boating. The rapids above South Alexandria are the most challenging, but the nearby Smith River Road provides an easy retreat. Below South Alexandria the pitch is more moderate, and civilization is less evident from the river. The gorge and waterfall at the end of the trip deserve exploration, on foot.

There is a hand-painted gauge on the left abutment of the Cass Mill Road bridge in South Alexandria. It is possible to scratch down the river with a water level of − 0.5. Medium water is considered to give a reading of 0.5; high water is 1.0.

The best access is off the old highway, now called Smith River Road, although part of it may be snow-covered in early spring. The upper end of it can be reached by turning off NH 104 at Murray Hill Road. To reach it at South Alexandria, turn off at Cass Mill Road.

Below the NH 104 bridge there is ¼ mile of Class III ledges, including an old dam: then there is ¾ mile of smoothwater to the bridge on Murray Hill Road.

Below the Murray Hill Road bridge (1 mile) there is a short stretch of flatwater; then comes the first rapid in a left-hand bend. This is the first of two brief Class III rapids, each followed by quiet stretches. Next comes a Class IV section, full of small rocks and crosscurrents, which rushes past a picnic area on the right shore and down to the next bridge (1¾ miles) on Smith River Road. For a shorter and slightly easier run, this bridge is a possible put-in.

Below the second bridge there is 1 mile of continuous Class III–IV rapids with a very fast pace in high water. At the end of this mile there is a short drop in a right turn, with a large rock and hole sitting in the center, forcing boaters to one side or the other. The left side is preferable, although another rock upstream of the main hole must be avoided. Below this drop the river divides around an island just before the Cass Mill Road bridge. The right side contains the hardest rapids on the river, a tough Class IV over large rocks and ledges; it should be scouted before running. The left side descends much more gradually and is much easier to navigate.

The first ½ mile below the Cass Mill Road bridge in South Alexandria (3 miles) contains Class III–IV rapids, and it is often run with the stretch above. A set of power lines (3½ miles) marks the point where the rapids moderate. This power line crossing can be reached from Smith River Road, which follows the left bank from South Alexandria.

Below the power lines (3½ miles) there are 2 miles of Class III rapids, then ½ mile in which the rapids diminish to mere current. At this point the river passes the bridge to Smith River Campground (6 miles). Then there are 2 miles of smoothwater to a broken dam (8 miles), which can be run on either side at certain water levels. **Caution!** It is best to take out above the dam: the river below is more suitable for sightseeing than boating.

Shortly below the broken dam (8 miles), the Smith River foams through Profile Gorge, a 150-yard rock-walled stretch that can be viewed from a high cement bridge at the gorge entrance. Moderate rapids follow to a bad drop just above the NH 3A bridge. Beneath the bridge is the beginning of Profile Falls (8½ miles), where the Smith River slides over ledges for 100 yards before plunging down a 30-foot vertical drop. A road on the left bank leads to a parking area at the foot of the falls. The river from there to the Pemigewasset River (9 miles) is Class II.

## WINNIPESAUKEE RIVER                                    NH

The Winnipesaukee is a river of intermittent rapids, and some are long and difficult. The water is clear, although rebar is a threat below Tilton. This lower section, therefore, is not recommended. A new hydro dam in Tilton further complicates the run. The upper part, from Silver Lake to Tilton, is excellent for training beginners, as the lakes in the headwaters provide a dependable flow. The river below Tilton is isolated and flows through a narrow, wooded valley with continuous Class III–IV rapids below the Cross Road bridge. River flow is controlled by Lochmere Dam, located between Winnisquam and Silver lakes. Each fall the Water Resources Board draws down the levels of Winnipesaukee and Winnisquam lakes about 3 feet, which provides medium to high water levels for several weeks, generally after Columbus Day.

### NH Rte. 140–Franklin                                    6 mi

| | |
|---|---|
| Description: | Flatwater, Class I–II, III–IV |
| Date checked: | 1984, ST |
| Navigable: | High water (late March to early April) |
| | Medium water (late April, May, and annual fall drawdown) |
| Scenery: | Forested, settled, town |
| Map: | USGS Penacook 15 |
| Portage: | 2¼ mi L **dam in Tilton**—long and difficult, not recommended |

This description begins very close to Exit 20 off I-93. There is a launching ramp on Shaker Road just east of the NH 140 bridge that provides access to Silver Lake, located upstream.

The first ½ mile is flat, followed by ½ mile of Class I–II below the I-93 bridge, followed by more flatwater, followed by easy Class II to Tilton. Take out on the left in Tilton (2¼ miles). If you wish to continue, carry across the bridge, down NH 3, and put in below the hydro dam. Ask permission. A 100-yard Class II rapid leads to smoothwater, punctuated by another Class II.

The difficult rapids begin at the Cross Road bridge (4½ miles), where the river enters a steep, narrow valley. At first there is a series of rapids and pools as the river flows over runnable, washed-out dams and past ruined factories. There are many turns in the river, and the rapids get longer and harder, up to Class IV, as you approach and pass under a covered railroad bridge (5¹/₂ miles). Class IV rapids continue and end abruptly at a millpond just below the NH 3 bridge in Franklin. The presence of industrial debris, including rebar, in this section detracts from what could be a superb whitewater experience.

## CONTOOCOOK RIVER                                              NH

The Contoocook River is one of the principal tributaries of the Merrimack River. It rises in Rindge east of Mount Monadnock and flows generally northeast to join the Merrimack in Penacook.

The greatly differing sections of the Contoocook hold appeal for both flatwater and whitewater paddlers. In the upper section there are easy rapids, but only in high water, in the early spring. Much flatwater follows as the river's volume increases. Heavy rapids above Henniker give way to pleasant flatwater, with a few rapids near the confluence. The calm stretches and even some of the rapids provide opportunities for summer boating.

### Jaffrey–Peterborough                                        6¾ mi

| | |
|---|---|
| Description: | Class II |
| Date checked: | 1988, PB |
| Navigable: | High water (late March to early April) |
| Scenery: | Forested |
| Maps: | USGS Monadnock 15, Peterborough 15 |
| Portages: | 2 mi   L   **Class IV gorge** 400 yd |
| | 5 mi   R   Noone Dam 10 yd |
| | (6¾ mi   L   **Peterborough Dam** 30 yd) |

From Jaffrey the Contoocook flows through easy rapids interrupted only by a small gorge. These rapids are a good training ground for beginning whitewater paddlers. This section, very small and winding, contrasts noticebly with the lower river in breadth and volume.

There is a dam at the outlet of Cheshire Pond, and a put-in is possible from the US 202 bridge just below. Easy Class II rapids start immediately. The river crosses several times beneath the railroad and the old US 202 bridges. The old road can be followed beside the river. After 2 miles the river makes a sharp right turn into a hemlock grove, and there is a wooden bridge 30 yards beyond.

**Caution!** Make a steep, short take-out on the left above the bridge (2 miles) because there is a gorge below. The gorge contains difficult rapids that can be run at certain water levels. At higher levels the rapids are Class IV and can be navigated by closed boats. At somewhat lower levels open boats can proceed from drop to drop in the gorge, lining or lifting around any drops judged impassable. The gorge should be scouted, particularly since a fallen tree or jammed log would create a bad situation. To portage, carry down the road on the left for ¼ mile, and upon passing the first house on the right return to the river. A car certainly eases this portage.

Below the gorge are another 1½ miles of Class II rapids. For the next mile rapids alternate with smooth stretches to a side road bridge (4½ miles) above the millpond in Noone. The dam at Noone (5 miles) requires a short portage on the right. Another mile of mixed rapids and flatwater continues to Peterborough, where there is a little drop next to the Peterborough Plaza. A take-out can be made at the new NH 101 bridge (6¼ miles) or, after a little more smooth paddling, at the dam above a stone bridge in Peterborough (6¾ miles).

## Peterborough–Bennington                                    12 mi

| | |
|---|---|
| Description: | **Flatwater,** quickwater, Class I |
| Date checked: | 1983 |
| Navigable: | Passable at most water levels, especially toward Bennington |
| Scenery: | Forested |
| Map: | USGS Peterborough 15 |
| Portages: | 2 mi   R   **North Village Dam** 10 yd |
| | (12 mi   R   **first of several dams in Bennington**) |

The paddle from Peterborough to Bennington is one of the prettiest on the river. Most of this stretch, particularly the second half, is navigable whenever the river is free from ice.

From the stone bridge and dam, it is a 2-mile paddle to the dam in North Village. Portage on the right. The Contoocook then flows under US 202 and snakes swiftly around some low islands. This portion might be impassable in low water. Smooth paddling for 5½ miles past woods and meadows leads to a small side road bridge (7½ miles). In another mile the Contoocook empties into Powder Mill Pond, the backup from a dam in Bennington. A half mile down the pond there is a covered bridge at a narrows (9 miles). Continuing down the pond, a railroad bridge crosses at another narrows (10¾ miles) and then comes to the first dam in Bennington (12 miles). Take out on the right bank.

## Bennington Portage                                    1½ mi

On the river through Bennington there are at least four dams and impassable rapids. In addition, the Monadnock Paper Mill sometimes diverts water and leaves the riverbed almost dry.

## Bennington–Hillsboro                                    12 mi

| | |
|---|---|
| Description: | **Flatwater,** Class I–II |
| Date checked: | 1988, PB |
| Navigable: | Passable at all levels |
| Scenery: | Forested |
| Map: | USGS Hillsboro 15 |
| Portage: | 12 mi **two dams in Hillsboro** ½ mi |

This stretch is not quite as appealing as that above Bennington. The current is slow and the river winds considerably.

Put in below the last dam in Bennington at the bridge near the Monadnock Paper Company which is visible from US 202. It is 2½ miles to Antrim and another 8¼ miles to the entrance of the North Branch of the Contoocook (10¾ miles). About half a mile past the North Branch, Class II rapids begin and continue right up to the dam (12 miles) in Hillsboro, making a difficult and dangerous approach.

Take out on the right where the river comes close to the road ½ mile above the dam and just before the mill buildings. It is also possible, with permission, to take out upstream before the rapids at private docks.

## Hillsboro–West Henniker                                    6½ mi

| | |
|---|---|
| Description: | Flatwater, quickwater, Class **III–IV** |
| Date checked: | 1988, PB |
| Navigable: | High and medium water (spring and after heavy rains) |
| Scenery: | Forested, settled |
| Map: | USGS Hillsboro 15 |
| Portage: | 6½ mi   R   **West Henniker Dam** 10 yd |

The heaviest rapids on the Contoocook are found in this section: the river at this point is one of the largest whitewater rivers in New England. The water level here is more reliable than it is on other rivers, making the rapids runnable all spring and after heavy rains.

There is a USGS gauge on the right bank 1 mile above the dam in West Henniker. When it read ups to 8.0, all rapids except Freight Train Rapids near the end are difficult Class III. Freight Train Rapids are always Class IV. At water levels above 8.0, all the rapids become more turbulent. This section can be run with open boats at water levels up to 9.5 with great care. At virtually any water level, capsizing in the Contoocook can lead to a long swim and a difficult rescue.

A mill dam directly under the NH 149 bridge in Hillsboro makes it advisable to put in just below the village. Reach the river from the left bank near the railroad trestle. The first ½ mile consists of Class III rapids, then the river becomes smooth, with one rapid shortly above the NH 202 bridge. From there quickwater continues to the bridge (3 miles). Access to the river is good from either old NH 202 on the right bank or from a dirt road on the left bank, which you can drive on in dry season with four-wheel-drive vehicles.

Another smooth ½ mile leads to the start of the rapids. Those just starting a trip can go through the woods and put in from old NH 202 at the beginning of the rapids. This is the usual starting point.

The first rapid of the lower section (3½ miles) begins in a slight left turn, where the current goes from being imperceptible to irresistible. There are no rocks here, but the waves can be very turbulent at high water. The river bends right with rapids and returns to the road (4 miles). The next left turn holds another difficult rapid, the shallowest in this portion: if this rapid is passable, then the whole stretch can be run.

When the river leaves the road, there is a very challenging rapid ahead. The right turn is the beginning of a heavy and continuous ½ mile rapid known as the "S-turn." In this rapid, swimming and rescue are extremely difficult. S-turn is the most technical rapid and is often scouted from the right. Easier rapids follow, with a USGS gauge on the right bank (5 miles). Those who wish to avoid the last and toughest of the Contoocook rapids should take out here where the road is near.

From this calm spot (5 miles) the river turns left with easy Class II rapids. Where it turns right the ferocious Freight Train Rapids begin, a Class IV pitch in medium water. Take out on the left bank at the turn to scout. The route is basically through the biggest waves and holes in the center. The last ½ mile is

quickwater running to the dam in West Henniker (6½ miles).
A take-out can be made on the right bank on old NH 202. This
dam is very dangerous, and take-out should be well upstream.

## West Henniker–Henniker                                          **2 mi**

| | |
|---|---|
| Description: | **Quickwater,** Class II–III |
| Date checked: | 1988, PB |
| Navigable: | Medium water |
| Scenery: | Settled, towns |
| Map: | USGS Hillsboro 15 |
| Portage: | 2 mi   R   **broken dam** 20 yd |

From the old NH 202 crossing in West Henniker (just below
the dam) only one rapid interrupts the smooth course to the new
covered bridge at New England College. Starting under the stone
NH 114 bridge just below, the river runs through a series of Class
II–III rapids for ½ mile to a broken dam. This dam is in the
process of washing out and should be inspected in advance from
the steel truss bridge 100 yards below.

## Henniker–Hopkinton flood control dam                            **6½ mi**

| | |
|---|---|
| Description: | **Flatwater,** quickwater |
| Date checked: | 1988, PB |
| Navigable: | Passable at all water levels |
| Scenery: | Forested |
| Map: | USGS Hopkinton |
| Portage: | (6½ mi   L   **two dams** ½ mi) |

Below the steel truss bridge the river flows sluggishly, with only
one rapid, just around the first corner, which is flooded out in
high water. At low water levels the pollution is noticeable, and
the attractiveness of the river depends on recent fluctuations in
the water level at the dam. This dam is one of the larger flood
control projects in New England and can potentially back up
water all the way to Henniker. The best access is at a boat ramp

on the right at the bottom of the southern loop, 3 miles above
the dam. Portage on the dirt road on the left, starting above the
second boom.

## Hopkinton flood control dam–Rowley Bridge                    ½ mi

The ½ mile section of Class II rapids running to the Rowley
covered bridge offers a place to practice technique in an enjoyable setting.

## Rowley Bridge–the "Island"                                  15¼ mi

| | |
|---|---|
| Description: | **Flatwater,** quickwater |
| Date checked: | 1988, PB |
| Navigable: | Passable at all water levels |
| Scenery: | Forested, settled |
| Maps: | USGS Hopkinton, Penacook 15, Concord |
| Portage: | 5 mi   R   **dam in Contoocook** 10 yd |

The Contoocook flows swiftly for only a short distance below
the Rowley Bridge, gradually slowing to the dam at a small park
with picnic tables in Contoocook Village. The dam is an easy
carry when the water is not too high.

Immediately below the dam, past a covered bridge where
canoes can be rented, there is a short Class I rapid. How difficult the rest of the river is depends on the water level: at low
water it is essentially flat, with some boat traffic; at high water
the current is swift, with considerable turbulence and strong
eddies.

The Warner River joins on the left (6 miles), and the Tyler
Bridge (7½ miles) offers access. On the south bank near the
bridge are Gould and Rattlesnake hills, where timber for the
Civil War warship USS *Kearsarge* was cut.

The riverbanks were uninhabited above the Blackwater River
(9 miles), but now a few cabins are seen on the way to a side road
bridge in the locality known as Riverhill (13¾ miles). The river
is lined with houses in the next 1½ miles to a park in Penacook

known appropriately as the "Island" (5¼ miles ). Reach the Island by taking Washington Street out of Penacook and following a marked turn-off. There is a public landing on the upstream tip of the island for easy take-out. Although it is possible to continue to the Merrimack, because of the dams and the rapids most paddler terminate their trip here.

## The "Island"–Merrimack River                                    2½ mi

There are dams on both sides of the Island, and each requires a short portage. The next mile to the US 3 and 4 bridge in Penacook (1¼ miles) has some Class II–III rapids. Just below this bridge is a broken dam that can sometimes be run as a stunt, but as a rule it should be portaged. In low water you can land on the right just above the dam to portage, but avoid this in high water when the current is stronger.

Easy rapids follow for ½ mile to another bridge (1¾ miles), where a take-out should be made on either side above the bridge. Directly below this bridge is an island with an old bridge abutment. To the left of the island, there is a very sharp drop, followed by an unrunnable dam. On the right side of the island, the descent is more gradual and possibly runnable, but a difficult Class IV. Look this over carefully. The right bank offers a long but gradual portage of 400 yards that avoids all the difficult rapids. When the two channels rejoin, there are more Class IV rapids, with a line of old mill buildings on the left bank. Rapids diminish quickly to the confluence with the Merrimack River, where the Contoocook splits to form Hannah Duston Island.

## WARNER RIVER                                                        NH

The Warner River flows eastward from Bradford toward Concord. It empties into the Contoocook River a little below the town of Contoocook. The upper part contains thrilling rapids for covered boats or open boats with maximum flotation, the middle portion has easy rapids, and lower down, the river meanders through wild swamps. It passes under two covered bridges and runs down the median of I-89.

## Bradford–Roby                                              6½ mi

| | |
|---|---|
| Description: | Quickwater, Class II–IV |
| Date checked: | 1988, KJ |
| Navigable: | High water (March) |
| Scenery: | Forested, towns |
| Map: | USGS Mount Kearsarge 15 |
| Portage: | 5 mi   R   **dam** |

Put in at the NH 114 bridge southeast of Bradford. The broken milldam at Melvin Mills (3 miles) can be run. After leaving the pond below the mill, the river flows through continuous Class III rapids that require many quick decisions. The river is small, and there are many sharp turns. In about 1 mile and around a left turn the river splits and part of it goes into an old millrace on the extreme left. Immediately below is the first tough rapid, with approximately ½ mile of uninterrupted Class IV drops terminating in a chute between cement abutments directly above a small bridge, which is easily visible from NH 103. Just above the chute between the cement abutments, approximately 150 feet, is a low dam that should be run in the chute to the far left in medium water but should be scouted. Just above the dam is a small pool (another 100 feet) and before that the worst of the drops in this section.

After this first difficult pitch the river eases to Class II for about ½ mile before entering the second and most difficult rapid, which is a series of five closely spaced Class IV drops in a gorge beyond an old mill site that ajoins a small picnic area. There is an old tar road on the left, which can be used for scouting or portage. Below the second difficult rapid the river eases up. Soon, behind some houses, there is a stretch of water that turns out to be a millpond. Portage the small dam by the abandoned mill on the right.

Below the dam (5 miles) there is quickwater for about 1 mile as the river meanders in a big loop, passing under NH 103 twice. At the second bridge another long section of Class III–IV rapids starts. These are beautiful and continuous rapids, with one-boat eddies. There are no pools for rescue, but there are no sharp drops either, except near the end where the river makes a sharp right turn and goes over a 3-foot ledge that is hard to diagnose from the boat and difficult to run without scraping. Directly below the ledge there is a bridge on a small dirt road (6½ miles).

## Roby–Warner                                            2½ mi

| | |
|---|---|
| Description: | Quickwater, Class I–II |
| Date checked: | 1988, KJ |
| Navigable: | Medium water (April) |
| Scenery: | Forested, settled |
| Map: | USGS Mount Kearsarge 15 |
| Portage: | 1½ mi   L   **dam in Waterloo** |

Below the bridge the rapids quickly lighten from Class II to quickwater. In 1½ miles, just below the covered bridge at Waterloo, there is a dam that is followed immediately by a short Class IV drop. Take out on the left and portage along the old railroad as far down the rapids as you wish. It is another 1 mile to the I-89 bridge (2½ miles).

## Warner–Contoocook River                                10 mi

| | |
|---|---|
| Description: | Quickwater |
| Date checked: | 1988, TG |
| Navigable: | High or medium water (April to end of May) |
| Scenery: | Forested, towns |
| Maps: | USGS Mount Kearsarge 15, Penacook 15, Hopkinton |
| Portage: | 7½ mi   L   **dam in Davisville** ¼ yd |

The river below here makes a very pleasant run, with only a few fallen trees to present problems. Put in a dirt road just east of I-89, near Exit 9 at the junction with Stevens Brook.

There are a few riffles through Warner and several bridges through the next 3 miles. The interstate highway crosses twice, and the river flows through for a while through its median. After a couple of miles through a swamp, where the insects can be vicious, then it reaches the bridge at Davisville (7½ miles). Portage ¼ mile down a road on the left bank to an old road leading directly to the river. This portage has been used for years but has recently been purchased and heavily posted with NO TRESPASSING signs. An alternative portage has not yet been discovered. This route bypasses an old, partly washed-out dam and the Class IV rapid below it.

From the dam (7½ miles) it is a pleasant 2½ miles to the Contoocook River (10 miles). Watch for frequent strainers. Paddle down the Contoocook for 1½ miles to the bridge at Tyler (11½ miles).


## BLACKWATER RIVER                                    NH

The sandy bottom of the Blackwater Valley is not as rich for farming as other parts of New Hampshire, which perhaps explains why this valley is so sparsely settled. The river rises in Wilmot north of Mount Kearsarge (Merrimack County) and flows southeast to meet the Contoocook River not far from Concord. Most of the river is a delightful, easy paddle in a scenic area. The Blackwater is one of the few large rivers that the New Hampshire legislature has designated as Class A, so the quality of its water is high.

Medium water levels, spring or fall season, are required. The river should be avoided in high water because the many fallen trees are definitely hazardous: inexperienced paddlers often have to be rescued from them.


### Wilmot Flat–Cilleyville                            3¼ mi

This upper part of the river makes a pleasant run when the water in the lower Blackwater River is too high. See USGS Mount Kearsarge 15.

Put in below the Tannery Pond dam at Wilmot Flat. To reach the put-in, take US 4 west for 4 miles from Andover Center. Take Village Road on the right approximately ½ mile to Tannery Pond on the right. Please note that this area is mostly private property, with no easy put-in. The brook is small, with a slow current and many downed trees. Some small bridges are low and require ducking or possibly portage in extremely high water. Before the covered bridge you pass the confluence with the North Branch on the left.

Take out near the covered bridge in Cilleyville above the broken dam.

## Cilleyville–West Salisbury                                    **9 mi**

| | |
|---|---|
| Description: | Flatwater, quickwater, Class I–II |
| Date checked: | 1988, MB |
| Navigable: | High water needed above Andover (early spring) |
| | Medium water (late spring and wet fall) |
| Scenery: | Forested, town |
| Map: | USGS Mount Kearsarge 15 |
| Portage: | (9½ mi **broken dam at West Salisbury**) |

Put in from the old NH 11 bridge just upstream of the old dam remains. Class III rapids run for 100 yards, then moderate into Class I, then II, to the covered bridge at Andover (3 miles). To avoid whitewater, put in here.

After the covered bridge there is a floating bridge across the river from a snowmobile path, followed by another bridge on Beech Hill Road, which has a hand-painted gauge on the left.

The current becomes slower, with occasional riffles, as the river wends its way, passing twice beneath US 4. After 4½ miles it enters the slackwater of the Bay, where the river broadens into a 1½-mile series of marshy ponds. You can take out at the end of the Bay on a dirt road to the left.

## West Salisbury–flood control dam                              12 mi

| | |
|---|---|
| Description: | Quickwater, flatwater, Class II |
| Date checked: | 1988, MB |
| Navigable: | Medium water (late spring and wet fall) |
| Scenery: | Wild |
| Maps: | USGS Mount Kearsarge 15, Penacook 15 |
| Portage: | 12 mi   L   **flood control dam** |

Put in at the end of the Bay, which can be reached by traveling west out of Salisbury Center on US 4. Take the first left (West Salisbury Road). This comes out at the end of the Bay.

There is a steep, rocky drop at the end of the Bay, then less than ½ mile to the next bridge, where there is a broken dam with jagged masonry in the river. The Class II rapids below the dam diminish to quickwater within the next mile to Peters Bridge, the best place to put in for this section.

From Peters Bridge (1½ miles) there are 4 miles of quickwater to Sawyers Bridge (5½ miles). It is a beautiful stream that meanders through a swamp above and below Sawyers Bridge, but there are many fallen trees. Some of them are dangerous in high water because you may be swept under them; others are a nuisance at low water because they must be lifted over.

The best take-out above the dam is on a dirt road on the right just east of Littles Hill (11 miles). Below are some Class II rapids, then backwater from the flood control dam.

## Flood control dam–Snyder's Mill                             4 mi

| | |
|---|---|
| Description: | Flatwater, **quickwater,** Class III–IV |
| Date checked: | 1988, MB |
| Navigable: | High water (April) |
| Scenery: | Forested |
| Maps: | USGS Penacook 15, Hopkinton |

This section is recommended only for covered boats, open boats with maximum flotation, and a strong party of at least four boats which has Class IV experience. People who never tip over in the Contoocook in Freight Train Rapids above Henniker often swim in one of the two Class IV rapids above Snyder's Mill.

Put in on the right at the foot of the cascade under Swett's Mills Bridge on NH 127. The put-in is just past the salt shed of the highway department on a dirt road next to the town hall and library. Below the cascade the river splits around an island where there is a shallow, rocky rapid. This is more water on the right. If you do not hit any rocks here, the rapids farther down the river past Dingit Corner will be extremely exciting. Below the island there is an easier put-in behind the Webster Elementary School (¼ mile).

The river then riffles through an attractive, forested area. One and a half miles below the school the river turns left and tumbles through a Class III rapid that has a couple of large rocks and a nice set of three-foot standing waves with a pool at the bottom.

At that point the river squeezes through a 15-foot-wide notch in a ledge and drops 4–5 feet into a messy hole, which is again only recommended for advanced closed boaters or those open boaters with maximum flotation. It should be scouted and/or portaged on the left. It is quite exciting and often results in nosestands and Eskimo rolls. The water below the hole is fast and deep. This can be seen upstream from Clothespin Bridge (2 miles).

Below Clothespin Bridge there is a Class III ledge. The river rounds a sharp left corner, passes the USGS gauge (2½ miles), and drops over a rocky Class III rapid best run near the left bank. The gauge can be checked from the road by taking Clothespin Bridge Road off NH 127. After crossing the bridge, follow the river ⅕ mile downstream. Pull over at a roadside pull-off. The gauge is located upstream from here, so take a common driveway and walk past the house on your left. The gauge is on the center driveway just past the house. It is not recommended that you run the river at a gauge reading of less than 3.3, or that any open boats do so at a reading over 3.9.

The first set of Class IV rapids (2¾ miles) is rocky and continuous, with only small eddies, big enough for one boat. This area can be scouted or portaged on the left side. There is a trail going upstream from Snyder's Mill on the left (downstream) approximately ¾ miles upstream for those who wish to view this very difficult set of rapids. The river swishes from side to side around the rocks like a downhill ski run. After rounding a sharp right turn, the river drops into a ¼-mile stretch of flatwater, the lull between storms. If the first rapids are not to your liking, do not run the next set.

The second set of Class IV rapids is very turbulent, tricky to run upright, and hardly enjoyable swimming. It could be described as a hard Class IV washing machine, followed by a 4-foot ledge onto a ¼-mile washboard which is made up of shallow, bony rapids that run down under Snyder's Mill Bridge (4 miles). There is a dirt access road on the right, which was the take-out until it was marked as private property. Instead, take out on a small trail directly downstream from this road, or take out at the bridge. Neither option is a great take-out, however.

### Snyder's Mill–Contoocook River                          6 mi

| | |
|---|---|
| Description: | Flatwater, quickwater |
| Date checked: | 1988, MB |
| Navigable: | Medium water |
| Scenery: | Forested |
| Maps: | USGS Penacook 15, Hopkinton |

The lower section of the Blackwater is a pleasant run, with the only hazard being occasional fallen trees. Bridges cross at 4½ miles and 5½ miles. There is no access at the confluence (6 miles), but in any case many paddlers will want to continue 3¼ miles down the Contoocook to Broad Cove, on the right, or paddle the Contoocook upstream 1¼ miles to the bridge that can be reached by taking Tyler Road off NH 127, to Snyders Mill Bridge. Cross one bridge over the Blackwater, then the second bridge. The confluence with the Contoocook River is 4 miles downstream.

## NORTH BRANCH, BLACKWATER RIVER          NH

This is an easy trip, possible in wet summers, and ideal for beginners or bird watchers.

Start at the launching ramp above the dam at Cilleyville near the junction of NH 11 and NH 4A on the right bank. Paddle upstream for about a mile through Bog Pond and then on upstream another 1½ miles to the bridge at West Andover near Winslow Eaves Sculpture Studio. Then return. You may encounter beaver dams at the north end of Bog Pond, but they are a minor problem.

## SOUCOOK RIVER          NH

North of Loudon near Pearls Corner, Bumfagon Brook and Gues Meadow Brook join to form the Soucook River, which flows south to the Merrimack River below Concord. It is a pleasant, winding stream, with a good current and largely undeveloped banks.

It is possible to begin ¾ mile upstream from Pearls Corner at the second bridge on Pearls Corners Road, but that section has Class II rapids that remain blocked by deadfalls.

The last 11 miles beginning at the US 4 bridge east of Concord are especially recommended because there are no carries. This lower portion of the Soucook is more difficult at medium water levels, when there are several Class II rapids and innumerable riffles. At high flows many of them are washed out, so there are only occasional rapids. If there is not enough water to run the rock dam just above the bridge, the river below is too low for an enjoyable trip.

### Pearls Corner–US Rte. 4 Bridge                                    11 mi

| | |
|---|---|
| Description: | Quickwater, flatwater, Class II |
| Date checked: | 1988, RM |
| Navigable: | High water (April) |
| Scenery: | Forested, towns |
| Maps: | USGS Gilmanton 15, Suncook |
| Portages: | 5 mi   L   **dam at Loudon** 50 yd |
| | 8½ mi   R   **Cascade Camping Area** 200 yd |

Put in below the confluence at a bridge on a side road east of Pearls Corner. There are 2½ miles of good current in a winding meadow stream to the first bridge, then another 2½ miles, half of which is deadwater, to the dam in Loudon. The first NH 106 bridge is just before the dam. Take out on the left and carry across the road. Put in on the right. The short, rocky Class II rapids below can be lined if necessary. The portage trail goes to the end of the rapids. Immediately following the end of the rapids, the river is blocked by downed trees. There are 2½ miles of good current and occasional rapids between wooded banks to the new (second) NH 106 bridge, which is just before the dam.

Below the NH 106 bridge (7½ miles) there is about 1 mile of flatwater to a rocky Class IV rapid that can be run only under favorable conditions. Portage 200 yards on the right through the Cascade Camping Area to a pool below. It is ½ mile to the next side road bridge (9 miles), below which the river forms the eastern boundary of the city of Concord. In 2 miles there is a 1-foot dam at a gauging station just above the US 4 bridge. The gauge house no longer has a readable gauge.

## US Rte. 4 Bridge–Merrimack River                                    11 mi

| | |
|---|---|
| Description: | **Quickwater,** Class I–II |
| Date checked: | 1988, RM |
| Navigable: | High water (April) |
| Scenery: | Forested, rural |
| Maps: | USGS Suncook, Concord |

Below the US 4 bridge the river passes almost immediately under an old truss bridge, and just under the new NH 393 bridges is a Class II rapid. More quickwater flows as the river winds behind steep, wooded banks that are often 100 feet high. Watch out for fallen trees, particularly at high flows when the water is strong. Just before the river passes under Pembroke Road, on the Concord/Pembroke town line, there is a new gauge on the left bank. To reach the gauge, travel east on NH 9 in Concord and take Pembroke Road to the Concord/Pembroke town line. When you cross the river, look upstream and you will see the gauge on the right side. However, you cannot read the gauge from this distance and must travel up Pembroke Road a little farther and enter the trailer park on the left. Follow the trailer park road to the gauge. A reading of 4.8 makes for an enjoyable trip; 4.4 is considered too low. The original covered bridge that was directly upstream of this new bridge is no longer there.

After the NH 106 bridge (4¾ miles) Class II rapids occur more frequently, ending with a fast Class II drop at a ledge ½ mile above the high US 3 bridge (7½ miles).

Occasional Class I–II rapids start 2½ miles below the US 3 bridge. Just beyond the old railroad grade you reach the Merrimack River (11 miles).

Take-out is on the left bank ½ mile below the confluence and is reached from a side road in Suncook.

## SUNCOOK RIVER                                                      NH

The Suncook River flows from Crystal Lake in Gilmanton through the two Suncook lakes and then southwest to the Merrimack River at Suncook. Although there are four dams, there is some fine quickwater in the 29¼ miles described below. There is also a substantial amount of flatwater that can be run throughout the paddling season.

## Lower Suncook Lake–Pittsfield                              7¾ mi

| | |
|---|---|
| Description: | Lakes, quickwater, Class I–II |
| Date checked: | 1983 |
| Navigable: | High water needed for rapids (April) |
| Scenery: | Forested, towns |
| Map: | USGS Gilmanton 15 |
| Portages: | 4¼ mi e **dam in Barnstead** 50 yd |
| | (7¾ mi   R   **dam in Pittsfield** 300 yd) |

The river becomes runnable below Lower Suncook Lake. Put in from a side road upstream of NH 28. There is ½ mile of Class II water to the NH 28 bridge. From the bridge there are 1¼ miles of Class I rapids that lead to an old dam site just above the first bridge in Center Barnstead (1¾ miles). There is a Class II rapid for a short distance in the vicinity of that bridge. The current gradually eases off in the next ½ mile, and then there are 2 miles of flowage to the dam in Barnstead.

Below the dam (4¼ miles) there are some rapids for 1½ miles to a 2-mile backwater behind the Pittsfield dam (7¾ miles).

There is access to the river at several points above both dams from side roads.

## Pittsfield–Epsom Circle                                   8¾ mi

| | |
|---|---|
| Description: | Quickwater, Class I–III |
| Date checked: | 1983 |
| Navigable: | High water (April) |
| Scenery: | Forested, towns, settled |
| Maps: | USGS Gilmanton 15, Gossville |

In medium water it is possible to relaunch above the bridge. In high water carry across the bridge and relaunch below or put in 200 yards downstream from the Pittsfield dam on the left. The river is small and fast, and there is evidence of beaver activity. It is an easy Class II run for the first 2 miles to a sharp left turn at a ledge. Below that the rapids become more difficult. Between the power line and the bridge at Webster's Mills is the most difficult drop, a Class III rapid that is best to run on the right in high water.

Below the bridge (3 miles) the river broadens. There are big waves in high water, but in medium water the river is scratchy. Class II rapids continue for 1 mile before ending abruptly, followed by 1½ miles of quickwater to the bridge at North Chicester (5½ miles). Just below the bridge a low dam can be run under favorable conditions.

In the last 3¼ miles to Epsom Circle (8¾ miles), meandering through meadowland, the river is easy and enjoyable.

## Epsom Circle–Short Falls                                  4 mi

| | |
|---|---|
| Description: | Flatwater, quickwater, Class II–IV |
| Date checked: | 1983 |
| Navigable: | High water needed for rapids (April) |
| Scenery: | Forested, settled |
| Maps: | USGS Gossville, Suncook |
| Portage: | 1¼ mi   R   **dam at Bear Island** |

After ¼ mile the Little Suncook River comes in on the left. The river becomes ponded by a dam, which is 1¼ miles below the bridge near Epsom Circle. This dam is located at the head of Bear Island on the topographic map.

The island is about a mile long. The channel on the left starts by going over a low dam and has a number of tricky Class III and IV drops that local covered boaters find exciting. The right-hand channel requires a portage around a dam on the right. The rapids on this side of the island are Class II.

The rapids end shortly below the island. Fast water continues for about 1¾ miles to the bridge at Short Falls, where there is a riffle just above the bridge (4 miles), with some small surfing waves.

## Short Falls–Suncook                                          8¾ mi

| | |
|---|---|
| Description: | Flatwater, quickwater |
| Date checked: | 1983 |
| Navigable: | Spring, summer, fall |
| Scenery: | Forested, settled |
| Map: | USGS Suncook |
| Portage: | 4 mi e **dams at NH Rte. 28 bridge** |
| | (8¾ mi **dam at Suncook**) |

Below the bridge the water is ponded, and there are big estuaries at the mouth of all the tributaries. The left bank is mostly wild, but in many places on the right there are cottages and trailer parks.

In 4 miles a bridge on NH 28 is followed by an island with a dam on each side. Take out on either side of either dam. The best portage is on the island. There is current only for a short distance before you reach a backwater that extends for the remainder of the 4½ miles to the US 3 bridge (8½ miles) in Suncook. Below the bridge are a small pond and a high dam (8¾ miles).

From the dam the river drops nearly 100 feet in the first half of the remaining mile to the Merrimack River.

## LITTLE SUNCOOK RIVER                                    NH

This small, exciting stream is the outlet of Northwood lake in Northwood. It flows almost due west to the Suncook River just below the traffic circle in Epsom. US 4 follows nearly on the right bank, but the highway is usually out of sight. See the USGS Gossville map.

The first convenient put-in is the NH 107 bridge ½ mile below the outlet from Northwood lake. Since you immediately encounter numerous blind turns and narrow Class III–IV rapids that are frequently blocked by downed trees and barbed wire fences, this put-in is not recommended. A better choice is a roadside picnic area on US 4, where the river approaches the road. From here there is ½ mile of quickwater to a small concrete dam (½ mile), which is visible down a side road from US 4. Below this dam are rocky Class III–IV rapids that require just the right water level, which is found only a few days of the year after heavy rains and during the annual drawdown of Northwood Lake. There are many sharp corners, which sometimes hide a snowmobile bridge or a fallen tree. Take out at the bridge in Gossville (1¾ miles), since the next ½ mile to the Suncook River is congested with fallen trees, alder thickets, and grapevines in the middle of a swamp.

There is an annual fall drawdown of Northwood Lake by the Water Resources Board (603-271-1110).

## PISCATAQUOG RIVER                                       NH

The Piscataquog River is formed west of Goffstown by the union of the North Branch, which rises in Weare, and the South Branch, which rises in Francestown. The main river then flows eastward to the Merrimack in Manchester. The rapids can be run later in the year than those on the branches, and the smooth sections can run whenever they are free from ice.

## Confluence–power dam                                              3 mi

The first 1½ miles to Goffstown is described under both the North and South branches because it would be run as a continuation of one of those trips. The first dam lies just below the bridge in Goffstown. Water is backed up by the second, a high power dam, forming the recreational Glen Lake.

## Power dam–Grasmere                                                1 mi

Description:      Flatwater, quickwater, Class II–III
Date checked:     1983
Navigable:        High to medium water
Scenery:          Settled
Map:              USGS Goffstown

Below the power dam, which can be reached from the south, there are continuous rapids that are Class II in medium water and generate very large waves in high water. It is best to run this stretch when the upper river is low.

## Grasmere–Merrimack River                                          6 mi

Description:      **Flatwater, quickwater,** Class I–III
Date checked:     1988, GT
Navigable:        Spring, summer, fall
Scenery:          Settled, forested
Maps:             USGS Goffstown, Manchester South
Portages:         4 mi   L   **Kelleys Falls dam**

The rapids ease at Grasmere Bridge. The next 2½ miles are mostly quickwater, with occasional Class I rapids between attractive wooded banks to the backwater from the Kelleys Falls dam, where cottages line the shore.

The dam is located almost beneath the Pinard Street bridge. Take out at the boat ramp on the left, or continue below the railroad bridge to portage.

Below Kelleys Falls the river runs briskly through a ravine so deep that the houses in Manchester can scarcely be seen on the banks above. The river drops over a series of ledges separated by quickwater. The third ledge, a mile down, contains the remnants of an old dam, which can be scouted or carried on the right.

Several islands can be run on either side, including the large one at the confluence. The banks of this lower section are littered with shopping carts and other debris. None of the lower bridges offers access, but a convenient take-out is on the left bank of the Merrimack under the Queen City Avenue bridge. A road heading into the old factory area south of Queen City Avenue leads under the bridge. A more pleasant take-out is on the Merrimack from side roads near the I-293 bridge 2¼ miles downstream.

## SOUTH BRANCH, PISCATAQUOG RIVER          NH

The South Branch rises southwest of Concord in Francestown and flows east and northeast to join the North Branch just above Goffstown. The upper river has too many obstructions to be popular, but the lower river is frequently used as a whitewater practice run. Someone who is going to "run the Piscataquog" is usually referring to the section below New Boston.

### Francestown–old bridge                              7½ mi

This section is not popular because it contains a mixed selection of water, including two gorges. See the USGS Peterborough 15 and New Boston quadrangles.

Put in at the NH 136 bridge east of Francestown. Following a steep rapid below the bridge, the river winds through a marshy area with beaver dams. Shallow, pleasant Class II rapids, with steep drops between two bridges, are interspersed with fallen trees. Easy rapids, and occasional more difficult spots, continue to the second NH 47 bridge (3¾ miles), becoming smooth as they approach a bridge on a side road (4¼ miles). Take out here, since the unrunnable gorge starts above the next bridge (5 miles), and the portage is difficult. Carry by car to the next bridge.

One-quarter mile below the end of the gorge is an old mill site. A large boulder in the center and a large drop may have to be lifted over or portaged. Shallow rapids lead into quickwater through a swampy area. Rapids start again above the next bridge, and continue intermittently to a small bridge (6½ miles) at an old paper mill site. The bridge spans an awkward chute that reputedly contains old machinery. Portage to the right. It is another mile to the usual put-in for the run to New Boston.

## Old bridge–New Boston                                    3½ mi

| Description: | Class I–II |
| Date checked: | 1988, GT |
| Navigable: | High water (March to early April) |
| Scenery: | Rural, towns |
| Map: | USGS New Boston |
| Portages: | ¾ mi   R   **small dam** |
| | 2½ mi   R   **first dam in New Boston** 50 yd |
| | (3¼ mi   R   **second dam in New Boston** 300 yd) |

This abandoned bridge can be reached by a side road to the west of NH 13 a mile south of New Boston. Proceed for approximately 2 miles, crossing the river midway. Put in whenever it is convenient, by either the abandoned bridge or the midway bridge.

From the abandoned bridge there is ¾ mile of Class I rapids to a small dam that is washing out, followed by another ½ mile to the side road bridge crossed en route to the put-in. Below this bridge Class II rapids lead in 1¼ miles to a dam, which should be portaged on the right. Rapids continue for ¼ mile to the NH 13 bridge, just below which there is a millpond. Carry the dam in the center of New Boston (3¼ miles) on the right, go down the street for 300 yards, and put in near the next NH 13 bridge. In ¼ mile, the river passes a bridge by the old railroad station (3½ miles).

## New Boston–Goffstown 7½ mi

| | |
|---|---|
| Description: | Quickwater, Class **I–II** |
| Date checked: | 1983 |
| Navigable: | High water (March to early April) |
| Scenery: | Rural, towns |
| Maps: | USGS New Boston, Weare, Goffstown |

The most convenient starting point in New Boston is the old railroad station across the second bridge below the dam. In about ¼ mile there is a side road bridge.

For the next 5 miles NH 13 is often in sight on the right bank. Many of the rapids in this section are artificial because rocks have been placed in the river to improve the fish habitat. The rocks present no problem in high water, but they require careful route selection at lower levels. It is 2½ miles to the next bridge. The Middle Branch enters below on the left (3 miles). The next 1½ miles to a bridge (4½ miles) and a gauging station are somewhat easier. This is a popular take-out spot.

One mile below the gauging station the road leaves the river, and the rapids end. This is the last take-out before Goffstown. The river meanders, with a fast current, fallen trees, and many channels. The North Branch (6 miles), indistinguishable from other channels, enters on the left. From there it is 1½ miles to the bridge at Goffstown (7½ miles).

## MIDDLE BRANCH, PISCATAQUOG RIVER NH

The Middle Branch rises in Francestown and flows northeast to a marshy area, where it makes an abrupt turn and flows south to meet the South Branch about 2 miles below New Boston.

**Five Corners–South Branch**                                    **5¾ mi**

| | |
|---|---|
| Description: | Flatwater, quickwater, Class I–III |
| Date checked: | 1983 |
| Navigable: | High water (April) |
| Scenery: | Forested, marsh |
| Map: | USGS Concord 15 |
| Portage: | 5 mi e **dam** 50 yd |

Put in below the gorge at the five corners over a mile west of NH 77. The trip starts slowly, then a gorge follows, with some Class II–III rapids and a sharp right turn. Below the NH 77 bridge a steep drop may have to be lined or carried. After a few more rapids, the river enters a swamp where two other brooks join and makes its turn to the south. A small bridge on a closed road crosses at the end of the marsh, and the going is easy down to the backwater of a dam. Easy rapids continue below the dam for the ¾ mile to the South Branch.

## NORTH BRANCH, PISCATAQUOG RIVER          NH

The North Branch rises southwest of Concord in Deering and flows east and south to join with the South Branch just above Goffstown. The upper part is steep and rocky, with many ledges and old dam sites, and the lower portion is a pleasant quickwater run. The two are separated by a large flood control dam in Everett.

**Lake Horace–Everett Dam**                                     **9 mi**

| | |
|---|---|
| Description: | Class II, **III,** IV |
| Date checked: | 1983 |
| Navigable: | High water (April) |
| Scenery: | Forested, towns |
| Map: | USGS Hillsboro 15, Weare |
| Portages: | 2¼ mi   R   **dam at North Weare** 50 yd |
| | (9 mi **flood control dam**) |

All but one of the twenty-two milldams that formerly obstructed the river are gone, but the steep drops that engendered them remain. Since the old sites are still in the process of change, and the problems are different at different water levels, this section should only be run by competent parties who are willing to assess the problems as they come up. Almost everything can be run at the right water level, but many people would prefer to line or carry some of the drops.

Put in just below Lake Horace. The river is very small, with some overhanging bushes. Two old dams are located above the bridge a short way down. Then a series of more than six ledges follows to the millpond of the dam in North Weare, which sits atop a complicated ledge.

Another ledge lies under the New Boston road, and then easy Class II rapids run to the gorge below the old NH 77 bridge. There are a few more steep drops, then some easier drops (Class II + ) and some quickwater past the bridge on the road to the reservoir (6 miles) bring you to the old abutment (7¼ miles). The river splits around a complicated island, where the route is not obvious. Take out from the old road on the left near Choate Brook (7¾ miles). You can reach this point from Pages Corner, turning south on Sugar Hill Road and continuing past the ROAD CLOSED sign.

## Everett–Goffstown                                     8½ mi

| | |
|---|---|
| Description: | quickwater |
| Date checked: | 1983 |
| Navigable: | High or medium water (spring and after moderate rains) |
| Scenery: | Rural |
| Maps: | USGS Weare, Goffstown |
| Portage: | 5¼ mi   R   **dam in Riverdale** |

Put in just below the flood control dam by carrying past the ROAD CLOSED sign. The bridge ½ mile below is an alternate

put-in. The river winds with gentle current through meadowland
to Riverdale, where the dam above the bridge should be carried
on the right. Be considerate of the landowner.

Below the dam (5¼ miles) there are 1¼ miles of easy river
to the NH 114 bridge (6½ miles), where there is a boat ramp,
and to another bridge at Goffstown (8½ miles) 1½ miles below.


## COHAS BROOK                                                    NH


Cohas Brook flows along the south end of Manchester and
enters the Merrimack at Goffs Falls. The banks are so thickly
wooded that nearby settled areas are usually out of sight, but I-
93 is audible for a portion of the trip. See the USGS Manchester
North map.

The upper portion is a nightmare of dense thickets, fallen
trees, wire mesh, and electric fence. Also in store is a mile
of paddling in the median strip of I-93. The median strip can
be paddled upstream and back from the Bodwell Road bridge,
just after the river leaves the median. Small beaver dams, fallen
trees, and some low brush are encountered.

An acceptable, 4-mile portion begins at the second Bodwell
Road bridge. Expect a few fallen trees and/or log jams. The
stream, soon enlarged by the outlet of Massabesic Lake, passes
under I-93 in ¾ mile. Shortly after passing the NH 28A bridge
(1¼ miles), the stream meanders through a large wet marsh west
of NH 28A. Around the corner below is a Class II–III rapid
that runs continuously for about 100 yards and is runnable only
in high water. Take out on the right just after these rapids where
Goffs Falls Road approaches on top of a high steep bank (4¼
miles).

The lower portion is not recommended. It contains smoothwater and rapids. In the middle of a Class III–IV rapid (5¼
miles) there is a difficult access on the left from Perimeter Road
just opposite and downstream of the north end of the Manchester
Municipal Airport's main runway. This rapid can be portaged on
the right. Smoothwater and rapids continue to Pine Island Pond

(5¾ miles), which can be accessed publicly only via Perimeter Road up a very high bank. Below the dam (6½ miles) there is ¼ mile of unrunnable cascades to the Merrimack River.

## SOUHEGAN RIVER                                                    NH

The Souhegan rises in the Pack Monadnock and more southerly ranges and flows north and east to the Merrimack River between Manchester and Nashua. The upper portion offers a good intermediate whitewater trip; farther down, the river has a mixture of smoothwater and rapids. Riverbanks are usually unsettled except near towns.

Although it may be possible to canoe above Greenville, it is not recommended because there is an impassable gorge above the old power station below town. Although old rebars have been removed from the gorge, it is reported that there is a partly submerged pipe that presents a dangerous hazard.

### Greenville–NH Rte. 101 Bridge                              5¾ mi

| | |
|---|---|
| Description: | Class II–III |
| Date checked: | 1988, BL |
| Navigable: | High water (late March to early April) |
| Scenery: | Forested |
| Map: | USGS Peterborough 15 |

This is a very popular section of rapids, because the parts are of consistent difficulty and the road is close by, offering opportunities for scouting and rescue.

Put in at the site of the old hydroelectric plant on a short side road off NH 31 a mile north of Greenville and ¼ mile north of a railroad overpass. The rapids exposed by the removal of this dam should not be attempted because of the hazard from a partially submerged pipe.

The first mile to the NH 31 bridge is the most difficult (Class III). The rapids are rocky, with several small ledges, and they generate considerable waves in high water. Eddies are small, and rapids are continuous.

Below the bridge, the river follows the road closely for a while. The first drop is rocky, then the river becomes slightly easier, offering choices among the rocks.

Where the river turns away from the road, a huge boulder sits in the river to the right. A sharp left turn shortly below concerns boaters, but the large rock on the right has a pillow that makes it easy to miss.

At the large island, the left-hand channel tends to be blocked by fallen trees. The right-hand channel has a ledge where a zig-zag course may be easier to plan after scouting.

Below the island, the river becomes easier, splitting again in several places. Many parties take out at a girder bridge on a side road (4½ miles), since access is good and the rapids diminish to the NH 101 bridge.

## NH Rte. 101 Bridge–Wilton                                          1¼ mi

| | |
|---|---|
| Description: | Class **III**–IV |
| Date checked: | 1988, BL |
| Navigable: | High water |
| Scenery: | Forested |
| Maps: | USGS Peterborough 15, Milford |
| Portages: | ¾ mi **ledge**—lift over |
| | 1 mi   L   **first dam in Wilton** |
| | (1¼ mi **second dam in Wilton**) |

The Class III rapids beginning at the NH 101 bridge are more difficult than those below the old power station. Paddlers must dodge rocks in a very swift current. In ¾ mile there is a sharp Class IV drop over a ledge, which is best to run on the left. A dirt road that leads away from the river on the left can be used for scouting, carrying, or taking out.

After the second section of difficult rapids there is ¼ mile of fast water to the first dam in Wilton (1 mile). Portage on the left and continue through ¼ mile of rocky Class III rapids to a bridge and the mouth of Stony Brook on the left. The second dam is just below.

## Wilton–Milford                                              5¾ mi

| | |
|---|---|
| Description: | **Quickwater,** Class II |
| Date checked: | 1988, BL |
| Navigable: | High water |
| Scenery: | Forested, towns |
| Map: | USGS Milford |
| Portage: | (5¾ mi   R   **first dam in Milford**) |

At the second dam there are two options. You can carry ½ mile along the road through Wilton to the bridge at the east end of town. Doing this avoids a series of dams and a stretch of river that is often dry because of the diversion of the water into a power canal that parallels the river. However, if there is water in the river, you can put in below the final dam by following a steep dirt road over the railroad tracks and run ½ mile of Class II rapids to the bridge mentioned above, near which the power canal rejoins the river.

From the bridge at the east end of Wilton, Class II rapids continue for ¾ mile, ending just past the truss bridge at Jones Crossing. This marks the end of the rapids on the upper river, and it is the usual take-out for paddlers interested primarily in whitewater.

From Jones Crossing (1¼ miles), there are 4½ miles of winding stream, with a fast current and a few fallen trees, to Milford (5¾ miles). Take out at the ballfield off NH 101.

## Through Milford                                              1 mi

To avoid the carry around two dams, it is recommended that you portage by car, since buildings and retaining walls make hand-carrying each dam difficult.

## Milford–Turkey Hill Bridge                                   **10 mi**

| | |
|---|---|
| Description: | Flatwater, **quickwater,** Class I–II |
| Date checked: | 1983 |
| Navigable: | High water (spring) |
| Scenery: | Rural, towns |
| Maps: | USGS Milford, South Merrimack, Nashua North |

Put in by carrying down between the houses opposite the A&P on NH 101A. Except for a rocky Class III rapid beneath the high NH 101 bridge, this section begins with 2 miles of quickwater.

Below the NH 122 bridge (2 miles), there are 5½ miles of meandering quickwater past two more bridges to a sharp right turn, where there is a Class II ledge. The river then splits around two low islands, below which is Indian Ledge, a Class III rapid that should be scouted. The best carry starts on the right above the islands, but you can also run the Class II rapids on the left and then line the main drop down a side channel. Then there are 2¼ miles of smoothwater to the Turkey Hill bridge.

The Turkey Hill bridge (10 miles) is a recommended take-out point if you wish to avoid the portage at Wildcat Falls farther downstream.

## Turkey Hill Bridge–Merrimack                              **3¼ mi**

| | |
|---|---|
| Description: | **Quickwater,** Class II–III |
| Date checked: | 1983 |
| Navigable: | Medium water |
| Scenery: | Forested |
| Map: | USGS Nashua South |
| Portages: | 2 mi   L   **Wildcat Falls** ¼ mi |
| | (3 mi **dam at Merrimack**) |

Three-quarters of a mile below the Turkey Hill bridge there is an easy Class II rapid, followed by 1¼ miles of deadwater to Wildcat Falls (2 miles). Take out on the left and carry ¼ mile around the falls, which are doubly hazardous because they are likely to be jammed with debris. Then it is ¼ mile with two short Class II rapids to the high Everett Turnpike bridge, under which there is a short Class III rapid. One-half mile farther is the dam and the US 3 bridge at Merrimack (3 miles). Only ¼ mile of fast water brings you to the Merrimack River (3¼ miles).

## STONY BROOK                                                  NH

Stony Brook, a small stream west of Manchester and Nashua, is a tributary of the Souhegan River. Because of its size, it is less reliable and less frequently runnable than the Souhegan. When there is enough water, Stony Brook provides a short run comparable, in the last part, to the tougher stretches of the Souhegan.

### South Lyndeboro–Wilton                                     **3 mi**

| | |
|---|---|
| Description: | Class II–III |
| Date checked: | 1983 |
| Navigable: | High water (late March to early April) |
| Scenery: | Forested |
| Maps: | USGS Peterborough 15, Milford |
| Portage: | 2¾ mi   L   **sawmill** 20 yd |

From the put-in at the NH 31 bridge just below South Lyndeboro, there are 1½ miles of Class II rapids to the next NH 31 bridge. The river then turns left under a railroad bridge and drops through Class III ledges, which should be looked over from the highway nearby. The next mile has many more such ledges, all runnable at the right water levels but cautiously.

The dam at the sawmill (2¾ miles) above Wilton can be portaged on the left. More rapids continue to Wilton (3 miles). Take out on the right where there is an artificial embankment made of stone.

In the next 100 yards to the Souhegan River there is a dam that necessitates a short, steep portage on either side. Most boaters will not want to make this portage.

## NASHUA RIVER                                    MA, NH

The Nashua River is formed by the junction of the North and South branches at Lancaster Common, Massachusetts, and flows northeast to the Merrimack River at Nashua. Most of the Nashua flows through Massachusetts, and so that part of the river is described in the *River Guide* volume that covers Massachusetts. This volume describes the Nashua from its confluence with the Nissitissit River, which rises in New Hampshire and is frequently paddled.

Not long ago, the Nashua was extremely polluted, but great strides have been made in cleaning it up, and now much of it is a nice paddle.

### East Pepperell, MA–Mine Falls                              9¾ mi

| | |
|---|---|
| Description: | Flatwater, quickwater |
| Date checked: | 1983 |
| Navigable: | Spring, summer, fall |
| Scenery: | Forested, settled, towns |
| Maps: | USGS Pepperell, Nashua South |
| Portages: | 5¼ mi e **old dam at Ronnells Mills** |
| | 9¾ mi  R  **Mine Falls**—difficult |

From the Mill Street bridge in East Pepperell, where the put-in is below the dam, it is only ¾ mile to the junction of the Nissitissit. The current is moderate as far as the broken dam at Ronnells Mills, just below the NH 111 bridge. This dam can be run, but do not run it without careful scouting. Besides the more obvious problems, some spikes still protrude from the river.

From here to the first dam, about 1 mile west of Nashua, the current slows. The take-out at Mine Falls is a 700-foot carry, so it might be better to take out at the Horrigan Conservation Area off NH 111, about halfway down.

## Mine Falls–Merrimack River 5½ mi

| | |
|---|---|
| Description: | Flatwater, quickwater (rapids if desired) |
| Date checked: | 1983 |
| Navigable: | Spring, summer, fall |
| Scenery: | Forested, settled, urban |
| Map: | USGS Nashua South |
| Portage: | 3¾ mi e **dam—difficult footing** |

Portage Mill Falls on the right. This is the dam that forms the Nashua Canal, and the portage to the canal is easier than the one to the river (see the next section).

On the river, the first rapids below the dam are sharp drops over sharp ledges and are real boat-eaters. Where the river separates around an island, they become easier. A good path leads high above the river, with a trail down to the river almost at the end of the rapids; the carry is about ¼ mile.

Below the rapids the river wanders peacefully in two big loops to the left under the Everett Turnpike and under a prize-winning pedestrian bridge.

Just before the last loop a factory comes into sight on the right, with a solid line of factories around the next bend. Water from the canal exits under these factories. Below the stone arch Main Street bridge is another dam that can be portaged on either side, although the right is shorter; the bank is steep in either case.

The river is quickwater for the remaining 1¾ miles to the Merrimack; the chief obstructions are shopping carts in the river.

## Alternate canal trip about 3 mi

The portage into the canal on the right (east) side is much easier than the portage into the Nashua River. The canal is sluggish, passing under the same turnpike and pedestrian bridges as the river.

At the far end, the canal goes down the drain and emerges from underneath the factory. The paddler can carry right down to the Standard Hardware parking area by the river.

A more desirable carry is under a power line ½ mile upstream, where the river is only a short distance down the bank through the bushes.

## River/canal circle trip                                        about 6 mi

Put into the canal from the parking area behind the high school. This is also a convenient take-out for persons coming downstream, better than at Mine Falls. Paddle left—upstream—to near the dam where a carry can be made with some effort over to the river. This is the best approach for anyone who wishes to run the rapids. Continue downstream to where the factory comes into sight ahead and there is a culvert on the right (the upstream end of the oxbow shown on the maps). Carry up to the canal and paddle back to the start.

## NISSITISSIT RIVER                                        NH, MA

The Nissitissit River rises in Lake Potanaipo in Brookline, New Hampshire, and flows southeast into the Nashua River in Pepperell, Massachusetts. Although the entire river may be run in high water, the section from Lake Potanaipo to the MA 13 crossing is not recommended.

This is a trout stream of clean water within 50 miles of Boston. For paddling it ranks as Class I, with sharp turns, beaver dams, and fallen trees furnishing hazards.

## Brookline–West Hollis                                        4¾ mi

| | |
|---|---|
| Description: | Quickwater, Class **I** |
| Date checked: | 1983 |
| Navigable: | High water |
| Scenery: | Forested, rural |
| Map: | USGS Townsend |

The first good put-in is behind the fire station in Brookline, New Hampshire. Driving north on NH 13 from Townsend,

Massachusetts, take the first right after the Riverside Restaurant. If the water looks too low at this point you may wish to put in at Bohannon's Bridge about 2 miles farther downstream. A short distance before that bridge there is a single Class II drop that should be scouted and can be lined or portaged. From Bohannon's Bridge you will be out of sight of civilization for about 2½ miles, winding through Campbells Meadows and over a dozen or so beaver dams.

After 2½ miles the river turns right at a house on the bank. Below there is an old mill site with a drop that may be up to a Class II. The owner does not like persons trespassing on her property. Therefore parties who are incapable of running this drop without scouting from shore should take out on the conservation property upstream and portage by car to the West Hollis bridge ½ mile downstream. To reach the conservation land, from Brookline Street in Pepperell take Bemis Road, which leads to the pumping station. Turn right between two houses, where there is a conservation land sign on a tree. Continue straight as far as you can. Where the path turns left along an abandoned railroad, no more than two cars at a time can descend the cart path on the right to the river. Be sure to mark this point because it is not easy to recognize from the river.

## West Hollis–Pepperell                                            3½ mi

| Description: | **Quickwater,** Class I |
|---|---|
| Date checked: | 1983 |
| Navigable: | High water |
| Scenery: | Forested |
| Map: | USGS Pepperell |
| Portage: | 1¼ mi e **small dam** |
| | 3½ mi R **dam at Pepperell** |

Some paddlers consider this the best part of the river, with its good current and wooded banks. A small dam at a man-made pond can usually be run. Below the Prescott Street bridge (2 miles) there are some shallow rapids and then a long deadwater section above the dam, bordered by several houses. Take out on the right.

## Pepperell–Nashua River                                    1 mi

The rapids below the dam can be run. Most of them are Class II, and they end shortly below the MA 111 bridge. The next bridge, at Mill Street (¼ mile), is the last access before the Nashua River, which is an additional ¾ mile of pleasant quick-water paddling.

From the confluence it is another 4½ miles to the next bridge on the Nashua River, the NH 111 bridge just above a washed-out dam.

## SALMON BROOK                                            MA, NH

Salmon Brook is a very small stream that rises in Groton, Massachusetts, and flows northward to enter the Merrimack River in Nashua, New Hampshire. The section above Massapoag Pond is very difficult because of the obstructions and alder swamps. There are no real rapids. The river is of chief interest to swamp- and culvert-lovers.

## Massapoag Pond–Simoneau Plaza (Main Street)          6½ mi

| | |
|---|---|
| Description: | Flatwater, quickwater |
| Date checked: | 1983 |
| Navigable: | Anytime except extreme low water; high water is more difficult |
| Scenery: | Forested, rural, settled |
| Maps: | USGS Pepperell, Nashua South |
| Portages: | **frequent at bridges and culverts**—depends on water level |

Below the Massapoag Pond dam lies a lovely swampy pond—Lower Massapoag Pond—which has no development and no dam. The low culvert at MA 113 can be run. The next section is a nice marsh that gradually becomes very narrow; the brook meanders back and forth between high pine banks on both sides.

All the bridges are low, and some are so low that portages are mandatory. Most of the culverts can be run, though. The only bridge that presents a real problem is a stone bridge with a rapid above and parallel to it: take out above the rapid.

The mile above Harris Street is the least desirable and is also more obstructed by alders and meanderings. The last mile is nicer.

The river runs underneath Simoneau Plaza, so it is necessary to take out above the gate on the west side of Main Street or at the playground farther upstream.

The river is not particularly accessible for paddling for the remainder of its distance to the Merrimack. A stone at a little park near the Alds Street bridge marks where Hannah Duston spent the night on her return. The river then flows through a factory to the Merrimack.

The first settlement in Nashua was at the mouth of Salmon Brook, but it was later moved a mile north to the mouth of the Nashua River.

## BEAVER BROOK                                    NH, MA

Beaver Brook is a pleasant, winding stream that flows from Beaver Lake in Derry to the Merrimack River at Lowell. There is a good current for most of that distance, with lots of small beaver dams, some minor rapids, and occasional carries. The brook flows through several suburban communities, but few of the settled areas are visible from the river.

## Derry–West Windham                                              **7 mi**

| Description: | Flatwater, quickwater |
| --- | --- |
| Date checked: | 1988, RCG |
| Navigable: | High water (April) |
| Scenery: | Forested, towns |
| Maps: | USGS Derry, Windham |
| Portages: | 4 mi   R   **dam at Kendall Pond** 100 yd |
| | 7 mi   R   **dam at West Windham** 40 yd |

The original put-in on NH 28 is not recommended because of major sewer pipe construction and numerous deadfalls along the river. An alternative put-in is off Gilcrest Road in Londonderry. In less than 1 mile, Beaver Brook enters Kendall Pond (3½ miles). Gilcrest Road can be reached by taking Exit 4 off I-93 onto NH 102 toward Londonderry, and then taking the first left. Gilcrest crosses Beaver Brook just before intersecting with Kendall Pond Road.

One-half mile across the pond is the outlet (4 miles), where there are a dam and a bridge. Take out on the right and carry across the road. Beware of snowmobile bridges just past the dam. For the next 3 miles the stream winds through meadows where there are logjams and beaver dams. Portage the dam at West Windham (7 miles) on the right. The NH 128 bridge is just below it.

## West Windham–Second NH Rte. 128 bridge                         **3 mi**

| Description: | **Quickwater,** Class I |
| --- | --- |
| Date checked: | 1988, RCG |
| Navigable: | High water (March, April, or wet fall) |
| Scenery: | Forested |
| Map: | USGS Windham |

The river bottom is gravelly, and numerous rocks give practice in reading water, but the current is so slow that they present little hazard. Fallen trees in the river present another navigational problem for paddlers in this section. It is 1¾ miles to the NH 111 bridge, ¼ more to the next bridge, and then 1 mile to the second NH 128 bridge. The usual easy run on Beaver Brook is from Kendall Pond to this point.

## Second NH Rte. 128 bridge–Collinsville                         10½ mi

| | |
|---|---|
| Description: | Flatwater, **quickwater,** Class II |
| Date checked: | 1983 |
| Scenery: | Forested, towns |
| Maps: | USGS Windham, Lowell |
| Portages: | ¾ mi  L  **broken dam** |
| | 3¾ mi **small dam** |
| | (10½ mi  R  **dam in Collinsville**) |

This section of Beaver Brook is more demanding than the sections above; it has a few rapids and two interesting stone arch bridges.

A house marks a left turn at a broken dam. Although the locks are jagged, it can be run, or it can be lined or portaged on the left. Deal with it as you choose and continue on promptly. The second of two closely spaced bridges (Tallant Road) offers good access upstream on the left (1¼ miles). Quickwater follows 1½ miles to a bridge, now closed, and then for another mile to a small concrete dam (3¾ miles), which can be lifted over on either side or run in the middle.

One-half mile past the second dam a steel beam bridge (4¼ miles) on NH 111A may have to be carried at high water because of low clearance. It is ¾ mile to a stone arch bridge and another ½ mile to the bridge on Bridge Street (5½ miles) opposite the shopping center in Pelham.

From the shopping center it is ¾ mile to the Willow Street bridge, and from there the river winds for 4½ miles mostly through meadowland. There are some Class II rapids above the dam and bridge at Collinsville (10½ miles) in Dracut. Take out 200 yards above the dam, on the right, at a launching map.

## SPICKET RIVER                                          NH, MA

The Spicket River rises in Island Pond in Hampstead and flows
south to reach the Merrimack at Lawrence. The upper and lower
parts are not practical to paddle, but the middle section offers a
more pleasant quickwater run than might be expected in such a
settled area.

### Town Farm Road–Methuen, MA                          8 mi

| | |
|---|---|
| Description: | Quickwater |
| Date checked: | 1988, RD |
| Navigable: | High water (March and April or after rain) |
| Scenery: | Wooded, settled |
| Maps: | USGS Ayers Village, Lawrence |

A start can be made at Town Farm Road, just below an alder
swamp, or at NH 97, 1 mile south. The brook is small, and it
wriggles back and forth among the trees, sometimes up to the
backyards of houses. The least attractive section is through the
trash generated by the shopping center along NH 28 (5 miles).
After another mile the new river channel parallels I-93, with
access to the old channel through a culvert. The river passes
under the interstate ramp (7 miles) and under a railroad bridge.
Take out, with permission, on the left above the highway bridge.

Below here there are two dams, close together, and the river
runs over at least two more dams, one of which is confined
between factory walls, before reaching the Merrimack 4 miles
below.

## LITTLE RIVER                                          NH, MA

This stream is runnable from Plaistow, New Hampshire, to
within a mile of the Merrimack River in Haverhill, Massachusetts,
at which point it runs into a culvert. It is a small quickwater stream
that is runnable only at high water.

Begin the run from Main Street in Plaistow (NH 121A) just
east of NH 125. In ½ mile the stream passes beneath Westville

Road, and within another ½ mile beneath two bridges, the second of which is NH 125. It passes under NH 121 (1½ miles) just above the state line. The stream remains small until it passes underneath I-495 (3 miles) and enters the backwater of a dam in Haverhill. Much of this flowage is paralleled by railroad tracks. The best take-out points in Haverhill are at a playground (5 miles) on the right 150 yards past a railroad bridge and ½ mile above the dam, or at Benjamin and Apple streets just above the dam. See the USGS Haverhill map.

## POWWOW RIVER                                    NH, MA

This small stream in southeastern New Hampshire has two sections that offer pleasant canoeing in largely isolated areas. See the USGS Kingston, Exeter, and Newburyport West maps. The take-out in the first section is now posted as available only to residents of Kingston per order of the selectmen.

The second section begins off NH 107A on Chase Road. Put in where the river comes close to the road a short way south of the Chase Road bridge. The first 1½ miles are through fine woods. Access is available where Dugway Road crosses near the end of the woods. Then 1 mile of marsh and pond brings you to Tuxbury Pond, where there is 1 mile of lake paddling to the dam at the outlet (3½ miles). The parking lot at the dam is along Newton Road in Amesbury, Massachusetts. This section may be extended (scouted only) by putting in through large open meadows 2½ miles to the bridge at West Whitehall Road. One can take out here or continue down Lake Gardner 2 miles to the dam just off High Street in Amesbury (8 miles).

# Chapter 6

# Piscataqua Watershed

# PISCATAQUA WATERSHED

NH ¦ ME

Milton Mills

Farmington •
Milton •
Lebanon •
North Rochester
Little River

Rochester •
Salmon Falls River
Cocheco River
North Berwick •

Isinglass River
Somersworth •
Great Works River

Dover •

Bellamy R.

Deerfield •
Nottingham •
Oyster R.
Piscataqua River

Lamprey River
North River

Newmarket •
Piscassic R.
Great Bay

Raymond •

Chester •
Brentwood •
Exeter •
Sandown •
Exeter River

Scale in miles

0    5    10    15    20

The Piscataqua Watershed is bypassed by many paddlers on their way north. The rivers are generally small, and since they do not rise from snowy heights as the Saco does to the north, they have a short runoff. During a peak of three weeks, however, they offer quickwater and Class I–II rapids in channels that are narrower and more intimate than those familiar to most paddlers.

The North and Little rivers offer by far the best Class II water in the spring, although portions of other rivers have shorter stretches of rapids worth exploring. The Cocheco from Farmington to Rochester and the last 5 miles on the Exeter to Fremont are the best of many quickwater stretches.

Summer canoeing is quite limited. Portions of the Exeter, Lamprey, Salmon Falls, and Great Works rivers offer flatwater except in dry summers, but the tidewater portions of the Exeter and Salmon Falls, as well as the nearby York River in Maine, are of course always runnable.

The Piscataqua River itself is a tidal estuary, formed by the confluence of the Cocheco and Salmon Falls rivers, which continues the line dividing Maine and New Hampshire that the Salmon Falls River previously marked. It drains both these rivers and several others that flow into Great Bay. The upper part is wide, with moderate current. Below Dover Point, where Great Bay empties into the river, it is marked by one of the strongest tides on the eastern seaboard.

## COCHECO RIVER                                          NH

The Cocheco River rises above Farmington, becoming runnable there as several smaller branches join forces. It is a pleasant paddle to Rochester.

Its course through Rochester to tidewater at Dover is marked by dams, waterfalls, dangerous gorges, and pollution. Therefore the lower section is not recommended.

## Farmington–Rochester                                    10½ mi

| | |
|---|---|
| Description: | Flatwater, **quickwater,** Class I |
| Date checked: | 1988, TQ |
| Navigable: | High water (later March to early May) |
| Scenery: | Rural, urban |
| Maps: | USGS Alton 15, Berwick 15 |
| Portage: | 1½ mi **culverts** 50 yd |

Put in at the NH 153 bridge ½ mile south of the center
of Farmington. A flood control and river-grading project has
given the section near town an aseptic look. Soon the river
begins twisting and turning, with a moderate current. Watch
out for fallen trees and overhanging bushes in this area. In
1½ miles the river disappears into a pair of culverts placed
there by the Vickers Gravel Company. **Caution!** If the river is
high, these culverts may be entirely underwater and hazardous
because they create a strong suction. Take out with care and
portage.

The next 5 miles are ideal for the beginning whitewater paddler,
as they offer many sharp turns with a moderate current, plus a
number of riffles and Class I rapids. The current slows down
near a bridge (6½ miles) on a back road connecting Chestnut
Hill Road with NH 11. This is the recommended take-out, on
the east side of the river (parking is available).

The remaining 4 miles are through an urban section of
Rochester, and most are in the backwater of the first dam. If
you are continuing through, be careful to take out at or above
the NH 11/US 202 bridge (10½ miles) because there is a dangerous waterfall 40 yards beyond this bridge.


## EXETER RIVER                                              NH

The Exeter River was known in early times as the Squamscott
River and is still so named on its lower, tidal section. It rises in
Chester and flows 34 miles before reaching tidewater at Exeter,

a trip the proverbial crow would make in only 15 miles. Because the river doubles back on itself so much, it does not pick up many feeder streams, so it remains narrow for its entire length.

## Chester–Sandown                                                                    **4 mi**

This section is no longer navigable. The river is but a very small stream that has brush and trees all along the bank. When the water is high enough to run, it flows through the brush creating dangerous strainers.

## Sandown–Fremont                                                                   **12½ mi**

| | |
|---|---|
| Description: | Flatwater, **quickwater,** Class I |
| Date checked: | 1988, AS |
| Navigable: | High water (late March to late April) |
| Scenery: | Rural |
| Maps: | USGS Haverhill 15, Mount Pawtuckaway 15 |
| Portages: | 1 mi e **gorge at mill site** |
| | 1¼ mi e **dam** |
| | 1¾ mi e **mill site** |
| | (12¼ mi   R   **Fremont Dam** 10 yd) |

Much of the first 7 miles below Sandown is through marshes where perseverance, a map, and a compass are all helpful. There are also a few snowmobile bridges that may have to be lifted over.

The last 5 miles to Fremont are the finest on the river for scenery as well as being hazard-free, and constitute probably the best quickwater in the Piscataqua Watershed.

From Sandown, where the put-in is on NH 121A just north of town, the river flows gently for ¼ mile to Lily Pond, which is ¼ mile long and easier to paddle than the name implies. There is no dam at the outlet.

Below Lily Pond there are Class I rapids for ½ mile to an old mill site (1 mile) and a gorge that is unrunnable. The gorge can be inspected in advance from the bridge just below.

After another ¼ mile a small backwater above a dam can be portaged on either side. Shortly below there is another gorge at an old mill site that has some interesting stonework remaining. There is another bridge just beyond.

Below the second bridge (1¾ miles) the river enters a large swamp where the route is difficult in low water. The old railroad grade is used as a snowmobile trail, and the river is spanned at the crossings by sagging bridges. In the next 3 miles it flows under two more road bridges, followed by 3 miles more of brushy meadow.

After passing under the seventh bridge (7½ miles), the river becomes narrow and quick. There is some brush to be avoided and an occasional tree across the stream, but from here past 3 more bridges there are no impassable or dangerous sections. There is a short slackwater behind the dam at Fremont, which is located about ¼ mile after the first houses appear on the left bank. Portage on the right. The remaining 500 yards to the center of Fremont are flatwater.

## Fremont–Brentwood                                    5½ mi

| | |
|---|---|
| Description: | Flatwater, **quickwater,** Class II |
| Date checked: | 1988, AS |
| Navigable: | High water (late March to early May) |
| | Medium water (moderate summer rainfall) |
| Scenery: | Forested, towns |
| Map: | USGS Haverhill 15 |
| Portage: | 1 mi   R   **second dam in Fremont** 20 yd |
| | 4½ mi   R   **West Brentwood Dam** 20 yd |
| | (5½ mi   L   **waterfall** 150 yd) |

There are mile-long millponds on both ends of this run. The connecting 2½ miles of quickwater are passable frequently during the summer. There may be trees down that have to be lifted over. The Class II rapids, all between the West Brentwood dam and NH 125, are short but exciting in high water.

From the bridge next to the general store in Fremont, the river goes through 100 yards of Class I rapids to a lake that extends for 1 mile to a dam. Portage on the right. The next 2½ miles are quickwater, with one short swampy section. There has been recent beaver activity, so a few lifts may be required. Just below a campground on the right bank there is a crude rock dam that is runnable in high water.

The last mile to West Brentwood is backwater from the dam (4½ miles) with many cottages on both banks. **Caution!** The dam is just above the second bridge in West Brentwood. Take out on the right. In high water you can continue immediately below the dam, putting into a 50-yard Class II rapid. After a brief pause there is a second Class II rapid, also about 50 yards long.

**Caution!** Take out on the left above the NH 125 bridge: a Class III rapid begins directly under the bridge and leads immediately to a 10-foot waterfall under a second bridge 200 yards downstream.

## Brentwood–Exeter                                    **12 mi**

| | |
|---|---|
| Description: | **Flatwater,** quickwater, Class I–II |
| Date checked: | 1988, AS |
| Navigable: | High water (late March to early May) |
| | Medium water (moderate summer rainfall) |
| Scenery: | Forested, settled |
| Maps: | USGS Haverhill 15, Exeter |
| Portages: | 5 mi  R  **Pickpocket Dam**–cross bridge, |
| | put in  L  50 yd |

The backwater from Pickpocket Dam dominates the middle of this section, both by slowing the flow of water and by making the course far from obvious. Above this, however, there are 2 miles of pleasant quickwater through dense second-growth forest, and below the dam there are several challenging Class II rapids that are runnable in high water.

Put in at least 50 yards below the waterfall. Easiest access is from the left bank. The first 100 yards are Class II, followed by quickwater and occasional Class I rapids to a bridge 2 miles below. Most of the next 3 miles are in the backwater behind Pickpocket Dam (5 miles). The course is hard to follow here. **Caution!** Portage the dam and the chutes below it, because they are more dangerous than they appear to be. Put in near the bridge below.

The first 150 yards past Pickpocket Dam are Class II rapids, which can be run in fairly high water. Then there are intermittent Class I and II rapids to the NH 111 bridge (6 miles) a mile below the dam. One-quarter mile downstream, around a blind right turn, is a 75-yard Class II rapid that is especially difficult in high water.

The remaining 6 miles to Exeter have little current. The river passes under a railroad bridge 1 mile below NH 111, a back road bridge another mile farther, and the NH 108 bridge ¾ mile beyond that. There has been recent beaver activity in this area, so be ready to climb over some of their dams. The final 3 miles to Exeter involve much sharp meandering and confusing junctions with side channels. Careful observation of the current will get you through.

**Caution!** There is a 10-foot dam just below the first bridge in Exeter with no adequate access near it. Take out on the right 50 yards above the bridge, just when it first becomes visible; or take out ½ mile above the bridge at the public park on the left, adjacent to the Phillips Exeter Academy playing fields.

Below Exeter, the river is called the Squamscott and is tidal. In 6 miles it enters Great Bay (18 miles).


## GREAT WORKS RIVER                                    ME

This unassuming little river claims the distinction of having the first water-powered mill in the United States, in the section of South Berwick called Great Works. Mills existed there for over three hundred years, until the 1940s, when the remaining few fell into disuse.

## North Berwick–South Berwick                        11½ mi

| | |
|---|---|
| Description: | **Flatwater,** quickwater, Class I |
| Date checked: | 1983 |
| Navigable: | High water (late March to mid-May) |
| | Passable at most water levels for last 3½ mi |
| Scenery: | Forested |
| Maps: | USGS Kennebunk 15, York 15, Dover 15 |

The first 5 miles to Emerys Bridge on Hooper Sands Road are narrow and winding, and the river shallows out early in the season. The next 3 miles to Junction Bridge, at the west end of Emerys Bridge Road, hold water a little longer. Both sections are prone to blowdowns.

The final 3½-mile section from Junction Bridge to the village of Great Works is runnable except in very dry summers, and it is entirely flatwater. Take out at the Brattle Street bridge (11½ miles), ¼ mile below the ME 236 bridge.

**Caution!** Below the Brattle Street bridge there is a series of falls and rapids called Rocky Gorge. Stay well above it. Continuing to the Salmon Falls River, into which the Great Works River flows, is not feasible because this obstruction requires a mile-long portage.

There is a dam on the Great Works River at the confluence with the Salmon Falls River.

## ISINGLASS RIVER                                          NH

The Isinglass River flows from Bow Lake in Strafford to the Cocheco River in Rochester. At one time it provided water power for several mills in Barrington, but all that remains today is the small dam above the US 202 bridge. The banks are mostly wooded, and there are only a few houses within sight of the river.

The river itself is quite clean, and there is an attractive waterfall near the end.

The first 2 miles can be done only in very high water. Check the old mill sluice above the US 202 bridge which can be seen from the bridge or reached by a short trail starting from the southwest corner of the bridge. If there is enough water here, the rapids above, which are considerably easier, will be runnable. Very high water in the river downstream tends to make Class I rapids easier and Class II rapids harder.

## NH Rte. 126–Cocheco River                                    10½ mi

| | |
|---|---|
| Description: | Flatwater, **quickwater,** Class I–II |
| Date checked: | 1988, TQ |
| Navigable: | High water (late March to end of April) |
| Scenery: | Forested, rural |
| Maps: | USGS Mount Pawtuckaway 15, Dover West, Berwick 15 |
| Portage: | 8 mi   R   **waterfall** 125 yd |

There is good current for about 1½ miles below the NH 126 bridge in Barrington. Then there are three short, easy Class II pitches as the river parallels US 202. Stay to the left of the island. Just above the US 202 bridge there is a quiet pool behind an old dam. **Caution!** The sluiceway is runnable, but it must be scouted, for there are some sharp boulders to avoid. When the water is really high, there are powerful currents that make it difficult to control a boat in the narrow channel.

The river below the US 202 bridges (2 miles) is mostly quickwater, with a few Class II rapids, for 2½ miles to a small iron bridge beside a house on the right. In this section there are two pairs of bridge abutments that predate the Revolutionary War. Past the bridge the river is sluggish for ½ mile, below which there is another ½ mile of Class I and II whitewater. Halfway down the rapids at a sharp right turn there is a Class II + ledge passable on the left which stretches almost all the way down the river. The rapids end 50 yards below the Berrys Hill bridge (5½ miles). The remaining two miles to NH 125 contain flatwater.

Below the NH 125 bridge (7½ miles) there is a ½ mile slack current to a 25-foot waterfall. **Caution!** At a stone abutment on the right 20 yards above the first sign of rapids, take out on the right and carry 125 yards along an old road. This is a good picnic and rest spot, for the falls shoot out between massive rocks and make an impressive sight. The next ¼ mile is Class II–III: difficult in very high water, scratchy in moderately high water, and impassable in anything else. The rapids end with an S-turn between high banks, followed by a rock garden that is likely to add a few scratches to your boat. The next 1½ miles to the Rochester Neck Road bridge are a pleasant quickwater run over a sandy bottom; catfish are often visible here.

One-half mile below the Rochester Neck Road bridge (10 miles), the Isinglass empties into the Cocheco River. It is 1¼ miles down the Cocheco to the next crossing, a bridge on County Farm Road (11¾ miles). This section is all flatwater except for the last 100 yards, where there is an easy Class II rapid.

## LAMPREY RIVER                                          NH

The Lamprey is one of the longest rivers in the Piscataqua Watershed, and it is probably the flattest. The section above Raymond offers Class I rapids for spring paddlers. Below town the river can be run for most of the year because there are few rapids. Packers Fall, Class II or III, depending on the water level, is runnable well into the summer by kayaks and canoes.

### Deerfield–Raymond                                    9 mi

| | |
|---|---|
| Description: | Flatwater, quickwater, Class I–II |
| Date checked: | 1988, GT |
| Navigable: | High water (late March to early May) |
| Scenery: | Forested, settled |
| Map: | USGS Mount Pawtuckaway 15 |

Three-quarters of a mile above Raymond, a tributary named Cider Ferry enters on the right, flowing from Onway Lake. The name came from a barrel of cider that slipped and burst as it was being taken over the stream by some early settlers before there was a bridge. "But," as some remarked, "as fish do not drink cider, no harm was done."

Put in 2 miles south of Deerfield Center at the junction of NH 143 and 107. The Lamprey is at this point a narrow trout stream, with Class I–II rapids, shallow riffles, and quickwater. Beavers have made a strong resurgence on this part of the river, and you will surely encounter several of their dams. One and a half miles below, before the first bridge, are two ledges. The first is runnable on the left in very high water; the second must be lined or carried. From the first bridge to NH 27 is 2½ miles, largely quickwater with a few Class I rapids, including a 100-yard stretch that ends right of NH 27.

From the NH 27 bridge (4 miles) the next 1½ miles are flat and wide: follow a straight course here. Then there are more Class I rapids in the next mile to the Langsford Road bridge (6½ miles), with a Class II–III ledge just below. The rapids end in another ¼ mile, and the final 2¼ miles to Raymond (8 miles) and the side road bridge east of town are once again flat and wide. Take out at this bridge, since there is a gorge in the next mile.

### Raymond–NH Rte. 102/107 bridge                                    1 mi

Most of this distance is flatwater or quickwater. The gorge is within sight upstream from the bridge. It can be lined in low water, but it is difficult to portage.

### NH Rte. 102/107 bridge–West Epping                             3½ mi

| | |
|---|---|
| Description: | Flatwater, quickwater, Class I |
| Date checked: | 1988, GT |
| Navigable: | Medium water |
| Scenery: | Forested, settled |
| Map: | USGS Mount Pawtuckaway 15 |
| Portage: | (3½ mi  L  **dam**) |

Put in either at the bridge or, if the 50 yards of Class II rapids are too low, into Dead Pond. The pond is a pleasant paddle for a mile past some cottages. Then the river narrows again and drops over some easy rapids past a small bridge (1¼ miles) where there is an easy put-in but not much room for parking. This bridge is 1 mile down Prescott Road, which goes east off of NH 107. In another ¾ mile the river passes the NH 101 bridge and then continues for a couple of miles to the backwater of the dam, which is below the next bridge.

## West Epping–Wadley Falls                                        12 mi

| | |
|---|---|
| Description: | **Quickwater,** Class II |
| Date checked: | 1988, GT |
| Navigable: | High to medium water (spring) |
| Scenery: | Forested, town |
| Map: | USGS Mount Pawtuckaway 15 |
| Portage: | (12 mi   R   **dam at Wadley Falls**) |

Below the dam in West Epping is a short pool easily accessed from a dead-end road along the left bank. Class II ledges begin under the next bridge and continue for ½ mile, gradually becoming easier. The river passes a few rock dams, and the final ledge is underneath the first bridge in Epping (3½ miles). All three bridges in Epping offer easy access and parking.

Below Epping (4 miles) the river meanders for 3 miles to the NH 87 bridge. After the bridge a long, smooth stretch twists, with numerous log-jams, through old pastures and woods for another 5 miles past the mouth of the North River (10¾ miles) to the Wadley Falls dam (12 miles).

## Wadley Falls–Newmarket                                          10½ mi

| | |
|---|---|
| Description: | Flatwater, **quickwater,** Class I–III |
| Date checked: | 1988, GT |
| Navigable: | High water (late March to early May) |
| | Medium water (average summer rainfall) |
| Scenery: | Forested |
| Maps: | USGS Mount Pawtuckaway 15, Dover 15 |
| Portage: | 7¼ mi   L   **Wiswall Falls Dam** 50 yd |

For a quiet retreat into the woods, the first 4 miles are superb. Paddlers continuing below the bridge on Lee Hook Road may have a scratchy time in moderately high water because the rapid starting under the bridge, and another shorter one a mile farther, need rather high water to run well.

One feature of the lower stretch is Packers Falls, which are not actually falls but rather one of the most challenging rapids in the Piscataqua Watershed. It is a roaring Class III run in early spring and is often well run into summer as a Class II drop. There are well-developed portage trails for those who want to run Packers Falls several times.

Below the dam at Wadley Falls there is a brief rapid, then 4 miles of quiet paddling past densely forested banks of hemlocks and hardwoods to the Lee Hook Road bridge. Below the bridge are 200 yards of easy Class II rapids with large combers in high water. At the end of the rapid, there is a broken dam that cuts diagonally across the river; it can easily be run by following the current rather than the shore. A combination camp and trailer park extends for the next mile along the left bank to a short rapid on either side of an island (5 miles).

It is another 2¼ miles to the Wiswall Road bridge and Wiswall Falls Dam (7¼ miles). Below the dam there is a 200-yard Class II rapid, which, if unrunnable, can be carried on the left. Another ¾ mile brings you to Packers Falls (8 miles).

**Caution!** Take out on the left at least 20 yards above the bridge and scout Packers Falls. This run is a difficult Class III in high water, and a moderate Class II, with some scratching at the bottom, in medium water. There are two more short Class II rapids just below Packers Falls, then 2½ miles of flatwater to Newmarket, where the route through the flowage may be obscure. The Piscassic River 9¾ miles) enters on the right just above the dam (10½ miles).

## LITTLE RIVER                                                    ME

The canoe season is short but exciting on the Little River. Canoe it early in the morning or on an overcast day because it heads into the afternoon sun for most of its length.

## Lebanon–Salmon Falls River                          11¼ mi

| | |
|---|---|
| Description: | Flatwater, quickwater, Class I–II |
| Date checked: | 1983 |
| Navigable: | High water (late March to early May) |
| Scenery: | Forested |
| Map: | USGS Berwick 15 |

The usual put-in is below the broken dam beside an old mill in Lebanon. In high water the river can be run above the mill, either from Fall Road (a mile upriver) or from ME 11/US 202 (3 miles above the mill). Determined explorers occasionally start even higher up. The river above the mill is quite narrow, with Class I and II rapids.

From the mill there are two rapids, with one at a broken dam, in the first mile. In the next 1 mile, from the Lord Road bridge to the bridge on Little River Road, the river is smooth and winding. The next 4¼ miles to Stackpole Bridge pass through an area known as the Marshes, where the river maintains a good current around numerous tight turns and twists. Occasional breakthroughs create some confusion, but careful observation of the current will guide you through easily.

Whitewater enthusiasts frequently begin at Stackpole Bridge (6¼ miles), under which there is a small drop over a ledge. The next 2 miles are smooth and slow until the river reaches a small Class I rapid, followed soon after by ¼ mile of Class I rapids up to Messenger Bridge, where Pine Hill Road and Little River Road meet.

Below Messenger Bridge (8½ miles) there is another Class I rapid, then an easy Class II rapid. The river is narrow enough that you must pick either the right or left side, since there is no room for a middle route, and the only clear passage involves switching occasionally from a course down one side to a course down the other. Stop and scout frequently unless you like piling up onto ledges and into impassable rock gardens. One particularly interesting spot has a car-sized boulder perched on top of a ledge left of center; the usually runnable channels lead you within an arm's length of it.

The long rapid ends with a small ledge in a sharp right turn. The last ½ mile of this rapid, down a back-road bridge (9½ miles), is very scratchy when the rapids above are marginally runnable. Flatwater follows. One-half mile above the Hubbard Road bridge (11¼ miles) there is a broken dam at the end of a sharp S-turn that can be run with extreme caution or lined from the right bank.

The Little River empties into the Salmon Falls River (11¼ miles) just below the Hubbard Road bridge. Somersworth is 5 miles downstream (16¼ miles).

## NORTH RIVER                                              NH

The North River is a short tributary of the Lamprey River above Wadley Falls. Its paddling season is brief, but it definitely offers the best whitewater run in the Piscataqua Watershed, a 2½-mile continuous Class II run above NH 152.

There is a lot of beaver activity, so be aware of downed trees on all sections of the river.

In very high water it can be run from the back-road bridge near the outlet to Pawtuckaway Pond or from NH 152 at a point 2½ miles north of Nottingham; both of these branches are somewhat overgrown but runnable, and both have quick-water and Class I rapids. The usual put-in is by the school in Nottingham.

### Nottingham–Wadley Falls                              8¾ mi

| | |
|---|---|
| Description: | Flatwater, quickwater, Class II |
| Date checked: | 1988, LTW |
| Navigable: | High water (late March to early April) |
| Scenery: | Forested |
| Map: | USGS Epping 7.5 |
| Portage: | 4 mi   R   **NH Rte. 152 bridge** 30 yd |

The first 1½ miles are flat, with a fair current. About 100 yards above the Merellis Road bridge, Class II rapids begin.

The most difficult rapid is 80 yards below the bridge. It is Class II–III and must be taken in the center. Class II rapids continue with only brief pauses for 2½ miles to Harvey's Shingle Mill (long since abandoned) at the next bridge, NH 152.

**Caution!** Take out in the eddy on the right just above the NH 152 bridge (4 miles), because there is a Class IV rapid below the shingle mill. The drop has a rusted turbine in the middle of the drop. Put in on the left below the mill. The mile to Birch Hill Road bridge is swift running, with Class I rapids. Recent beaver activity has created seasonal logjams on this section that may require lifting or portaging. Along this stretch there are some incredible stands of sycamores, which are uncommon in New Hampshire. In the next 1½ miles to the NH 125 bridge (6½ miles), the river flows with a moderate current past a stand of maple trees, on the left. Take out at the bridge.

Below NH 125 there is one mile of flatwater to the Lamprey River (7½ miles), with another 1¼ miles down that stream to the dam at Wadley Falls (8¾ miles).

## PISCASSIC RIVER                                             NH

The Piscassic River is a large brook that flows eastward from Fremont and Epping to the Lamprey River just above Newmarket. The section above NH 87 is extremely difficult and is not recommended unless you enjoy hacking your way through thick alder and vine tangles. Below NH 87 the river is more open, and it has many narrow, tight turns in quickwater. There are a number of downed trees.

**Newfields–Newmarket**                                    **5¾ mi**

| | |
|---|---|
| Description: | Flatwater, **quickwater,** Class I–II |
| Date checked: | 1988, LTW |
| Navigable: | High water only (late March to mid-April) |
| Scenery: | Rural |
| Map: | USGS Dover 15 |
| Portage: | ¼ mi   R   **rapids** 100 yds |
| | 4 mi   R   **rapids** 100 yards |
| | 5 mi   L   **rapids** 40 yds |

Put in at the NH 87 bridge. Just below there is an old mill site some steep, narrow Class II rapids, which can be run solo or carried 100 yards on the right. In ½ miles you pass an old railroad bridge, and in another 1½ miles a bridge (2 miles) on a back road. The river is swift and meandering there, with many downed trees and bushes that narrow passages and challenge your steering.

In the next mile there is good farm scenery, but beware of wire fences across the river. This brings you to the bridge southeast of Four Corners. In ¼ mile, there is another bridge (4 miles) where there is a Class II rapid that is sometimes runnable, even at reasonable water levels. In 1 mile there is another sharp Class II drop that cannot be seen ahead of time; it should be carried 40 yards on the left. The three rapids should all be portaged, as paddlers will not want to swim rapids that may have barbed wire running across the river. Shortly after that, the river reaches the NH 152 bridge. From there ¾ mile remains to the high dam (5¾ miles) just west of Newmarket.

If you continue, it is ¾ mile farther to the Lamprey River and another ¾ mile to the dam at Lamprey River Falls (7¼ miles) in Newmarket.

# SALMON FALLS RIVER                    ME, NH

The river flows south from Great East Lake and forms part of the boundary between Maine and New Hampshire.

Three sections of the river are not recommended. Above Milton Mills it is a very small stream with shallow rapids that are seldom deep enough to run and a thick alder swamp where the channel is difficult to follow and frequently blocked by debris. Portions of the river immediately below Milton and from Berwick/Somersworth to South Berwick also are not recommended because of unrunnable rapids and dams.

## Milton Mills–Milton                    9 mi

| | |
|---|---|
| Description: | Lakes, flatwater, Class II |
| Date checked: | 1988, TQ |
| Navigable: | High water (early Spring) |
| Scenery: | Forested, settled |
| Maps: | USGS Newfield 15, Berwick 15 |
| Portages: | 1 mi   L   **secon dam in Milton Falls** |
| | 1¼ mi   L   **third dam in Milton Falls** |

Below the first dam just north of town, bear right for almost a half mile. The rapids, when runnable, are nearly continuous and very heavy. In ½ mile there is an old mill site with abutments and then a short stretch of rapids before a second mill site. Both should be lined, lifted over, or carried. The last ¼ mile is mostly backwater behind the second dam (1 mile). Take out on the left immediately below the bridge. After this dam there is a short Class II rapid, then flatwater to the third dam. Land on the left well above the bridge.

A boat can be put in just below the third dam (1¼ miles). Paddle under the bridge and parts of the mill buildings. The first

¼ mile is an alder tangle, but paddling improves as you proceed downstream. The river meanders extensively, and it is still somewhat impeded by fallen trees.

The river enters the extreme northern end of Northeast Pond (4¾ miles), from which it is 2½ miles to the bridge (7¼ miles) between Northeast Pond and Townhouse Pond, and an additional ¾ mile to the southeastern end where there is a good take-out. From the bridge it is 1¾ miles to the dam at Milton (9 miles).

## North Rochester–Somersworth                          14½ mi

| | |
|---|---|
| Description: | **Flatwater,** quickwater, Class I–II |
| Date checked: | 1988, TQ |
| Navigable: | High water (late March to early May) |
| | Passable at all water levels, below Little River |
| Scenery: | Rural, towns |
| Map: | USGS Berwick 15 |
| Portages: | 4½ mi   R   **East Rochester Dam** 100 yd |
| | 11½ mi **dam** |

The heavy use of the river for water power in the nineteenth century is evident in dams (and in factory buildings above the put-in) below the take-out and halfway down when the river passes through East Rochester. Quickwater enthusiasts will find a pleasant paddle above East Rochester but must be prepared to run over 50 yards of Class II rapids entering town. The next 2 miles to Step Falls, like the first 4½ miles, are good only in high water. In contrast, the remaining 8 miles are flat and runnable all summer.

Put in behind the Spaulding Paper Products plant just off NH 16. If your boat makes it over the first riffles 10 yards below the put-in bridge, you will have easy going all the way to East Rochester, even though the river seems shallow.

The river meanders through sandy areas of marginal farms and suburban sprawl, but it has a beauty of its own. The rapids are small and minor until you reach East Rochester, where a Class

II rapid begins 40 yards above an abandoned iron bridge. The most difficult section is directly beneath the bridge, and it should be scouted. The US 202 bridge is immediately below this rapid. **Caution!** There is a 10-foot dam 100 yards below the bridge Portage on the right.

Below the dam in East Rochester (4½ miles), there are heavy Class II rapids for 75 yards, then primarily quickwater until Step Falls (6½ miles), which is a series of ledges that are runnable under proper conditions. Below this point the river is almost without current for the remaining 8 miles to Berwick/Somersworth.

Five miles from East Rochester, the Little River enters on the left (9½ miles). A bridge on Hubbard Road 400 yards up this stream offers access to the Salmon Falls River and is especially useful for summer paddling.

Two miles past the Little River there is an 8-foot dam. You can take out here, at the Rochester Street bridge (13 miles), or a Parson's Park (14½ miles), ½ mile above the center of Berwick/Somersworth. **Caution!** There is no adequate take-out in town, and there is a dam 10 yards below the bridge connecting the twin towns of Berwick and Somersworth.

## Somersworth–South Berwick                                    5¼ mi

The next 5¼ miles are not recommended. First, there is the dam ½ mile below the last take-out suggested. Then there is a ¾-mile section of the river behind the General Electric plant in Somersworth which contains unrunnable rapids and dams. Determined paddlers can put in below this obstacle, but they will have a 100-yard portage within the first mile. Below, the river is pleasant for 3 miles to Salmon Falls (19¾ miles), a 15-foot drop just above a railroad bridge. Another portage is necessary here, because there are 150 yards of unrunnable rapids below Salmon Falls. Finally, there is ½ mile of flatwater to the ME/NH 4 bridge (21¼ miles), immediately below which there is a 10-foot dam.

# TIDEWATER CANOEING                          NH

An exception to the rule that water always flows downhill is found in the tidewater portion of coastal rivers. Tide introduces an entirely different dimension into canoeing.

The Atlantic Ocean has water even when all the interior rivers are dry and provides it to the lower parts of rivers in the Piscataqua Watershed on an inflexible but precisely calculated schedule. Since the tide reverses every six and a quarter hours or so, return trips traveling with the tide both ways are possible, so there is no need to spot cars.

On the negative side, the tide must always be taken into account when you plan trips. The tide's rise and fall leaves a soft, slippery deposit of mud on the shores below the level of high tide, so landing anywhere, even at a prepared launching ramp, is difficult. Because sewage from towns upstream ends up in the harbor, the water is not clean enough for enjoyable swimming, which detracts from summer trips.

Tidewater paddlers should know something about "the rules of the road" for navigation and about the markings on buoys. Although hand-driven craft may have the right of way, arguing the point is unprofitable. At low tide much of the upper tidal area is shallow, even for a canoe, so you may wish to follow the channel. The canoe's shallow draft gives it an advantage, so it is courteous to stick to the side of the channel, in file astern, and leave the center for deeper-draft boats.

The rivers of the coastal plain are the only ones in New Hampshire that reach the ocean within the state boundary. All the drops on the rivers that flow into Great Bay were once harnessed for power, so the head of tidewater is at a dam in all cases. The upper tidal portions seem little different from the nontidal portions, except for a different kind of grass, a preponderance of oaks and pines, and the exposed flats at low tide. Although there are some developed areas and motorboats, much of the shore is still wooded and looks as it did centuries ago, except that the trees are now smaller.

Descriptions for the following rivers start from the dam at head of tidewater. The approximate tide correction that should be added to the Portsmouth tide time is given for this point from both high and low tide. Note that the time the tidal current reverses does not necessarily correspond to the time of high or low tide. At Dover Point, for instance, the current will still be running in well past the time of high tide.

The river descriptions are arranged clockwise, starting at the southwest.

## Maps

All of these rivers are on the USGS Dover 15-minute quadrangle except for the upper part of the Squamscott River, which is on the Exeter quadrangle, and the lower part of the Piscataqua, which is on the York, Maine, quadrangle. Also consider using navigation maps.

## Tide Information

Tide charts for the whole eastern seaboard are computed and printed months in advance; copies may be available in libraries, where you would look under "Tides." Local tables covering a short period are often available free from marinas and banks. Daily tide information is published in local newspapers and broadcast on some radio and television stations.

## EXETER/SQUAMSCOTT RIVER

**Exeter–Great Bay, 6½ mi**            **Tide correction: +2 hr**

The Exeter River changes its name to the Squamscott River when it passes the last cascade in Exeter and becomes tidal. Put in from a road on the left bank ½ mile downstream of the second bridge in Exeter. The shores are high marsh grass and almost entirely undeveloped. The "Oxbow" is an island of grass marked by a clump of trees. It can be rounded only at fairly high tide, which flows in from both directions. A marina is downstream from the last bridge.

When approaching the Squamscott River from Great Bay, you can recognize the railroad bridge at the mouth all the way from Adams Point. The dark wood of the two spans of bridge pilings makes a checkerboard against the island and the white rock fill of the causeways at each end.

## LAMPREY RIVER

**Newmarket–Great Bay, 1½ mi**          **Tide correction: +1¾ hr**

A state boat-launching ramp is located on the right bank. The Lamprey has the shortest tidal section of any of the big rivers, coming in near the Squamscott River at the southwest end of Great Bay.

## OYSTER RIVER

**Durham–Greay Bay, 2¾ mi**          **Tide correction: +1¼ hr**

Put in from the left bank at a park in Durham, downstream from the NH 108 bridge. Many boats are anchored nearby. At low tide even a canoe will need to follow the channel, which meanders back and forth across the mud flats and is marked by poles with yellow flags. Durham Point is on the right at the mouth.

## BELLAMY RIVER

**Sawyer's Mill–Little Bay, 4 mi**          **Tide correction: +1¼ hr**

To put in on the Bellamy River, drive through the Sawyer's Mill parking area off NH 108. Bear left around the mill building, and continue past the old mill houses to a second mill and dam ½ mile downstream. Put in below the second dam from the left bank. The river is very small. Low tide exposes a short rapid. One mile downstream, a road on the left bank leads down to some houses. Near the mouth on the right bank there is a wildlife refuge.

## GREAT BAY

Great Bay, a 3-by-6-mile triangular body of water, has many of the characteristics of a shallow lake of the same size, with the added complication of the tide. A navigable channel snakes back and forth like a river meandering across a floodplain. Your paddle will often touch bottom, even in the center. The prevailing wind is from the southwest, and when a heavy wind opposes the tide, the water is rough and makes for a less than enjoyable paddle.

## DOVER POINT

Dover Point, central to the tidewater of the area, is a neck of land extending southward between the Piscataqua River and Little Bay, which leads from Great Bay. The point is traversed by US 4, which crosses to the south shore on a pair of high bridges. Hilton Park, on the tip, is accessible from both lanes. It has rest rooms (open only in summer). A picnic area with fireplaces, on the west side, and a launching ramp with parking, on the east side, are connected by an underpass. This park is a good starting point, lunch spot, or end point for these tidewater trips.

From the Dover Point launching ramp, to the left (north) is "upstream" on the Piscataqua River, which is formed by the confluence of the Cocheco and Salmon Falls rivers 4 miles above. To the right (southeast) the Piscataqua flows to the Atlantic Ocean, 8 miles away. The channel underneath the bridges leads west to Little Bay and from there to Great Bay.

Underneath the bridges, the three northernmost spans are blocked by rocks at low tide. The tidal current flows at up to 8 knots, with considerable turbulence and eddies at most stages, and is strongest at half-tide. Canoes will find it necessary to pass this point with the tide. Ahead is Little Bay, with Goat Island in the center. Go right, under the low US 4 bridge, to reach the Bellamy River; bear left for Great Bay. The Oyster River is on the right just as the bay starts to widen. To reach the Lamprey River follow the western shore. The checkerboard light-and-dark at the southwest end of the bay is the railroad trestle at the mouth of the Squamscott River. Great Bay itself is interesting to explore.

The paddler can leave the launching area at Hilton Point on the incoming tide nearly two hours past the tide in Portsmouth, explore around in the bay and any of the rivers, and return on the outgoing tide. Or for variety, go down one river with the outgoing tide and up another with the returning tide (spotting cars, of course).

## COCHECO RIVER

**Dover–Piscataqua River, 3 mi**            **Tide correction: +1½ hr**

The dam and mill over the Cocheco River adjacent to NH 108 are worth stopping to see. At high water a rainbow appears in the spray. Put in below the mill from a side road on the left bank or at one of the various marinas. The river leaves the road immediately, with only occasional farms along the shore. In two places it cuts a narrow gorge through steep cliffs. The junction with the Salmon Falls River forms the Piscataqua River.

## SALMON FALLS RIVER

**Portland Road bridge–
   Piscataqua River, 4 mi**            **Tide correction: +1½ hr**

Put in from the left bank below the mill at the second dam below Salmon Falls. Blueback herring are often found here. Past the first mile of farmland, the dam on Great Works River is on the left. In another ½ mile the lawns of Hamilton House extend to the river. Downstream there are wooded cliffs, with a historical trail along the shore. At the picnic area downstream to the left of Eliot Bridge you can listen to the clatter of cars crossing. The confluence with the Cocheco forms the Piscataqua River.

## PISCATAQUA RIVER

**Confluence–Atlantic**
**Ocean, 12 mi**          **Tide correction: Dover Point, +1¼ hr**

The Piscataqua is a large river from the start, and an adverse wind can cause much trouble. Dover Point is 4 miles down the right. Below Dover Point there are docks for ocean-going ships, tankers, and pleasure boats of all sizes. This trip will be enjoyable for people who like to ride bicycles in rush-hour traffic. Huge eddies swirl around piling and buoys, and in addition to the wind and the tide, wakes from large boats come from all directions, raising a tremendous chop. Paddlers should keep well out of the channel and avoid big boats. This is obviously no place for a novice. However, experienced paddlers, fortified with favorable wind and tide, can have an interesting trip that differs from paddling inland rivers.

Since the wind is most often from the south and strongest in the afternoon, the best plan is to start from Hilton Park, going down on a noon low tide and returning in the afternoon with the wind and tidal current behind. On the right below Dover Point, oil company piers have pilings that have to be avoided by those hugging the shore. The river narrows and races past rocky cliffs and under the high I-95 bridge (4¼ miles). Two more bridges carry US 1. Immediately below the lower bridge is Four Tree Island Park (5½ miles), which has covered picnic tables, grills, and rest rooms. The launching ramp is under the bridge to the right.

Farther down the Piscataqua River there are many docks, and a prison rises conspicuously. Just at the point, on the right, stand a Coast Guard station and Fort Constitution (no public facilities).

For a better canoe trip, take the more intimate right-hand route at Four Tree Island and go down among the islands. Strawberry Banke is on the right. The large white building on the left by the bridge is Wenworth-by-the-Sea. Fort Stark is on the point at the left.

If the wind is onshore and the tidal current running in, it is farily safe and a lot of fun to ride the swells just inside the breakwater. Keep clear of the channel.

# Chapter 7

# Saco Watershed

Grey area not covered in this book.

# SACO WATERSHED

Bartlett

Saco River

E. Branch

NH
ME

Bearcamp River

Swift River

Whittier

Silver River

Conway

Center Conway

Old Saco R.

Fryeburg

Ossipee Lake

Pine River

Ossipee River

Saco River

Kezar Falls

Hiram

Little Ossipee River

East Limington

Bonny Eagle

Saco River

Biddeford

Saco

Scale in miles

0   5   10   15   20   25   30

Clean water, a mountain setting, and relative proximity to population centers have always made the Saco River and its tributaries some of New England's most popular rivers for paddling.

The headwaters, with their spring whitewater runs, lie mostly in New Hampshire; below the Maine line the river becomes more placid, flows more smoothly, and is marked by a number of dams. This book includes only the Saco River and tributaries that lie in New Hampshire. The Saco River downstream from Fryeburg, Maine, which includes the parts usually run in the summer, is described in the companion volume, the AMC River Guide: Maine.

For whitewater thrills the upper Saco and the Swift rivers rate among the best and most difficult in New England. Nice runs with easier rapids can be found on parts of the Bearcamp and Ossipee rivers, and on the Saco below Bartlett. The Pine River offers the most secluded setting but is not an easy run. It is occasionally choked with alders and blocked by fallen trees, and much of it is impassable in low water. Only the last few miles of the Bearcamp, Ossipee, and Pine rivers can be run in low water. However, two tributaries of Ossipee Lake, the Pine River and the Silver River, benefit from annual fall drawdowns of the lakes from which they flow.

## SACO RIVER                                    NH, ME.

The Saco River begins at Saco Lake at the north end of Crawford Notch and drains the southern slopes of the Presidential Range through the Mount Washington Valley. From Conway it winds generally southeast into Maine and reaches the Atlantic Ocean south of Portland, Maine.

In its upper reaches, the Saco River drops steeply, providing excitement for expert paddlers. As it approaches Bartlett, the difficulty diminishes and canoeing becomes less demanding.

Below North Conway there are fewer rapids and more sections of quickwater.

## Davis Path–Sawyer's Rock                                        4½ mi

| | |
|---|---|
| Description: | Class III–IV |
| Date checked: | 1988, BL |
| Navigable: | High or medium water (mid-April to mid-May) |
| Scenery: | Forested |
| Map: | USGS Crawford Notch 15 |

This section, commonly known as the Upper Saco, is one of the most exciting whitewater runs in central New England. In addition to its continuous rapids, the river passes through beautiful White Mountain scenery. Since the Saco drains the steep-sided Crawford Notch region, runoff takes place rapidly, and warm, sunny days or spring rains can lead to a rapid rise in the level of the river.

From the Davis Path footbridge there is a short stretch of easy rapids leading to a very difficult Class IV gorge at the mouth of Nancy Brook. The gorge is extremely narrow, less than a boat-length wide, with turbulence off the walls.

Since the portage around the gorge is very difficult, most groups prefer the put-in off US 302 about 1 mile south of the Inn Unique at Notchland. This put-in is posted, and boaters should ask permission at the Inn Unique before going onto the property. Pull off the road into a dirt parking area, then cross the railroad tracks, and carry or line down to the river.

From the put-in, the rapids are continuous and generally Class III, but some are Class IV in high water. The first mile is particularly shallow and twisty and requires constant maneuvering except in very high water. Class III rapids continue to the entrance of the Sawyer River (2¾ miles), where there is a Class III drop and a small beach on the right that makes a good lunch or resting spot. There is then another ¾ mile of rapids to a railroad bridge (3½ miles), followed shortly by a Class III drop in a sharp left turn. At this point US 302 is visible high on the right bank. In the next broad right turn lies a Class IV stretch with large waves.

The difficulty diminishes again as the river approaches US 302 near Sawyer's Rock Picnic Area (4½ miles).

## Sawyer's Rock–Bartlett                                    2¾ mi

| | |
|---|---|
| Description: | Class II–III |
| Date checked: | 1988, BL |
| Navigable: | High water (late April to early May) |
| Scenery: | Forested |
| Map: | USGS Crawford Notch 15 |

This section is usually run in conjunction with the one above or below and ranks between them in difficulty.

There is ½ mile of Class II rapids to another railroad bridge (4¾ miles) with a wavy ledge underneath. The large hydraulic found there can be skirted on the left side. This hydraulic is a keeper and should be avoided at all costs. One hundred yards below the railroad bridge is a right turn with large rocks on the outside: many inexperienced boaters have left their boats on these rocks.

Another Class III rapid lies about 1 mile farther. From above this rapid only swift, shallow rapids to a blind left turn are visible. Most boaters should scout the passage between the large rocks in the turn and ledge-and-waves combinations below. The Saco then passes through shallow riffles, where the river has been bulldozed for flood control, to the iron bridge in Bartlett (7¼ miles), where there is parking and access on the left bank.

## Bartlett–Humphrey's Ledge                                    8¼ mi

| | |
|---|---|
| Description: | Class I–II |
| Date checked: | 1988, BL |
| Navigable: | High water (early May) |
| Scenery: | Forested |
| Map: | USGS Crawford Notch 15 |

The Saco from Bartlett to North Conway is a popular white-water run of medium difficulty. The current is swift, and there are intermittent Class II rapids, some of which have heavy waves in high water. The riverbed is wide most of the way, with fine houses along the banks.

The Saco's current is strong enough to undercut its sand and gravel banks and to topple the trees growing on them. Sometimes the water is high enough to remove the debris, but frequently it is not. Therefore, low-lying tree trunks are an ever present hazard, especially at the outside of the turns where the main current flows under them. There are always a few such obstacles to quench the enthusiasm and dampen the finesse of inexperienced and inattentive boaters.

In the first 8¼ miles to Humphrey's Ledge, the current is swift, with frequent Class I and II rapids. **Caution!** Be alert for fallen trees that block the main current at the outside of the turns. After about ½ mile the river divides. The old, open channel goes to the right, and a new, narrower one continues straight into the forest. The latter was scoured out during the flood of July 1973, and it is more easily blocked by fallen trees than is the old route. There is a difficult Class II rapid that begins about ¼ mile above the US 302 bridge (4½ miles).

There are more rapids below US 302, with a Class II rapid in ½ mile just above the Rocky Branch, which enters on the left. Beyond the railroad bridge (6 miles) easier intermittent rapids continue to the Ellis River, which enters on the left just before a railroad embankment. In ¾ mile the West Side Road follows along the right bank beneath Humphrey's Ledge.

## Humphrey's Ledge–North Conway                                    3½ mi

| | |
|---|---|
| Description: | **Quickwater,** Class II |
| Date checked: | 1988, BL |
| Navigable: | High to medium water (May) |
| Scenery: | Forested, rural |
| Map: | USGS North Conway 15 |

Below Humphrey's Ledge the river is smooth, but in high water the current is still very fast. In 2 miles, when a house appears high on a bank ahead, be prepared for an S-curve at Lucy's Rock. To either side of the large rock in the center the channel is relatively unobstructed, but there may be trees and other debris on the left at the outside of the turn. The river flows quietly again to the North Conway bridge, whose easternmost span crosses the main river.

## North Conway–Conway                                              8 mi

| | |
|---|---|
| Description: | **Quickwater,** Class I |
| Date checked: | 1983 |
| Navigable: | Medium water (May) |
| Scenery: | Forested, rural, settled |
| Map: | USGS North Conway 15 |

This section is easier than the ones above and below, and it contains no notable difficulties. However, it is wide and shallow, so it is not usually passable in summer without considerable wading.

The AMC Moose Campground (reservations required) is 2 miles down on the right and difficult to spot from the river. There is a railroad bridge at 4½ miles.

There is a possible take-out on the left before the turn above the Swift River where the rapids start. However, at most water stages the wavy rapid provides an exciting finish to the trip. Take out on the left below the covered bridge.

## Conway–Center Conway                                    2¾ mi

| | |
|---|---|
| Description: | Quickwater, Class I–III |
| Date checked: | 1983 |
| Navigable: | Medium water (May, sometimes passable in wet summers) |
| Scenery: | Forested, towns |
| Maps: | USGS North Conway 15, Ossipee Lake 15 |

Class II rapids start within sight of the covered bridge. A trip beginning here can also start on the Swift River, at the bridge ¼ mile above the confluence, which is immediately above the covered bridge and enters in the middle of the rapid.

Below the NH 16 bridge (¼ mile) there is another easy Class II rapid, and around another corner there is a short but difficult Class III rapid that can kick up 4-foot waves when the water is high. After a brief respite, a long rapid starts and is heavy at the beginning but less so as it continues until it eases off under the US 302 bridge (2½ miles). Good access can be had on the left at the old covered bridge site.

## Center Conway–Swans Falls                    10 mi

| | |
|---|---|
| Description: | Quickwater, Class II |
| Date checked: | 1983 |
| Navigable: | Spring, summer, fall |
| Scenery: | Forested, settled |
| Maps: | USGS North Conway 15, Ossipee Lake 15 |
| Portage: | (10 mi   R   **Swans Falls** 300 yd) |

This start is usually possible in summer. Shortly after the put-in there is a ledge, followed by some Class II rapids that can be bony in the summer. The riffles end by the Saco Bound put-in (3¼ miles).

Quickwater continues to the Weston's Bridge in Fryeburg (6¾ miles). The river meanders slowly to the dam at Swans Falls, where there is an access, a portage trail, parking, and an AMC campground.

In the summer the Town of Fryeburg sets up docks and rafts just downstream of Weston's Bridge. Keep to the extreme right to avoid swimmers.

For the remainder of the Saco River see the companion volume, *AMC River Guide: Maine*. The most popular summer quickwater run is from Fryeburg to Hiram.

## EAST BRANCH, SACO RIVER                    NH

### Benchmark 784–Lower Bartlett                    3 mi

This small stream is recommended only for closed boats. Under the right conditions it can be run down to the Saco River near Humphrey's Ledge in late April or early May. The rapids are continuous, and many are Class IV. They should be scouted carefully because precise and quick maneuvering is necessary. Fallen trees may present more than the usual hazard since it is hard to get out of the river once you have put in.

Scouting is possible on the north bank of the river from a paved road that leaves NH 16A in Lower Bartlett. The suggested put-in is at the first wooden bridge above the highway near Benchmark 784 on the USGS North Conway 15 map.

## SWIFT RIVER                                          NH

The beautiful Swift River rises in the west end of Albany Intervale and flows eastward to meet the Saco River in Conway. Most of the river can be paddled, and there are many challenging rapids to be negotiated. From Rocky Gorge to Darby Field, the Swift is suitable only for covered boats or those smaller open boats with thigh braces and maximum flotation.

Because of the large, high-altitude drainage, the Swift River tends to hold water fairly well and is normally runnable from mid-April to the end of May. The Kancamagus Highway runs through the Swift River Valley, providing convenient access at many points.

### Pine Bend Brook–Rocky Gorge                       8½ mi

| | |
|---|---|
| Description: | Quickwater, Class III |
| Date checked: | 1988, BL |
| Navigable: | High to medium water |
| Scenery: | Wild, forested |
| Maps: | USGS Crawford Notch 15, Mount Chocorua 15 |
| Portage: | (8½ mi   R   **Rocky Gorge** 200 yd) |

The rapids in this section are all or nothing! The quickwater is very wild and attractive, but access at either end is difficult unless you run the rapids.

Put in at the bridge over Pine Bend Brook from the Kancamagus Highway. The river starts with steep ledges and fast turns, and some scouting and perhaps lining or carrying is in order. After about 2 miles the rapids end, and the river enters a complicated beaver swamp, followed by about 2 miles of quickwater away from the road with mountain views.

The quickwater continues beyond Bear Notch Road (5¼ miles) for nearly 3 miles. The rapids start again abruptly ¼ mile above the first road access and continue for ½ mile. The most difficult drop is the double ledge visible from the Kancamagus Highway. Take out on the right above Rocky Gorge.

## Rocky Gorge–Lower Falls                              2½ mi

| | |
|---|---|
| Description: | Class III |
| Date checked: | 1988, BL |
| Navigable: | High to medium water (mid-April to mid-May) |
| Scenery: | Forested |
| Maps: | USGS Crawford Notch 15, North Conway 15, Ossipee Lake 15 |
| Portage: | 2½ mi   R   **Lower Falls** 200 yd |

This stretch is commonly referred to as the Upper Swift. It contains continuous, difficult rapids to challenge paddlers seeking whitewater sport. Expert open boaters will be able to navigate this stretch.

A put-in is possible over a smooth ledge right by the wood bridge at Rocky Gorge (also known as Upper Falls). Class III

rapids begin just below the gorge and continue for about 1 mile.
Then there are a couple of rapids that are more difficult: first
through some large boulders in a left bend, and then two ledges
after a right turn. These two ledges, sometimes known as the
Washboard, are right next to the Kancamagus Highway. Rapids
continue at a Class III pace, reaching Class IV in a bouldery
stretch just above Lower Falls.

Boaters should take out when they spot the recreation buildings on the right shore. Lower Falls is another 10-foot fall over
ledges, although it is more gradual than Upper Falls. It has occasionally been run on the far left as a stunt, but it should generally
be portaged. The picnic and parking areas here have been used
to take out or to put in for the stretch below.

## Lower Falls–Darby Field                                    6 mi

| Description: | Class **IV** |
|---|---|
| Date checked: | 1988, BL |
| Navigable: | High to medium water (mid-April into May) |
| Scenery: | Forested |
| Map: | USGS Ossipee Lake 15 |

This section is one of the most difficult uninterrupted runs in
all of New England. The stretch from the gorge, 2 miles below
Lower Falls, is often referred to as the Lower Swift. It provides
excellent sport for skilled boaters, but it is not a good run for
inexperienced paddlers. When the water is up, a damaged boat
and a long, exhausting and dangerous swim could result from
any tip-over.

At the bottom of the gorge, there is a hand-painted gauge on
a rock on the right. A reading of 1.2 on this gauge is a medium,
runnable level for this section.

The pool below Lower Falls makes a good put-in for this run. However, there is little chance to warm up for the rapid below the falls, which is a rocky, turbulent Class IV. Easier Class III rapids follow to the covered bridge on Dugway Road (½ mile). Another 1½ miles of shallow Class III rapids follow; this section can be very scratchy in medium water.

The next major rapids are at the Gorge (2 miles), where the river drops very steeply and the road is high on the right bank. To recognize the Gorge, look for three cottages on the left bank and pull out above the next left turn to scout (best done from the road on the right). The sharp left turn and right turn dump paddlers into a short pool right above the Gorge. There are various routes through the Gorge at different water levels, and paddlers unfamiliar with the Swift should pick one from the shore, since huge rocks in the Gorge make channel choosing difficult.

Rapids continue below the Gorge, with a Class IV drop ¼ mile farther along. More Class III–IV rapids continue to a left turn just above the Staircase (2¾ miles), where the boater should pull out and scout on the left. The Staircase is a short, steep, 50-yard drop over large boulders. It is Class IV at medium levels and Class V in high water. For those who do not wish to run these rapids, it is possible to carry or line down to the left of a rock island on the left.

Below the Staircase (2¾ miles) difficult rapids continue for another ½ mile to the site of an annual slalom race (for details, contact Saco Bound, Box 113, Center Conway, NH 03813). The race course is set up in a Class IV section where the Swift drops, around many large boulders. More rapids follow, with Class IV and slightly easier rapids very close together. The last of the difficult rapids is at a spot where the Swift approaches the road, splits around a rock the size of a small house, and drops 2 feet into a hole (5½ miles). This last hole is formed by a V-shaped ledge whose apex extends upstream. This is the largest, widest hydraulic on the river, and it can hold a boat even at medium water.

The last ½ mile to the Darby Field Inn sign is a Class III with shallow rapids. The sign is painted differently every year; boaters can also recognize the spot by the river's sharp turn away from the road and a side road leaving the Kancamagus Highway. Take out on the right.

## Darby Field–Conway                                        2¾ mi

| | |
|---|---|
| Description: | Quickwater, Class II–III |
| Date checked: | 1988, BL |
| Navigable: | High to medium water (mid-April into May) |
| Scenery: | Forested |
| Map: | USGS Ossipee Lake 15 |

This section of the Swift River is away from roads for much of the run. There is more hazard from fallen trees here than in the more difficult rapids above.

From a put-in near the Darby Field sign, there are continuous rapids for about ¾ mile. These rapids are scratchy Class III, with many sharp turns required. The rapids moderate to Class II and later to snaky quickwater. The river continues its twisting until a bridge on West Side Road and a covered bridge, at which point there is another Class II–III rapid (2½ miles). The Swift River enters the Saco River at a covered bridge over the latter in Conway, where there is another rapid.

Take out at the NH bridge just below the covered bridge over the Saco (2¾ miles). Cars can reach the river by following a dirt road behind the shopping center.

## OSSIPEE RIVER                                        NH, ME

The Ossipee River flows east for 17½ miles from Lake Ossipee across the Maine border and into the Saco River near Cornish. It has a dependable flow in the spring, but by summer the water is too low to run the lower section.

## Ossipee Lake–Kezar Falls 10¾ mi

| | |
|---|---|
| Description: | **Quickwater,** Class I–II |
| Date checked: | 1988, WH |
| Navigable: | High and medium water (spring) |
| | Low water, passable, some lining required at rapids |
| Scenery: | Forested, rural, towns |
| Maps: | USGS Ossipee Lake 15, Kezar Falls |
| Portages: | 10½ mi **first dam at Kezar Falls** across island |
| | 10¾ mi   R   **second dam at Kezar Falls** 30 yd |

Quickwater characterizes this section, although there is one very nice rapid just above the NH 153 bridge in Effingham Falls. There are several more short rapids before Kezar Falls, but for most of the distance the river is smooth. Anyone seeking a paddle in remote surroundings will not find it here: vacation cottages line the banks near the beginning, and below East Freedom there are more cottages and houses, with a main highway close by on the left bank for much of the distance.

The dam at the outlet of Ossipee Lake is at the end of a side road ½ mile west of the junction of NH 25 and 153 in Effingham Falls. Put in below the gatehouse and run down the sluiceway to a pool of slackwater. A section of Class II–III rapids follows for another ¼ mile; these are the most difficult rapids of this river. They lead up to the NH 153 bridge (½ mile).

Then there are 1½ miles of quickwater past the NH 25 bridge (2 miles) to East Freedom, where ¼ mile of Class II rapids leads under a bridge (4½ miles) to the Maine border. The remaining distance to Kezar Falls is mostly quickwater, with two short Class II rapids, one before and one after the ME 160 bridge in Porter (7¾ miles).

In Kezar Falls, go to the right of the island and take out at a small bridge (10½ miles). If you are continuing downstream, carry across the island to the foot of the main dam and continue

¼ mile through the town to the second dam (10¾ miles). Take out on the right, carry across the canal, and put in below the dam.

## Kezar Falls–Saco River                                            6¾ mi

| | |
|---|---|
| Description: | Quickwater, Class I–II |
| Date checked: | 1988, WH |
| Navigable: | High water, recommended (early spring) |
| | Medium water (late spring) |
| Scenery: | Forested, rural |
| Maps: | USGS Kezar Falls, Cornish |

Below the second flood dam in Kezar Falls, the Ossipee River takes on a different character. It is a very scenic run past forests and farms almost all the way to the Saco River, with quickwater or rapids for the entire distance.

When the water level is up, the run from Kezar Falls to the ME 5 and 117 bridge over the Saco can be made in a little over an hour, but if you continue down the Saco for another 14 miles to the ME 25 bridge, you can make a long, scenic trip of mixed flatwater and rapids. Note, however, that Limington Rips, which begin just above the bridge, are very severe rapids in high water.

A small sign is now posted on the right bank just above the Central Maine Power dam. It informs the paddler of the portage path, which is a wide and easy ¼ mile long. One can put in just below the dam to take advantage of the Class II rips or continue below to the powerhouse. To reach the dam by car, travel ½ mile east of the ME 25 bridge in Kezar Falls, turn north onto Garner Avenue and take the first right. Bear left at an old building to reach the dam, or turn right to reach the power station.

Below the dam there are nice Class I and II rapids for 1 mile to Which Way Rapids, where the river abruptly divides around an island. Quickwater and Class I rapids continue to the first bridge (3½ miles), with more quickwater to the second (5½ miles). Below the second bridge and past a few cottages there are some easy Class II rapids that lead almost to the Saco River (6¾ miles), only ½ mile above the ME 5 and 117 bridge east of Cornish.

## SILVER RIVER                                              NH

The Silver River, also called the West Branch on some maps, flows from Silver Lake in Madison to the north end of Ossipee Lake. It provides a secluded two- to three-hour run in high water. It has a good flow in the spring and also in the fall, when the level of Silver Lake is drawn down. Note, however, that this lake is not controlled by the Water Resources Board.

The first 2½ miles to Ossipee Lake Road are the most pleasant because the current is faster and the banks of the river are more open. The lower portion is entirely wooded, and there are a few trees blocking the stream.

### Silver Lake–Ossipee Lake                              6 mi

| | |
|---|---|
| Description: | Flatwater, **quickwater** |
| Date checked: | 1983 |
| Navigable: | High water, recommended (spring and mid-fall) |
| | Medium water, some wading required (late spring and early summer) |
| | Dam controlled (annual fall drawdown of Silver Lake) |
| Scenery: | Forested |
| Map: | USGS Ossipee Lake 15 |

The dam on Silver Lake is next to Silver Lake Road, which leaves NH 41 on the right just over 2 miles north of West Ossipee. A marina at Westward Shores on Ossipee Lake (west of the mouth of the river) can be reached by turning east off

NH 16 onto Nichols Road, which is 2 miles south of West Ossipee.

The quickwater at the beginning slackens somewhat as the stream enters a broad, open valley. Soon you reach the first of a score of beaver dams that dot the entire length of the river. Many of them can be run in high water. The banks become wooded again as you pass a sawmill on the right shortly before the Ossipee Lake Road bridge (2½ miles). In the remaining 3½ miles the river winds more, and there are a few obstructions.

## BEARCAMP RIVER                                    NH

The Bearcamp River flows eastward into Ossipee Lake, draining a large portion of the valley between the Sandwich and Ossipee ranges. Since much of the drainage area is mountainous, the runoff from rain and melting snow takes place quickly. The upper section is an easy paddle through meadowland, the middle section provides some fine whitewater in the early spring, and the last 9 miles are usually passable whenever the river is free of ice.

The countryside is relatively unsettled, and there are occasional views of the Sandwich Range to the north and the Ossipee Mountains to the south.

### Bearcamp Pond–Bennett Corners                    2¾ mi

| | |
|---|---|
| Description: | Quickwater |
| Date checked: | 1988, WH |
| Navigable: | High water (April) |
| Scenery: | Forested, rural |
| Map: | USGS Mount Chocorua 15 |

This is the most scenic portion of the river. For much of the distance the river flows through meadows. Watch out for fallen trees.

Bearcamp Pond Road leaves NH 25 on the north side ½ mile east of the NH 25 and 113 junction at Bennett Corners. In less than a mile it crosses the river just below the pond.

The Bearcamp winds through meadows for 1¾ miles to the Cold River, which enters on the left and approximately doubles the flow. After another mile of meandering between tree-linked banks, you reach the NH 113 bridge at Bennett Corners (2¾ miles).

## Bennett Corners–Whittier                                    3¾ mi

| | |
|---|---|
| Description: | Quickwater, Class **II, III, IV** |
| Date checked: | 1988, WH |
| Navigable: | High water (April) |
| Scenery: | Rural, towns |
| Map: | USGS Mount Chocorua 15 |
| Portage: | 1¾ mi   L   **old dam at South Tamworth** 20 yd |

This popular whitewater section is good training ground for intermediate paddlers if the water is not too high. Most of the hard rapids are visible from the road, so you can judge the difficulty before you begin. An aggressive party that scouts the bad drops during the car shuttle can make the run in an hour; a large and poorly organized group can easily take all day.

Below the NH 113 bridge at Bennett Corners, there is ½ mile of smoothwater with a slow current that ends up at a rocky rapid 100 yards long and rated Class II–III. A wood road on the left bank can be used as a portage if necessary. Soon there are two shorter, easier Class II rapids, followed by more smoothwater to South Tamworth. The road comes near the river (1 mile), and anyone who has had difficulty with the run up to this point should consider taking out.

A long rapid begins behind the post office, and ends below the next bridge (1½ miles) with a difficult Class III–IV ledge. One popular route involves hugging the right bank above the bridge, then moving quickly left underneath, either running the ledge on the left or stopping in the eddy just past the bridge. There is a wooded road on the left bank for portage.

**Caution!** Just around the next corner to the right is Bearcamp Gorge, a narrow Class III–IV chute that consists of 30 yards of turbulence between low ledges. It should be scouted. A large pool below the ledges vanished when the remainder of the dam upstream washed out. There is now a 4–5-foot drop at the end of the gorge, with a huge rock on the left at the bottom. An alternate watercourse has been created to the left of the gorge. The pool is greatly diminished.

The dam at South Tamworth can be inspected by walking upstream from a log yard off NH 25. It consists of a number of concrete piers supporting old timbers, a definite hazard to boaters. Portage to the left. Below the dam, the rapids are continuous; the next difficult pitch is a series of ledges just above a former bridge (2½ miles). There are more easy rapids, followed by a sharp Class III rapid containing a moderate hydraulic. Easy rapids continue past the NH 113 bridge in Whittier (3¾ miles). In another ½ mile, just past a cemetery, there is a good place to take out. To find the take-out, look for a burned-out house on the left of old NH 25, about ¾ mile below the Whittier Cash Market, where you can also park vehicles.

### Whittier–Ossipee Lake                                    10½ mi

| | |
|---|---|
| Description: | **Flatwater,** quickwater, Class I |
| Date checked: | 1988, WH |
| Navigable: | Passable at most levels |
| Scenery: | Forested, rural, settled |
| Maps: | USGS Mount Chocorua 15, Ossipee Lake 15 |

Except at the beginning, this section is passable for most of the paddling season. The bottom is sandy for many miles as the Bearcamp winds through woods and farmland.

There are many cottages and a large campground along the river in the 3 miles from NH 25 to NH 16, but the rest is isolated and very attractive.

Below the NH 113 bridge in Whittier, Class II rapids continue for ½ mile, after which there is about 1 mile of occasional riffles that are shallow in low water. To avoid these, start 1½ miles east of Whittier on NH 25 where the road comes close to the river. After that there are only a few shallow sections, all short. Pass under a covered bridge (4¼ miles), NH 25 (5¼ miles), and NH 16 (8¼ miles). Under the latter, on the right, there is a convenient take-out point.

## PINE RIVER                                        NH

The Pine River is a small stream of moderate length that flows into Ossipee Lake from the south. Although it is crossed by two highways and three side roads, only short portions of them follow its secluded banks. For most of its length it flows in narrow valleys, alder swamps, or wide meadows. Few streams in New Hampshire offer the river traveler such clean water and unspoiled scenery.

The river is narrow and occasionally choked with alders. When it flows through woodland, it can be easily blocked by fallen trees. For years there were many such obstacles, which made passage down the river difficult and frustrating. However, in the fall of 1986 all the obstructions, except those at low water level, were removed with a chain saw. You should nonetheless allow more time to run this river than your experience on others might indicate that you need.

Because of the gentle gradient and gravel bottom, parts of the Pine River provide year-round canoeing, and even the steepest sections are passable in medium water. Each fall the Water Resources Board (603-271-1110) draws down the level of Pine River Pond, and usually beginning in mid-October there is enough water in the whole river for one and a half weeks or more.

## Pine River Pond–Granite Road                                    5 mi

| | |
|---|---|
| Description: | **Quickwater,** Class II |
| Date checked: | 1983 |
| Navigable: | High water (April) |
| | Medium water, recommended (May and midfall) |
| | Dam controlled (annual fall drawdown) |
| Scenery: | Forested |
| Map: | USGS Wolfeboro 15 |

The Pine River begins as a small stream confined between two low, glacial ridges. In this section particularly, there are many places where alders choke the stream, and in other sections low limbs and overhanging trees are hazardous in the fast-moving current of high water. In less than medium water levels, some walking may be required.

If the stream looks passable in the first few yards, there is sufficient water for the entire trip to Ossipee Lake. In the fall, when the level of Pine River Pond is being drawn down, the effect will be less noticeable below Granite Road.

In Wakefield a road east from NH 16 near the Ossipee/Wakefield town line leads in about 1 mile to the Pine River just below the pond. For about 1 mile it flows through woods before it enters an alder swamp, where there are several beaver dams. Then the current picks up again and soon flows past a gravel pit, where there is a bridge. Just after a pumping station a short portage may be necessary where the river passes under a road in three culverts. NH 16 (3 miles) is a short distance beyond, near a railroad crossing and the entrance to the gravel pit.

This section between the two NH 16 bridges begins with some quickwater through some woods. Then the current slackens where the river is backed up by beaver dams in an alder swamp, but it picks up in the woods beyond.

From the second NH 16 bridge there is good current as the river flows through another alder swamp and over some beaver dams. It flows through attractive woods for a short distance above the Granite Road bridge (5 miles).

## Granite Road–Ossipee Lake                    15 mi

| | |
|---|---|
| Description: | **Flatwater,** quickwater |
| Date checked: | 1983 |
| Navigable: | High and medium water (April, May, and midfall) |
| | Passable at most water levels, below Elm Street |
| | Dam controlled (annual fall drawdown of Pine River Pond) |
| Scenery: | Wild, forested |
| Maps: | USGS Wolfeboro 15, Ossipee Lake 15 |

Halfway between Granite Road and Elm Street there is a 2-mile section of quickwater where the river flows through a very attractive wooded valley. Large pines and hemlocks grow along the banks between ridges that rise steeply from the flat bottomlands.

Below the Elm Street bridge the river is flat as it wanders through a wide valley of conifers and swamp maples. Occasionally there are places where people have camped in the past. From the mouth of the river at the south end of Ossipee Lake, there is a nice view of the Sandwich Range and the Moats.

Granite Road leads from NH 16 at a crossroads about 1½ miles south of the junction of NH 16 and 28 in Ossipee. In the first 3 miles the river wanders through an alder swamp, where the flatwater is interrupted by an occasional beaver dam. Then there are 2 miles of quickwater, after which the river meanders through an open meadow where there are views of Green Mountain to the northeast.

The river enters the woods again about ½ mile above the Elm Street bridge (8 miles). For the rest of the way the current is weaker. The river passes under NH 25 (14 miles), and a mile beyond that it empties into the lake (15 miles).

A road from NH 25 a short distance east of NH 16 leads past the Pine River and along the southwest shore of Ossipee Lake.

# Chapter 8

# Androscoggin Watershed

*Grey area not covered in this book.*

# ANDROSCOGGIN WATERSHED

# ANDROSCOGGIN RIVER                              NH, ME

All of the big lakes in the upper drainage area of the Androscoggin River—Rangely, Mooselookmeguntic, Richardson, Umbagog, and Aziscohos—have been made even bigger artificially by dams, so the volume of ponded water makes high water in the Androscoggin rapids very dependable in the summer. The attractive valley and clean water also contribute to the river's popularity. The James River Corporation provides a number of campsites for a fee. The sites on Umbagog Lake and the upper river are administered from the Brown Owl, 4 miles north of Errol on NH 16.

## Umbagog Lake–Errol                             3¾ mi

| | |
|---|---|
| Description: | Flatwater |
| Date checked: | 1983 |
| Navigable: | Spring, summer, fall |
| Scenery: | Forested |
| Map: | USGS Errol 15 |
| Portage: | 3¾ mi   L   **dam in Errol** |

The Androscoggin River is formed at the confluence of the Magalloway River and the outlet from Umbagog Lake. This point is now lost in the marshes and backwater from the dam in Errol. It can be reached from Umbagog Lake from approaches to the south, or by paddling 3 miles downstream on the Magalloway River from NH 16.

Below Umbagog Lake the river is wide, with extensive marshes on either side and a very slow current. In 3 miles it reaches NH 16, where there is a launching ramp, and in another ¾ mile it comes to Errol Dam, where there is another launching ramp on the left.

## Errol Rapids                                   ¾ mi

The short Class III rapid below the dam is best reached by parking on NH 16 at the pool just below and portaging up to it. Below the pool there is ¼ mile of Class II rapids past the

bridge in Errol. A large, slow-moving pool provides an opportunity for rescue at the mouth of Clear Stream. This is a popular
spot, and many people spend the day running and rerunning the
rapids. The lower part is an excellent spot to practice swimming
in rapids, which is something whitewater boaters should become
accustomed to under favorable conditions.

## Errol–Mollidgewock Campground                        3¼ mi

| | |
|---|---|
| Description: | Class I–II |
| Date checked: | 1987, ST |
| Navigable: | Spring, summer, fall |
| Scenery: | Forested |
| Map: | USGS Errol 15 |

To avoid the rapids, put in at the take-out for the rapids, using
the parking area at the NH 16 bridge. Or put in from the bridge
over Clear Stream.

The left side is wild, while the right side is paralleled by the
highway. The current is moderate and pleasant.

## Mollidgewock Campground–Seven Islands bridge      4¾ mi

| | |
|---|---|
| Description: | Class I–II |
| Date checked: | 1987, ST |
| Navigable: | Spring, summer, fall |
| Scenery: | Forested |
| Map: | USGS Milan 15 |

Mollidgewock Campground is administered by the James River
Corporation and is located on an old section of NH 16 along the
river that was cut off when the road was straigthened. Besides
being a lovely camping spot, it provides access to the river at
the start of the rapids.

The rapids are runnable in the summer, when the air and water
are warm, and are excellent for beginners, offering good-sized

waves with very few rocks underneath them. The rapids are continuous at first, then gradually interrupted with quickwater sections. Since the river is parallel to the road, access is possible at many points.

At the Seven Islands bridge there is a small drop to the left, the last one on this part of the river. A fast current running under the bridge offers a good place to practice eddies and ferries.

## Seven Islands bridge–Pontook Dam                                    9 mi

| | |
|---|---|
| Description: | Flatwater, quickwater |
| Date checked: | 1987, ST |
| Navigable: | Spring, summer, fall |
| Scenery: | Forested |
| Map: | USGS Milan 15 |
| Portage: | (9 mi   R   **Pontook Dam** 50 yd) |

The scenery is still beautiful, especially in spring when flora is abundant. At 3½ miles, the river passes the mouth of Bog Brook, which is a very rewarding side trip of approximately 1 mile. Many islands dot the river, providing a variety of passages. The river gradually slows to the ponding from Pontook dam. Take out at the road on the right bank.

## Pontook Dam–Berlin                                    12¾ mi

| | |
|---|---|
| Description: | Quickwater, Class II |
| Date checked: | 1987, ST |
| Navigable: | Controlled release; check at dam for schedule |
| Scenery: | Forested, town |
| Maps: | USGS Milan 15, Berlin |
| Portage: | (12¾ mi   L   **Berlin dams**) |

The 2¼ miles below Pontook Dam are the famous Pontook Rapids, and they are fairly continuous Class II. Put in at the dam, where there is a large parking area, rest rooms, and release information. The flow is entirely controlled by the dam, but the releases are posted well in advance.

There is a take-out on the right past where the road is near the river. Scout in advance so you'll recognize it from the river. Rapids then ease to quickwater. The next public access is on the left bank at the Dummer/Milan town line (3½ miles), and the next bridge is in Milan (6 miles). In Berlin, take out at the playground located on the left below the first bridge.

## Berlin–Shelburne Dam                                    11½ mi

A portage by car is recommended. The river valley is very attractive, with views of the Presidential Range to the southwest and lower mountains to the east, and much of the distance is quickwater and Class I rapids. However, the way is blocked by seven dams and marred by considerable pollution.

## Shelburne Dam–Gilead, ME                                8¼ mi

| | |
|---|---|
| Description: | Quickwater, Class I |
| Date checked: | 1987, ST |
| Navigable: | Spring, summer, fall |
| Scenery: | Forested |
| Map: | USGS Shelburne |

Put in at the bridge in Shelburne where the Appalachian Trail crosses. The view upstream, with the old log cribs and mountains, is outstanding. Pollution is still evident, but the river is delightful, with fast current and easy rapids dividing around islands. Mountain and bird watching are rewarding.

The next bridge is passed at 2¾ miles, and the Maine state line is reached at 6 miles. You can take out at the bridge in Gilead, Maine.

The following 31 miles to Rumford, Maine, are also pleasant. There are no dams and slightly fewer riffles, although there is still an occasional rapid.

# MAGALLOWAY RIVER                                     ME, NH

The Magalloway River rises in the most northwestern part of
Maine and flows south to join the Androscoggin River on the
west shore of Umbagog Lake.

## Aziscohos power plant–Wilson's Mills                    2½ mi

| | |
|---|---|
| Description: | Class III–IV |
| Date checked: | 1988, LT |
| Navigable: | Spring, summer, fall |
| | Dam controlled |
| Scenery: | Forested |
| Map: | USGS Oquossoc 15, Errol 15 |

A quarter mile below Aziscohos Dam, a side road from ME
16 reaches the river at the Aziscohos hydroelectric plant. A
trail from the plant leads 75 yards downstream to the put-in
just below an unrunnable 10-foot drop. The next 2½ miles to
Wilson's Mills is technical Class III–IV and is runnable at levels greater than 300 cubic feet per second. A scouting trail
runs the entire length of the rapids on the right. Take out on the right
just below the ME 16 bridge in Wilson's Mills. Flow through
this hydro plant and all other dams in the Androscoggin Watershed is controlled by the Androscoggin Reservoir Company in
Lewiston, Maine.

## Wilson's Mills–Lake Umbagog                             16¼ mi

| | |
|---|---|
| Description: | Flatwater |
| Date checked: | 1988, LT |
| Navigable: | Spring, summer, fall |
| | Dam controlled |
| Scenery: | Forested, rural |
| Map: | USGS Errol 15 |

Put in for the flatwater trip at a gravel parking area on the
right just below the ME 16 bridge in Wilson's Mills. Below the

put-in the river meanders for 2 miles; then it passes the Aziscohos Valley Camping Area and flows under a covered bridge. For the next 4¼ miles the river follows the road, meanders, and then meets the Diamond River. Three-quarters of a mile farther is a take-out on the left just below another ME 16 bridge. Below this point the Magalloway continues 9¼ miles to Umbagog Lake, where it joins the Androscoggin River. This section of the river has heavy powerboat traffic.

## DIAMOND RIVER                                                    NH

The Diamond River is formed by the union of the Swift and Dead Diamond rivers, and it flows through an impressive gorge into the Magalloway River. Dartmouth College owns most of the lower watershed of the Diamond and its branches. A good gravel road leaves NH 16 just east of Wentworth Location and passes through the gorge, with branch roads up the Swift and Dead Diamond rivers. The gate below the gorge is closed from May 1 to December 1, and it is usually impassable because of snow or mud at other times. Vehicle permits are issued only to members of the Dartmouth community, although foot and bicycle traffic is allowed. Further information can be obtained from the Director of Outdoor Affairs, Dartmouth College, Hanover, NH 03755.

### Confluence–Magalloway River                                    2 mi

| | |
|---|---|
| Description: | Class III–V |
| Date checked: | 1983 |
| Navigable: | High water |
| Scenery: | Forested, rural |
| Map: | USGS Errol 15 |

Take out on the left 100 yards below the confluence at Peaks Camp and carry ½–1 mile down the road to a suitable put-in. The first ¼ mile is no worse than Class III, but the next ¼ mile contains some drops that, if they are runnable, are Class

V, and they are nearly impossible to carry or line because of the cliffs on both banks.

After ½ mile along the road, the rapids diminish, and you can put in again whenever you decide that the road is close enough to the river. There is a good take-out just below the bridge (1 mile) adjacent to the road gate. After another mile of easier river, you reach the Magalloway River (2 miles).

## SWIFT DIAMOND RIVER                                        NH

This small stream rises in the Diamond ponds in Stewartstown and flows east to join the Dead Diamond. It is famous for fishing, but it is passable by canoe only for about two weeks during spring runoff, which is in early May, when access is likely to be poor. The upper end can be reached by a River Corporation road that follows Corser Brook north from NH 26 about 4 miles west of Errol. The lower end can be reached by a branch road from the Dartmouth road along Diamond River. Both roads are likely to be closed or unusable during mud season.

### Swift Diamond Farm–Diamond River                    9½ mi

| | |
|---|---|
| Description: | Class II–III |
| Date checked: | 1983 |
| Navigable: | High water only (May) |
| Scenery: | Wild |
| Map: | USGS Errol 15 |

Put in at a suitable point where the road approaches the river near Swift Diamond Farm. Pass under the access road in 1 mile. The run is mainly Class II, with a few harder spots that may be unrunnable depending on the water level. At the remains of Dixie Dam (2½ miles), line the dam and scout the two short drops below. Ellingwood Falls (6½ miles) consists of three narrow flumes that are difficult but runnable. There are 2 more miles of easy rapids, then 1 mile of difficult rapids, including a drop that is probably unrunnable, to the junction with the Dead

Diamond River (9½ miles). Take out 100 yards below on the left at Peaks Camp.

## DEAD DIAMOND RIVER                                    NH

This stream flows south from the most remote part of New Hampshire, the southeast corner of Pittsburg. The runnable portion lies almost entirely in the area known as the Second College Grant. The river is paralleled by a private Dartmouth College road that is not open to the public, so canoeing is infrequent, and then it is usually done in conjunction with fishing.

### Hell Gate–Diamond River                              12 mi

| | |
|---|---|
| Description: | Flatwater, quickwater, Class I |
| Date checked: | 1983 |
| Navigable: | High water (May) |
| Scenery: | Forested |
| Map: | USGS Errol 15 |

The usual put-in is at Hell Gate Camps, although the river above is runnable. The river meanders, with moderate current; the only difficult spot is at Half Mile Falls (5 miles). The current starts to pick up just below the bridge at the Management Center (11¾ miles). Take out at Peaks Camp, 100 yards below the junction with the Swift Diamond River (12 miles).

## UMBAGOG LAKE                                    NH, ME

Umbagog Lake is the largest "wild" lake in New Hampshire. Settlement is largely concentrated at the south end, where there is access from NH 26. The north end can be approached from the Magalloway or Androscoggin rivers, which come in from the west side. The northwest side is low and swampy. Campsites are managed by the Umbagog Lake Campground (Errol, NH; 603-482-7795). Reserve sites and pay a fee at the base camp located where NH 16 skirts the southern tip of the lake. The fee covers parking and a fire permit. See the USGS Errol 15, Milan 15, and Oquossoc 15 maps.

The lake offers clean warm water, fine scenery, excellent camp-sites, and wildlife, including loons, moose, and a pair of nesting eagles in its northern basin. Winds are mostly from the northwest and can easily kick up waves of 3 feet or more. An interesting side trip includes a paddle into Cedar Stump at the base of the Rapid River. Leave canoes at Cedar Stump and walk the well-worn trail along the Rapid. The trail is muddy and crosses over masses of tree roots before turning left and going uphill to meet a jeep trail running along the river. The Rapid is a spectacular Class IV river with a setting appealing enough to attract boat-ers from all over the country. A popular picnic spot is Smooth Ledge, about 1½ miles upstream from Cedar Stump. A large wooden sign is posted on a tree just to the right of the jeep trail. At the sign for Smooth Ledge, turn into the forest from the river and follow the trail for about 70 yards to the water. There is an osprey nest a little upstream of Smooth Ledge, and you might well see deer, moose, or bear visiting the river.

## CLEAR STREAM                                             NH

This mountain stream drains the eastern side of Dixville Notch. It is barely a canoe length wide throughout. Though seldom visible, NH 26 is nearby.

### Off NH Rte. 26–Androscoggin River               6½ mi

| | |
|---|---|
| Description: | Quickwater, Class I |
| Date checked: | 1983 |
| Navigable: | High water (early May) |
| Scenery: | Forested, rural |
| Map: | USGS Errol 15 |

Put in from a side road to a farm on the right off NH 26 about 5½ miles west of Errol. Above this point are more difficult rap-ids that require high water to run. Below here, the rapids are Class I, with perhaps one or two Class II rapids. In 1¼ miles

miles the river reaches the NH 26 bridge. Halfway to Errol the river begins to meander and the rapids spread out, although the current continues. Several small fallen trees partly or entirely block the channel. It is possible to take out at the NH 26 bridge in Errol (6¼ miles), but it is probably more convenient to paddle ¼ mile, mostly deadwater, to the Androscoggin River and then continue 200 yards upstream to the take-out below the rapids just downstream of the NH 26 bridge.

## MOLLIDGEWOCK BROOK                              NH, ME

Mollidgewock Brook flows from Mollidgewock Pond in Upton, Maine, northwest to the Androscoggin River opposite the campground of the same name. The canoeable portion is a small stream obstructed with alders and beaver dams. It can be ascended, possibly for 3 miles, from the Androscoggin; the distance varies directly with the paddler's desire to continue. It may be possible to reach the river at various points from a private road on the east side of the Androscoggin River.

This is also a good after-supper trip for people staying at the campground. See USGS Milan 15.

## BOG BROOK                                              NH

Bog Brook is a small stream that flows west from the north slope of Cambridge Black Mountain to the Androscoggin River near the Cambridge/Dummer town line. It is similar to but smaller than Mollidgewock Brook and can be ascended about 1½ miles from the Androscoggin. Nature loves who wish to canoe only Bog Brook will find the mouth within sight of a pull-off on NH 16. See USGS Milan 15.

# APPENDIX

## Safety Code of the American Whitewater Affiliation

*The following code, adopted in 1959 and revised in 1987, is reprinted with the permission of the American Whitewater Affiliation, 146 N. Brockton, Palatine, IL 60067.*

### I. PERSONAL PREPAREDNESS AND RESPONSIBILITY

1. **Be a competent swimmer,** with the ability to handle yourself underwater.

2. **Wear a life jacket.** A snug fitting, vest-type life preserver offers back and shoulder protection as well as the flotation needed to swim safely in whitewater.

3. **Wear a solid, correctly fitting helmet** when upsets are likely. This is essential in kayaks or covered canoes, and recommended for open canoeists using thigh straps and rafters running steep drops.

4. **Do not boat out of control.** Your skills should be sufficient to stop or reach shore before reaching danger. Do not enter a rapid unless you are reasonably sure that you can run it safely or swim it without injury.

5. **Whitewater rivers contain many hazards which are not always easily recognized. The following are the most frequent killers:**

   A. **HIGH WATER.** The river's speed and power increase tremendously as the flow increases, raising the difficulty of most rapids. Rescue becomes progressively harder as the water rises, adding to the danger. Floating debris and strainers make even an easy rapid quite hazardous. It is often misleading to judge the river level at the put in, since a small rise in a wide, shallow place will be multiplied many times where the water narrows. Use reliable gauge information whenever possible, and be aware that sun on snowpack, hard rain, and upstream releases may greatly increase the flow.

**B. COLD.** Cold drains your strength, and robs you of the ability to make sound decisions on matters affecting your survival. Cold water immersion, because of the initial shock and the rapid heat loss which follows, is especially dangerous. Dress appropriately for bad weather or sudden immersion in the water. When the water temperature is less than 50 degrees F, a wetsuit or drysuit is essential for protection if you swim. Next best is wool or pile clothing under a waterproof shell. In this case, you should also carry waterproof matches and a change of clothing in a waterproof bag. If, after prolonged exposure, a person experiences uncontrollable shaking, loss of coordination, or difficulty speaking, he or she is hypothermic and needs your assistance.

**C. STRAINERS.** Brush, fallen trees, bridge pilings, undercut rocks or anything else which allows river currents to sweep through can pin boats and boaters against the obstacle. Water pressure on anything trapped this way can be overwhelming. Rescue is often extremely difficult. Pinning may occur in fast current, with little or no whitewater to warn of the danger.

**D. DAMS, WEIRS, LEDGES, REVERSALS, HOLES AND HYDRAULICS.** When water drops over an obstacle, it curls back on itself, forming a strong upstream current which may be capable of holding a boat or a swimmer. Some holes make for excellent sport; others are proven killers. Paddlers who cannot recognize the differences should avoid all but the smallest holes. Hydraulics around man-made dams must be treated with utmost respect regardless of their height or the level of the river. Despite their seemingly benign appearance, they can create an almost escape-proof trap. The swimmer's only exit from the "drowning machine" is to dive below the surface when the downstream current is flowing beneath the reversal.

**E. BROACHING.** When a boat is pushed against a rock by a strong current, it may collapse and wrap. This is especially dangerous to kayak and decked canoe paddlers; these boats will collapse and the combination of indestructible hulls and tight outfitting may create a deadly trap. Even without entrapment, releasing pinned boats can be extremely time-consuming and dangerous. To avoid pinning, throw your weight downstream towards the rock. This allows the current to slide harmlessly underneath the hull.

6. **Boating alone is discouraged.** The minimum party is three people or two craft.

7. **Have a frank knowledge of your boating ability,** and don't attempt rivers or rapids which lie beyond that ability.

   A. Develop the paddling skills and teamwork required to match the river you plan to boat. Most good paddlers develop skills gradually, and attempts to advance too quickly will compromise your safety and equipment.

   B. Be in good physical and mental condition, consistent with the difficulties which may be expected. Make adjustments for loss of skills due to age, health, fitness. Any health limitations must be explained to your fellow paddlers prior to starting the trip.

8. **Be practiced in self-rescue,** including escape from an overturned craft. The Eskimo roll is strongly recommended for decked boaters who run rapids of Class IV or greater, or who paddle in cold environmental conditions.

9. **Be trained in rescue skills,** CPR, and first aid with special emphasis on the recognizing and treating of hypothermia. It may save your friend's life.

10. **Carry equipment needed for unexpected emergencies,** including footwear which will protect your feet when walking out, a throw rope, knife, whistle and waterproof matches. If you wear eyeglasses, tie them on and carry a spare pair on long trips. Bring cloth repair tape on short runs, and a full repair kit on isolated rivers. Do not wear bulky jackets, ponchos, heavy boots, or anything else which could reduce your ability to survive a swim.

11. **Despite the mutually supportive group structure described in this code, individual paddlers are ultimately responsible for their own safety, and must assume sole responsibility for the following decisions:**

   **A.** The decision to participate on any trip. This includes an evaluation of the expected difficulty of the rapids under the conditions existing at the time of the put in.

   **B.** The selection of appropriate equipment, including a boat design suited to their skills and the appropriate rescue and survival gear.

   **C.** The decision to scout any rapid, and to run or portage according to their best judgement. Other members of the group may offer advice, but paddlers should resist pressure from anyone to paddle beyond their skills. It is also their responsibility to decide whether to pass up any walk-out or take-out opportunity.

   **D.** All trip participants should constantly evaluate their own and their group's safety, voicing their concerns and following what they believe to be the best course of action. Paddlers are encouraged to speak with anyone whose actions on the water are dangerous, whether they are part of your group or not.

## II. BOAT AND EQUIPMENT PREPAREDNESS

1. **Test new and different equipment** under familiar conditions before relying on it for difficult runs. This is especially true when adopting a new boat design or outfitting system. Low-volume craft may present additional hazards to inexperienced or poorly conditioned paddlers.

2. **Be sure your boat and gear** are in good repair before starting a trip. The more isolated and difficult the run, the more rigorous the inspection should be.

3. **Install flotation bags** in non-inflatable craft, securely fixed in each end, designed to displace as much water as possible. Inflatable boats should have multiple air chambers and be test inflated before launching.

4. **Have strong, properly sized paddles or oars** for controlling your craft. Carry sufficient spares for the length and difficulty of the trip.

5. **Outfit your boat safely.** The ability to exit your boat quickly is an essential component of safety in rapids. It is your responsibility to see that there is absolutely nothing to cause entrapment when coming free of an upset craft. This includes:

   A. Spray covers which won't release reliably or which release prematurely.

   B. Boat outfitting too tight to allow a fast exit, especially in low-volume kayaks or decked canoes. This includes low-hung thwarts in canoes lacking adequate clearance for your feet and kayak footbraces which fail or allow your feet to become wedged under them.

   C. Inadequately supported decks which collapse on a paddler's legs when a decked boat is pinned by water pressure. Inadequate clearance with the deck because of your feet or build.

   D. Loose ropes which cause entanglement. Beware of any length of loose line attached to a whitewater boat. All items must be tied tightly and excess line eliminated; painters, throw lines, and safety rope systems must be completely and effectively stored. Do not knot the end of a rope, as it can get caught in cracks between rocks.

6. **Provide ropes** which permit you to hold on to your craft so it may be rescued. The following methods are recommended.

   A. Kayaks and covered canoes should have grab loops of ¼″ + rope or equivalent webbing sized to admit a normal-sized hand. Stern painters are permissible if properly secured.

   B. Open canoes should have secured anchored bow and stern painters consisting of 8–10 feet of ¼″ + line. These must be secured in such a way that they are readily accessible, but cannot come loose accidentally. Grab loops are acceptable, but are more difficult to reach after an upset.

**C.** Rafts and dories may have taut perimeter lines threaded through the loops provided. Footholds should be designed so that a paddler's feet cannot be forced through them, causing entrapment. Flip lines should be carefully and reliably stowed.

**7. Know your craft's carrying capacity,** and how added loads affect boat handling in whitewater. Most rafts have a minimum crew size which can be added to on day trips or in easy rapids. Carrying more than two paddlers in an open canoe when running rapids is not recommended.

**8. Car top racks** must be strong and attach positively to the vehicle. Lash your boat to each crossbar, then tie the ends of the boats directly to the bumpers for added security. This arrangement should survive all but the most violent accident.


## III. GROUP PREPAREDNESS AND RESPONSIBILITY

**1. Organizations.** River trips should be regarded as common adventures by all participants, except on specially designated instructional or guided trips. The group is collectively responsible for the conduct of the trip, and participants are individually responsible for judging their own capabilities and for their own safety as the trip progresses.

**2. River Conditions.** The group should have a reasonable knowledge of the difficulty of the run. Participants should evaluate this information and adjust their plans accordingly. If the run is exploratory or no one is familiar with the river, maps and guidebooks, if available, should be examined. The group should secure accurate flow information; the more difficult the run, the more important this will be. Be aware of possible changes in river level and how this will affect the difficulty of the run. If the trip involves tidal stretches, secure appropriate information on tides.

**3. Group equipment should be suited to the difficulty of the river.** The group should always have a throw line available, and one line per boat is recommended on difficult runs. The list may include: carabiners, prussick loops, first aid kit, flashlight, folding saw, fire starter, guidebooks, maps, food, extra clothing, and any other rescue or survival items suggested by conditions. Each item is not required on every run, and this list is not meant to be a substitute for good judgement.

4. **Keep the group compact,** but maintain sufficient spacing to avoid collisions. If the group is large, consider dividing into smaller groups or using the buddy system as an additional safeguard. Space yourselves closely enough to permit good communication, but not so close as to interfere with one another in rapids.

   A. **The lead paddler** sets the pace. When in front, do not get in over your head. Never run drops when you cannot see a clear route to the bottom or, for advanced paddlers, a sure route to the next eddy. When in doubt, stop and scout.

   B. **Keep track** of all group members. Each boat keeps the one behind it in sight, stopping if necessary. Know how many people are in your group and take head counts regularly. No one should paddle ahead or walk out without first informing the group. Weak paddlers should stay at the center of a group, and not allow themselves to lag behind. If the group is large and contains a wide range of abilities, a designated "sweep boat" should bring up the rear.

   C. **Courtesy.** On heavily used rivers, do not cut in front of a boater running a drop. Always look upstream before leaving eddies to run or play. Never enter a crowded drop or eddy when no room for you exists. Passing other groups in a rapid may be hazardous: it's often safer to wait upstream until the group ahead has passed.

5. **Float Plan.** If the trip is into a wilderness area or for an extended period of time, plans should be filed with a responsible person who will contact the authorities if you are overdue. It may be wise to establish checkpoints along the way where civilization could be contacted if necessary. Knowing the location of possible help and preplanning escape routes can speed rescue.

6. **Drugs.** The use of alcohol or mind-altering drugs before or during river trips is not recommended. It dulls reflexes, reduces de-

cision making ability, and may interfere with important survival reflexes.

7. **Instruction or guided trips.** In this format, a person assumes the responsibilities of a trip leader. He or she may pass judgement on a participant's qualifications, check equipment, and assume responsibilities for the conduct of the trip normally taken by the group as a whole.

   **A.** These trips must be clearly designated as such in advance, as they could expose the leader to legal liability. Trip or personal liability insurance should be considered.

   **B.** Even on trips with a designated leader, participants must recognize that whitewater rivers have inherent hazards, that each person is still responsible for their decision to participate and their safety on the water.

## IV. GUIDELINES FOR RIVER RESCUE

1. **Recover from an upset with an Eskimo roll** whenever possible. Evacuate your boat immediately if there is imminent danger of being trapped against rocks, brush, or any other kind of strainer.

2. **If you swim, hold on to your boat.** It has much flotation and is easy for rescuers to spot. Get to the upstream end so that you cannot be crushed between a rock and your boat by the force of the current. Persons with good balance may be able to climb on top of a swamped boat or flipped kayak and paddle to shore.

3. **Release your craft if this will improve your chances,** especially if the water is cold or dangerous rapids lie ahead. Actively attempt self-rescue whenever possible by swimming for safety. Be prepared to assist others who may come to your aid.

   **A. When swimming in shallow or obstructed rapids,** lie on your back **with feet held high** and pointed downstream. Do not attempt to stand in fast-moving water; if your foot wedges on the bottom, fast water will push you under and keep you there. Get to slow or very shallow water before attempting to stand or walk. Look ahead! Avoid possible pinning situations including undercut rocks, strainers, downed trees, holes, and other dangers by swimming away from them.

**B. If the rapids are deep and powerful,** roll over onto your stomach and swim aggressively for shore. Watch for eddies and slackwater and use them to get out of the current. Strong swimmers can effect a powerful upstream ferry and get to shore fast. If the shores are obstructed with strainers or undercut rocks, however, it is safer to "ride the rapid out" until a safer escape can be found.

4. **If others spill and swim, go after the boaters first.** Rescue boats and equipment only if this can be done safely. While participants usually assist one another to the best of their ability, they should do so only if they can, in their judgement, do so safely. The first duty of a rescuer is not to compound the problem by becoming another victim.

5. **The use of rescue lines requires training:** uninformed use may cause injury. Never tie yourself into either end of a line without a reliable quick-release system. Have a knife ready to deal with unexpected entanglement. Learn to place set lines effectively, to throw accurately, to belay effectively, and to properly handle a rope thrown to you.

6. **When reviving a drowning victim,** be aware that cold water may greatly extend survival time underwater. Victims of hypothermia may have depressed vital signs so they look and feel dead. Don't give up; continue CPR for as long as possible without compromising safety.

## V. UNIVERSAL RIVER SIGNALS

**STOP:** Potential hazard ahead. Wait for "all clear" signal before proceeding, or scout ahead. Form a horizontal bar with your outstretched arms. Those seeing the signal should pass it back to others in the party.

**HELP/EMERGENCY:** Assist the signaller as quickly as possible. Give three long blasts on a police whistle while waving a paddle, helmet or life vest over your head. If a whistle is not available, use the visual signal alone. A whistle is best carried on a lanyard attached to your life vest.

**ALL CLEAR:** Come ahead (in the absence of other directions proceed down the center). Form a vertical bar with your paddle or on one arm held high above your head. Paddle blade should be turned flat for maximum visibility. To signal direction or a preferred course through a rapid around obstruction, lower the previously vertical "all clear" by 45 degrees toward the side of the river with the preferred route. Never point toward the obstacle you wish to avoid.

## VI. INTERNATIONAL SCALE OF DIFFICULTY

This is the American version of a rating system used to compare river difficulty throughout the world. This system is not exact; rivers do not always fit easily into one category, and regional or individual interpretations may cause misunderstanding. It is no substitute for a guidebook or accurate first-hand descriptions of a run.

Paddlers attempting difficult runs in an unfamiliar area should act cautiously until they get a feel for the way the scale is interpreted locally. River difficulty may change each year due to fluctuations in water level, downed trees, geological disturbances, or bad weather. Stay alert for unexpected problems!

As river difficulty increases, the danger to swimming paddlers becomes more severe. As rapids become longer and more continuous, the challenge increases. There is a difference between running an occasional Class IV rapid and dealing with an entire river of this category. Allow an extra margin of safety between skills and river ratings when the water is cold if the river itself is remote and inaccessible.

## THE SIX DIFFICULTY CLASSES:

**Class I: Easy.** Fast moving water with riffles and small waves. Few obstructions, all obvious and easily missed with little training. Risk to swimmers is slight; self-rescue is easy.

**Class II: Novice.** Straightforward rapids with wide, clear channels which are evident without scouting. Occasional maneuvering may be required, but rocks and medium-sized waves are easily missed by trained paddlers. Swimmers are seldom injured and group assistance, while helpful, is seldom needed.

**Class III: Intermediate.** Rapids with moderate, irregular waves which may be difficult to avoid and which can swamp an open canoe. Complex maneuvers in fast current and good boat control are often required; large waves or strainers may be present but are easily avoided.

Strong eddies and powerful current effects can be found, particularly on large-volume rivers. Scouting is advisable for inexperienced parties. Injuries while swimming are rare; self-rescue is usually easy but group assistance may be required to avoid long swims.

**Class IV: Advanced.** Intense, powerful but predictable rapids requiring precise boat handling in turbulent water. Depending on the character of the river, it may feature large, unavoidable waves and holes or constricted passages demanding fast maneuvers under pressure. A fast, reliable eddy turn may be needed to initiate maneuvers, scout rapids, or rest. Rapids may require "must" moves above dangerous hazards. Scouting is necessary the first time down. Risk of injury to swimmers is moderate to high, and water conditions may make self-rescue difficult. Group assistance for rescue is often essential but requires practiced skills. A strong Eskimo roll is highly recommended.

**Class V: Expert.** Extremely long, obstructed, or very violent rapids which expose a paddler to above average endangerment. Drops may contain large, unavoidable waves and holes or steep, congested chutes with complex, demanding routes. Rapids may continue for long distances between pools, demanding a high level of fitness. What eddies exist may be small, turbulent, or difficult to reach. At the high end of the scale, several of these factors may be combined. Scouting is mandatory but often difficult even for experts. A very reliable Eskimo roll, proper equipment, extensive experience, and practiced rescue skills are essential for survival.

**Class VI: Extreme.** One grade more difficult than Class V. These runs often exemplify the extremes of difficulty, unpredictability, and danger. The consequences of errors are very severe and rescue may be impossible. For teams of experts only, at favorable water levels, after close personal inspection and taking all precautions. This class does **not** represent drops thought to be unrunnable, but may include rapids which are only occasionally run.

# INDEX

# ABOUT THE AMC

The Appalachian Mountain Club is a nonprofit volunteer organization of over 35,000 members. Centered in the northeastern United States with headquarters in Boston, its membership is worldwide. The AMC was founded in 1876, making it the oldest organization of its kind in America. It is committed to conserving, developing, and managing dispersed outdoor recreational opportunities for the public in the Northeast, and its efforts have endowed it with a significant public trust.

Twelve regional chapters from Maine to Washington, D.C., some sixty committees, and hundreds of volunteers supported by a dedicated professional staff join in administering the Club's wide-ranging programs. Besides volunteer organized and led expeditions, these include research, backcountry management, trail and shelter construction and maintenance, conservation, and outdoor education. The Club operates a unique system of eight alpine huts in the White Mountains; a base camp and public information center at Pinkham Notch, New Hampshire; five full-service camps; four self-service camps; and nine campgrounds, all open to the public. Its Boston headquarters houses a public information center and the largest mountaineering library and research facility in the United States. The Club also conducts leadership workshops, mountain search and rescue, and a youth opportunity program for disadvantaged urban youths. The AMC publishes books, maps, and America's oldest mountaineering journal, *Appalachia*.

*We invite you to join and share in the benefits of membership.* Membership brings a subscription to the monthly bulletin *Appalachia*; discounts on publications and at the huts and camps managed by the Club; notices of trips and programs; and association with chapters and their meetings and activities. Most important, membership offers the opportunity to support and share in the public service efforts of the Club.

Membership is open to the general public upon completion of an application form and payment of an initiation fee and annual dues. Information on membership as well as the names and addresses of the secretaries of local chapters may be obtained by writing to *Appalachian Mountain Club, 5 Joy St., Boston, MA 02108,* or calling during business hours, 617-523-0636.